Discipline That Works

Promoting Self-Discipline in Children

"If you manage a child, you should read *Discipline That Works*. You will find Dr. Gordon's non-coercive ideas useful from the first day they are applied. . . . He could have called his approach 'quality discipline.' Until we learn to use it, we will not have the quality society we all desire."
—William Glasser, M.D., author of
The Quality School

"This approach successfully nurtures self-discipline in young people, and it leads to families and homes in which openness, cooperation, and democracy may truly be practiced. You must read Gordon's book."
—Ron Miller, Ph.D., editor,
Holistic Education Review

THOMAS GORDON, Ph.D., is a clinical psychologist and founder and president of Effectiveness Training, Inc., a worldwide network of instructors offering training programs for parents, teachers, managers, young people, and others. He is the author of the best-sellers T.E.T. (Teacher Effectiveness Training) and P.E.T. (Parent Effectiveness Training). The latter has sold over 1¼ million copies in its Plume edition. He lives in Solana Beach, California.

OPPORTUNITIES FOR
BECOMING MORE EFFECTIVE IN
YOUR PERSONAL RELATIONSHIPS WITH CHILDREN

Readers who would like to acquire a higher level of effectiveness in applying the methods and skills described in this book have several options:

- You may enroll in the 24-hour P.E.T. course, which is taught by instructors who have been trained and certified by Dr. Gordon's organization, Effectiveness Training, Inc. Over a million parents have taken the P.E.T. course—in 31 countries, in 15 different languages.

- If you are a teacher, you may enroll in Dr. Gordon's *Teacher Effectiveness Training* (T.E.T.) course, which is also taught by certified instructors. Several hundred thousand teachers have taken T.E.T.—in 15 countries, in 8 different languages. Graduate credit is earned from taking T.E.T. in the United States. You may also purchase a T.E.T. book, the textbook for the course.

- You may purchase the *P.E.T. Video Program,* a self-instructional course for one parent, for spouses, or for a group of parents.

- You may purchase the audio-based *P.E.T. Home Program,* another self-instructional course.

- You may purchase Dr. Gordon's original *P.E.T.* book— 2 million copies sold in 15 languages.

- You may obtain a free *catalogue,* which offers many important books in the field of human relationship as well as descriptions of all of Effectiveness Training's courses.

Write or phone: INFORMATION
Effectiveness Training, Inc.
531 Stevens Avenue
Solana Beach, California 92075

(619) 481-8121

DISCIPLINE THAT WORKS

Promoting Self-Discipline in Children

(formerly titled
*Teaching Children
Discipline at Home
and at School*)

by

Thomas Gordon, Ph.D.

A Plume Book

To Linda,
my partner, friend, and wife

To Judy and Michelle,
my self-disciplined and lovable daughters

to the many thousands of instructors
teaching our courses
to parents and teachers
throughout the world

Permissions acknowledgments appear on page vii.

PLUME
Published by the Penguin Group
Penguin Books USA Inc., 375 Hudson Street, New York, New York 10014, U.S.A.
Penguin Books Ltd. 27 Wrights Lane, London W8 5TZ, England
Penguin Books Australia Ltd, Ringwood, Victoria, Australia
Penguin Books Canada Ltd, 10 Alcorn Avenue,
Toronto, Ontario, Canada M4V 3B2
Penguin Books (N.Z.) Ltd, 182-190 Wairau Road, Auckland 10, New Zealand

Penguin Books Ltd, Registered Offices: Harmondsworth, Middlesex, England

Published by Plume, an imprint of Dutton Signet, a division of
Penguin Books USA Inc. This is an authorized reprint of a hardcover edition
published by Times Books, a division of Random House, Inc.
The hardcover edition was published simultaneously in Canada by
Random House of Canada Limited, Toronto.

First Plume Printing, August, 1991
5 7 9 11 13 12 10 8 6

REGISTERED TRADEMARK—MARCA REGISTRADA
Library of Congress Cataloging-in-Publication Data
Gordon, Thomas, 1918-
[Teaching children self-discipline—at home and at school]
Discipline that works : promoting self-discipline in children :
(formerly titled Teaching children discipline at home and at school)
/ by Thomas Gordon.
p.   cm.
Reprint. Originally published: New York : Times Books, c1989.
Includes bibliographical references and index.
ISBN 0-452-26643-2
1. Discipline of children.   2. Self-control in children.
3. School discipline.   I. Title.
HQ770.4.G66   1991
649'.64—dc20   91-8547
                                                                 CIP

Printed in the United States of America
Original hardcover designed by Oksana Kusanir

Acknowledgments

I am grateful to a number of persons whose support and influence contributed to this project. Anyone who has read one or more of my other books already recognizes the strong influence of the late Carl Rogers on my thinking—particularly the emphasis on the necessity for parents and teachers to learn empathic listening skills, first employed by the counselors trained by Dr. Rogers at Ohio State University and the University of Chicago.

I wish to thank the instructors, parents and teachers who contributed many of the vignettes, dialogues and case histories that have been invaluable in illustrating the effective new ways to influence children to become self-disciplined and self-controlled at home and at school.

Peter Wyden, publisher of my previous books, frequently came through with strong support and wise counsel when I asked for his help with problems I encountered in organizing this book.

I am indebted to David Aspy and Flora Roebuck for their extensive research studies showing the positive effects on students of teachers who were trained in the various interpersonal skills I have described and advocated in this book; and I am similarly indebted to Bruce Cedar and Ronald Levant for their research that so clearly shows the positive outcomes of our P.E.T. course on both parents and children.

I am grateful to all the members of the staff of Effectiveness Training, the people who have provided the support, understanding, and affection that have sustained and nourished me over the years.

I thank Priscilla Lavoie and Diane Lucca for typing the manuscript throughout its many revisions. I also value highly the careful, sensitive and thorough editing performed by Sarah Trotta at Times Books.

T.G.

Contents

Introduction

The Discipline Debate

Discipline has recently surfaced as a very important issue in our nation—in fact, throughout the world. It is an issue that has captured the attention of the president, and has been debated in the highest court of our land and in Congress. It is the most frequent cause of disputes between spouses. It is the subject of spirited debates in PTA chapters, at school faculty meetings and within boards of education. Strict discipline, including the right (and duty) of parents to punish their children, is a critical plank in the platform of the Moral Majority and so-called family life advocates. And it has shown up in opinion polls as the number one concern of parents.

Clearly, discipline has become a political, legal, educational, religious, and family issue. It sharply divides parents, teachers, coaches, school administrators, and other caretakers of our children.

The shelves of our bookstores are loaded with parenting books with such titles as: *Dare to Discipline, Assertive Discipline for Teachers, Assertive Discipline for Parents, Parent Power, Parents on the Run: The Need for Discipline, Power to the Parents, Your Acting*

Up Teenagers, Survival Kit for Parents, Toughlove, and (believe it or not) *Spank Me If You Love Me*.

How pervasive the discipline debate has become also can be judged by the number of newspaper and magazine articles dealing with the subject. Just a small sample of titles and headlines I've collected about discipline and physical punishment in our schools includes the following:

Britain Ends a Painful Tradition of School Discipline
Thanks, No Spanks
Strap to Be Officially Banned November First
Santa Fe Schools Consider Ban on Spanking
Too Cruel for Criminals but OK for Children
Spanking Banned in Spokane Schools
Spare the Rod, Save Your Hide
Teacher Lets Class Join in Paddling of 11-Year-Old Girl
School Paddling Bill Has Uphill Fight
Teacher Paddling 29 Charged, Suspended
Mouth Taped
Suit Claims Coach Hit Teenager

It is also clear that the discipline issue causes an *inner* conflict for the majority of parents. In our Parent Effectiveness Training (P.E.T.) throughout the country, we find most parents start the class torn between being strict and being lenient. I recall one mother admitting, "With our first child I was strict and that didn't work, so when the second child came, I decided to be lenient." Another confessed: "I don't want to be an authoritarian and strict parent like mine were, but I find myself using the same methods—the same *words*—as my parents did; and I hate myself for it."

It's much the same dilemma for many schoolteachers. They start out wanting to be warm, friendly, and lenient with their students, only to see themselves turn into the traditional bossy, punitive teacher every one of us has suffered under at some time during the school years. It is still commonplace for teachers to be told, "Don't smile at your class until after Christmas."

Precisely how is the discipline issue defined? How is it expressed? What do proponents of the various approaches tell parents and teachers? Let's examine these questions more closely.

President Reagan trumpeted a call for "good old-fashioned discipline" at a national forum on educational excellence in the fall of 1983 in Indianapolis:

> American schools don't need vast new sums of money as much as they need a few fundamental reforms. First, we need to restore good old-fashioned discipline. . . . We need to write stricter discipline codes; then support our teachers when they enforce those codes. . . . (Cordes, 1984)

Soon after, in January 1984, President Reagan received a confirming report from a committee of officials from the departments of Education and Justice with representatives from the office of Management and Budget. Known as the Baver Report after its chairman, Deputy Director of Education Gary Baver, it dramatized the problem of violence and disorder in schools and stressed the need for firmer discipline—arguing for increased "authority" for teachers, principals, and administrators in dealing with discipline problems.

Some social scientists, however, especially psychologists, have said that stricter punitive discipline is *not* effective and is, in fact, harmful to children and youth. The chairman of a committee on discipline of the prestigious society of educators, Phi Delta Kappa, William Wayson, also a professor of education at Ohio State University, recently testified at a congressional hearing:

> If not accompanied by fundamental efforts to involve and serve the student, restrictive policies inevitably will lead to *worse* discipline and perhaps violence or to forcible removal from the school of students who most need and deserve educational attention. . . . (Cordes, 1984)

The report of that committee went on to explain that in fact good schools are characterized by: internal cooperation and cooperation between the schools and parents; democratic decision making; methods of making all students feel a sense of belonging and ownership; rules that promote self-discipline rather than rote reliance on adult rules; challenging and interesting curricula and instruction; the ability to deal with personal problems of students and staff; and the physical facilities and organizational structures that reinforce this approach.

Irwin Hyman, an educational psychologist who directs the National Center for the Study of Corporal Punishment and Alternatives in the Schools located at Temple University, testified to a House subcommittee:

> While there is violence against teachers, the punitiveness toward children that has pervaded American education is more a cause than a solution to classroom misbehavior. . . . "Good old-fashioned discipline" is the least effective way to change students' behavior. . . . (Cordes, 1984)

Dr. B. F. Skinner, considered the leading behavorial psychologist in the world, now professor emeritus of psychology at Harvard, recently joined the fight against corporal punishment in the schools. In a letter to California Assemblyman Sam Farr, September 16, 1986, he wrote:

> I hear that fundamentalist groups are organizing a campaign against the bill to abolish corporal punishment in California schools, misrepresenting the bill by charging that it would prevent action against terrorism and other forms of violence on school property. Of course that is not true. (How ironic that people should take that line and use that kind of strategy when they claim to speak for a God of love and truth.)
>
> Punitive measures, whether administered by police, teachers, spouses, or parents, have well-known standard effects: (1) Escape (education has its own name for that, truancy), (2) Counterattack (vandalism

> of schools and attacks on teachers), and (3) Apathy—
> a sullen do-nothing withdrawal. . . . One of the
> immediate effects of the bill would be to encourage
> teachers to look at other ways of controlling their
> students, which in the long run would be much more
> effective. (Skinner, 1986–87)

Clearly, Congress and state legislatures are getting a much
different picture of good old-fashioned discipline than that
provided by President Reagan and the Baver Report.

Discipline became a well-publicized issue after President
Reagan was shot, on March 30, 1981, by John W. Hinckley, Jr.,
the son of a wealthy and highly respected family in Denver,
Colorado.

Before the shooting, Jack Hinckley had adopted a strategy
of strict discipline with his son, eventually forcing him out of
the home to learn how to become financially independent. This
strategy was recommended by their son's psychiatrist. Many
months after young Hinckley's trial, his father and mother
admitted the "tough love" approach they had taken was wrong
and accepted full responsibility for their son's actions. In 1984
Jack Hinckley told a *Los Angeles Times* reporter:

> We were like so many conservatives still are today.
> They seem to think that the answer to our crime
> problem and violence problem is harsher and harsher
> punishment. . . . I now realize that's wrong. . . . In
> John's case, and in many other children's cases where
> they simply can't cope, and drugs and alcohol are not
> involved, we should have been all the more aware
> that something was seriously wrong. What I say in
> every talk is: For heaven's sake, don't kick somebody
> out of the house when they can't cope. (*Los Angeles
> Times*, February 23, 1984)

The Hinckleys have since sold their business and are engaged
in a nationwide crusade, educating the public about mental
health.

Discipline in the classroom was the issue in 1977 when

corporal punishment was challenged before the United States Supreme Court, in the case of *Ingraham* v. *Wright*. This case involved two teenagers who had been beaten by their school principal with wooden paddles, jokingly referred to in schools as "boards of education." Injury to the youngsters had been severe. In fact, the medical treatment required for the students was so extensive that, had it been their parents who wielded the paddles, the hospital would have been compelled by law to file reports charging the parents with child abuse. Despite this, the court decided by the narrowest of margins that the bodies of our schoolchildren should not be granted the same protection the Constitution already guarantees adults, including prisoners. Justice Black, writing for the majority, held that the schoolchild has little need for the protection of the Eighth Amendment, which forbids the use of cruel and unusual punishment in our land. Justice Lewis Powell claimed that the enforcement of due process procedures in schools would result in a "consequent impairment of the teacher's ability to maintain discipline in the classroom." He also noted: "Paddling of recalcitrant children has long been an acceptable method of promoting good behavior and instilling notions of responsibility and decorum into the mischievous heads of schoolchildren."

There is ample evidence that the court's decision is supported by the general public. Several Gallup polls have found that discipline is considered by parents to be the most pressing problem in schools, with a large majority supporting the legal use of corporal punishment; only a handful of parents (less than 20 percent) disapprove of its use by schools.

It may surprise some readers that in the United States only eight states have enacted laws that completely prohibit corporal punishment in the schools: California, Hawaii, Maine, Massachusetts, New Hampshire, New York, Rhode Island, and Vermont. Only six of those eight protect children in foster homes, child care institutions, or schools.

The discipline debate extends far beyond the borders of our own country. It is truly an international issue. It was hotly and widely debated in Sweden several years ago, when a bill was introduced in the Swedish parliament that not only would make spanking completely illegal, but also banned any insulting or injurious treatment by parents that could cause children mental distress. The bill passed against strong opposition. Corporal punishment in *schools* had long ago been declared illegal in Sweden.

In China, teachers who lose their tempers and use their hand in punishment are themselves liable to punishment. Singapore allows only principals or senior teachers to cane boys over ten years old for major school infractions, but girls are spared. The Japanese banned corporal punishment after World War II but the law is often overlooked in favor of "a question of degree of physical punishment." In Turkey, there is a familiar saying: "Where the teacher hits, a rose blossoms." In Latin America, while corporal punishment is officially taboo, the leather strap is used in some rural areas. In Kenya, corporal punishment is allowed but is so strictly regulated that it borders on ritual: it can only be done by the principal or headmaster, in the presence of witnesses; it must be recorded in a "punishment book" with such details as the number of cane strokes; and it can only be dealt out for exceptional violations such as lying, bullying or drunkenness. In Belgium, corporal punishment can draw a jail sentence. In Thailand, it has to be done with a stick no thicker than three quarters of an inch.

Most developed countries have abolished physical punishment of youngsters in their schools through laws prohibiting it. Among these are Austria, Belgium, Cyprus, Denmark, Ecuador, Finland, France, Iceland, Ireland, Israel, Italy, Japan, Jordan, Luxembourg, Mauritius, Netherlands, Norway, Portugal, Qatar, Romania, Spain, Sweden, Switzerland, Turkey, and the USSR (Bacon and Hyman, 1976). Poland, believe it or not, abolished physical punishment in its schools in 1783.

Someone once pointed out to me that, with few exceptions, it is those countries that at some time in their history came under the rule of the British Empire that still sanction corporal punishment in schools—i.e., Scotland, Wales, the United States, South Africa, Australia, Canada, Bermuda. (England itself finally ended corporal punishment in government-funded British schools in 1986.)

In Russia a controversy over discipline was ignited back in the 1930s as a result of the publication of a book by a distinguished Russian educator, A. S. Makarenko, entitled *The Collective Family: A Handbook for Russian Parents*. It became a best-seller in Russia, not unlike Dr. Spock's *Baby and Child Care* in this country. Makarenko's ideas were provocative and controversial, for he openly criticized the typical Russian family as having certain "unhealthy features," which he identified as (1) too much parental autocracy and (2) the reliance of parents on physical punishment (Makarenko, 1967).

Discipline has also become a prominent religious issue in the U.S., as everyone who watches television knows. Under the "Pro-Family" banner of the Moral Majority, evangelists strongly oppose the children's rights movement, labeling it "kiddie lib" and warning parents that children would be encouraged to sue them or choose to leave them. Pro-Family advocates typically condemn such things as long hair, sex education, freedom of speech, rock and roll music, and teenage sexual freedom, because they are seen as examples of the failure of parents to impose their "authority" on children. They strongly support patriarchal families in which the father is charged with not only the responsibility but the *duty* to discipline children and to keep them under strict control.

The Pro-Family group has its avid supporters, but also its severe critics, many of whom think that under the surface of this group's apparent concern for the American family lies another issue: power. One such critic is Letty Cottin Pogrebin, a founding editor of *Ms.* magazine and author of *Family Politics* (Pogrebin, 1983). She reports her firsthand observations of the Pro-Family Coalition's lobbying activities at the 1980 White House Conference on Families:

> I watched them not only condemn progressivism and feminism as usual, but capitalize on something extra: the delegates' pedophobic desire to keep children under control. . . . I heard many people wave off the subject of child abuse; they were far more interested in defending parents' rights to spank. Why is corporal punishment so important, I asked one man? "To teach them who's boss," he answered. Throughout the conference, parents complained openly that their

children talk back, care more about their friends than
parents, dress wildly, play loud music, watch TV, and
don't mind their parents. Parental frustration thick-
ened the air. They've lost their children and they
don't understand why. They don't know how to win
kids' respect except through the use of force and
publicly sanctioned power. *They have confused obedience
with love.* . . . The Pro-Family Coalition had all the
answers in the form of authoritarian certainties and
God-given rules. This was a national conference on
families derailed to questions of *control*, not *care*.
(Pogrebin, 1983)

The widely read Christian author James Dobson has become
a spokesman for strict punitive discipline of children. His views
have become known throughout the country, primarily through
his films and videos on parenting, which are rented or sold to
hundred of churches of many denominations. He too is obviously concerned about the integrity of the American family,
which he thinks can be preseved only if parents "dare to
discipline," which is the title of one of his books (Dobson, 1970).

Dobson reveals why discipline has become for him a religion-
related issue. He believes obedience to one's parents is a prerequisite to becoming obedient to all other adults and, ultimately,
to a supreme being as well. Anything but absolute obedience,
as Dobson sees it ("submission" and "yielding" are Dobson's
euphemisms), should not be tolerated by Christian parents.
Given such beliefs, it's easy to see why rebellion apparently is
considered the worst of evils: "[Parents] recognize the dangers
of willful defiance as expressed in 1 Samuel 15:23: 'For rebellion
is as bad as the sin of witchcraft, and stubbornness is as bad as
worshipping idols.' " (Dobson, 1978)

As a result of another set of events, discipline has emerged
as an important and widely discussed issue among health
professionals, too. In 1962, a physician, C. Henry Kempe, and
his associates published their classic work on "The Battered
Child Syndrome" in the *Journal of the American Medical Association*
(Kempe et al., 1962). That study opened the doors to later
investigations of the cancerous pathology in our society now

termed *child abuse*. By the end of the 1960s, all fifty states had
passed laws mandating the reporting of child abuse by physicians
and hospitals to law enforcement agencies. Now eighteen states
require anyone else who knows of abuse to report it. In 1974,
the National Center on Child Abuse and Neglect was established
by the federal government to increase and disseminate knowledge about the causes of violence toward children and to identify
preventive measures.

I became personally involved with the problem of child
abuse when I served as a member of the advisory board of the
National Committee for the Prevention of Child Abuse
(NCPCA), founded in Chicago by Donna Stone in 1972. I was
asked to write a booklet for them, *What Every Parent Should
Know*, which gives parents more than a dozen alternatives to
punitive discipline. It became one of a continuing series of
educational pieces published by NCPCA for parents and professionals. In this booklet I described the alternatives to physical
punishment we teach in my P.E.T. course and showed parents
how to use them (Gordon, 1975). It was during my tenure on
the board of this organization that I became painfully aware of
how widespread child abuse is in the United States, and how
frequently practiced.

Then, in 1980, a group of sociologists published a landmark
book. It presented the findings of eight years of interviews and
research on *all kinds of violence in families*, not just parent-child
violence.

Highly credentialed professionals, the authors and the
principal investigators in the study are Richard Gelles, chairman
of the sociology department of the University of Rhode Island;
Murray Straus, also a sociologist, a full professor at the University
of New Hampshire since 1968, and the author of many articles
on the family; and Suzanne Steinmetz, associate professor of
sociology at the University of Delaware. *Behind Closed Doors:
Violence in the American Family* is their brilliant exposé of the kind
and depth of this sort of violence today: parent-child, child-
child, child-parent, husband-wife, wife-husband. From the pu-
ritanical notion of "beating the devil out of the child" to today's
prevalent attitude that "a hit in the butt never hurt any child,"
this book traces the roots of family violence in America and

reports the findings of a survey of 2,143 parents from all walks of life (Straus, Gelles, and Steinmetz, 1980).

Among their startling findings from a large sample of American families:

- Seventy percent viewed slapping or spanking a twelve-year-old as "necessary," 77 percent as "normal," 71 percent as "good." Seventy-three percent admitted using some form of violence* on their child at some time in the child's life.
- Mothers who spank or hit their children do it more than once every other month—an average of 7.2 times a year.
- Eighty-six percent of three-year-olds had been victims of some form of parental violence, as had 82 percent of five-year-olds, 54 percent of those between ages 10 and 14, and 33 percent of those between 15 and 17.

Their study also found that a lot of physical punishment of children is far more severe than a "swat on the child's behind." Some findings:

- Between 3.1 and 4.0 million children have been kicked, bitten, or punched by a parent at some time in their lives.
- Between 1.0 million and 1.9 million were kicked, bitten, or punched in the year 1975.
- Between 1.4 and 2.3 million children have been *beaten up* sometime while growing up.

The authors of *Behind Closed Doors* admitted that the discovery that a child might be a victim of parental violence as often as once every other month came as a surprise to them. They were forced to conclude that "child abuse may be a chronic condition for many children, not a once in a lifetime experience for a rare few."

---

* Violence was defined in this study as "an act carried out with the intention of causing physical pain or injury." Abusive violence was defined as acts having a high potential for injuring another—such as punching, beating, kicking, biting, hitting with a hard object, stabbing, or shooting.

Your reaction to these findings may be similar to mine. I did not feel that these findings made us look like a nation that was too "permissive" with its children, one that was too "child-centered," as the dare-to-discipline advocates would have us believe. Quite the contrary. We are a nation in which most adults unquestioningly believe the old saying "Spare the rod, spoil the child." We are a nation of people who chuckle with approval at stories about fathers taking their kids (usually boys) behind the woodshed. We are a nation that makes jokes about mothers struggling to tear switches off the cherry tree. We are a nation that admires athletic coaches and Little League managers who have built a reputation for using strict discipline. We are a nation that applauds loud and strong those talk-show guests who advocate "tough love," strict discipline, and strong parental authority. We are a nation in whose schools 3.5 percent of students are paddled in a year—12.55 percent in Arkansas and over 10 percent in Florida, Mississippi, and Tennessee (Maurer, 1984).

Something about the idea of kids getting spanked or beaten seems almost cherished by adults: "It's good for what ails them"; "A little lickin' never hurt any kid"; "It was good enough for me, so why not for my kids?"; "Most kids need a little sense beat into them."

I've been told that among private schools in our country, the ones that boast of a policy of strict codes of dress and conduct, corporal punishment, and a "no-nonsense" philosophy, enjoy long admissions waiting lists. I suspect, too, there are more parents than we realize who secretly hope their youngsters will get drafted into military service, where, they believe, the kids will be "straightened out," "settled down," "taught respect for authority," "made a man of."

Although we are a nation obsessed with the idea that children *need* discipline, some parents do admit to having mixed feelings about punishing their kids. A mother in one of my early classes confessed: "I'm permissive with my kids until I can't stand them; then I get so authoritarian that I can't stand myself."

How many of us can recall being spanked by a parent, hearing at the same time the guilt-ridden expression "This hurts me more than it does you"? I have a suspicion that many parents, down deep inside, do hate to inflict physical punishment on their children. Who genuinely enjoys hitting someone much smaller and less powerful?

The authors of *Behind Closed Doors*, well aware of our nation's strong bias toward using physical punishment, argue passionately that it *must* be abolished:

> Despite the fact that physical punishment is viewed as necessary and beneficial by the majority of American parents, and despite the fact that many parents dogmatically cling to the notion that spankings are good for children, we *must* reduce and gradually eliminate the use of physical punishment and develop alternative technologies for child-rearing. It is possible to raise healthy, happy, well-behaved children without [using] violence. . . . In short, it is possible to eliminate the sequence of early experiences which teach millions of American children to use violence on those they love. (Straus, Gelles, and Steinmetz, 1980)

But not all psychologists are in agreement on this. Recently I was startled to find a book called *Parent Power* by an Oklahoma psychologist, Dr. Logan Wright. Dr. Wright received a distinguished-contribution citation in the 1977 Media Awards from the American Psychological Association for this book, the first two sentences of which tell parents:

> The order of the day for any parent who wants to retain some semblance of sanity is to get and maintain control. But the most important reason for seizing control is that *you must be able to control a child before you can really support and love him* [italics in the original]. (Wright, 1980)

Reading Wright's book had a profound effect on me. I recall dropping the book into my lap and thinking, "What's going on here? Why is a prominent psychologist advising parents to discipline and control their children as a prerequisite for loving them? It jarred me into beginning my own in-depth study of discipline, with the intention of sharing what I learned with parents and teachers.

I read all the power-to-the-parent and dare-to-discipline books, and I searched the psychological literature for all the reports of research studies I could find on discipline, punishment, power, styles of parenting, and so on. I found a surprisingly large number of such studies, as you will see throughout this book.

During the project I became increasingly aware of how very complex the subject of discipline really is. Over the course of unraveling these complexities and acquiring a deeper comprehension of the subject, I became determined to share what I learned with others who are also seeking an understanding of discipline and its effects on children. This book is the result, and Part I discusses discipline in depth. For example, I found that there are several quite different kinds of discipline—some good, some bad—a fact overlooked by many writers. I learned that discipline to most people means using rewards and punishments the same way we use them with our pets. I learned that rewards fail with older kids, and why, and why it is that for punishment to work it must be severe. Mostly, I ran into a lot of confused thinking, because books about discipline don't recognize there are several very different kinds of "authority"— some benign, some harmful. I found that punishment, especially if it is mild, can actually be rewarding to children sometimes, and rewards can sometimes be felt as punishing. I discovered the punishment is not the *cure* for children's aggression, like hitting baby brother, but is usually the *cause* of aggression toward others.

I'll offer numerous effective alternatives to punitive discipline at home and in schools, all of which are nonpower methods that will: greatly increase your overall effectiveness in dealing with the disruptive and unacceptable behaviors of youngsters; replace adult-imposed discipline with self-discipline; replace children's control by adults with children's self-control; replace unilateral setting of limits and rules by adults with limits and rules mutually arrived at by both adults and children; replace win-lose solutions to conflicts with no-lose (or win-win) solutions. Explaining and illustrating these more effective, more democratic, more humane methods is my objective in the second part of this book.

During my investigation of discipline, one fact became very clear: as a society we are employing the wrong strategies to reduce the self-destructive and socially unacceptable behaviors of young people that occur with shocking frequency—alcoholism, smoking, drug abuse, delinquent activities, dropping out of school, drunk driving, vandalism and other forms of violence, premarital pregnancies, rape, suicide. The ever-increasing frequency of these behaviors is certainly sufficient evidence that the way we have traditionally disciplined children at home and in our schools has not worked. In fact, disciplining children the way we do may be more a cause than a cure for these unwanted behaviors.

The usual strategies we see being employed to attack these serious problems are those that try to do something *to the child*. For example, the strategies consistently preferred by parents, school authorities, police, juvenile courts, and state and federally initiated programs to cure alcoholism, smoking, drug abuse, and drunk driving focus on the child: courses to educate and frighten youngsters as to the hazards of these self-destructive behaviors; programs to persuade kids to "say no"; laws to increase the severity of punishments for the youngsters; programs that offer counseling to them; programs that persuade parents to get tougher on kids (with love, of course) or to "know where your child is" or "be home when your child gets out of school," and so on.

The more I have learned about the principal causes of the behaviors that damage youth and weaken our society, the firmer my belief that our best hope for prevention is another kind of strategy—namely, helping adults who deal with children learn a new way to manage families, schools, and youth-oriented organizations. And that strategy will require teaching adults the skills required to govern their family, their classroom, their group more democratically, less autocratically—not the other way around as some are urging us to do.

PART
ONE

UNDERSTANDING
DISCIPLINE

chapter

ONE

Defining
Terms and
Clarifying Meanings

One of my favorite college professors badgered his students with the dictum: "Define your terms if you want an intelligent discussion." Yet I find that is exactly what people fail to do when they discuss discipline, resulting in a lot of misunderstandings. By clearing up these common misunderstandings in the pages ahead, I hope we can clarify the cloudier elements of the discipline issue.

THE NOUN AND THE VERB

It's important at the outset to look at the critical difference between the noun *discipline* and the verb *discipline*. As a noun, discipline is usually understood as behavior and order in accord with rules and regulations, or behavior maintained by training, as in "discipline in the classroom" or "the discipline of a good basketball team."

You seldom hear any controversy about the noun *discipline*. Everybody seems to be in favor of that kind. The word conjures up order, organization, cooperation, knowing and following rules and procedures, and a consideration for the rights of others.

The verb *to discipline* in my Random House Dictionary is defined as "to bring to a state of order and obedience by training and control" and "to punish or penalize; correct, chastise."

The teacher disciplined those children who talked by keeping them after school.

If kids are not disciplined at home they will be troublemakers at school.

In discussions of discipline, it is quite often assumed that the only way to get discipline (the noun), both at home and in the classroom, is for parents and teacher rigorously to discipline (the verb)—that is, control, punish, penalize, correct, and chastise children.

I have found considerable evidence refuting this widely held belief. In fact, I have discovered that disciplining children may be the *least* effective way to get discipline at home or in the classroom. Studies have shown that discipline in the classroom goes to pot whenever the teacher/disciplinarian leaves the room or faces the chalkboard. Everyone has seen this happen at home, too. Furthermore, because disciplining children involves using power, usually in the form of punishment or threats of punishment, children defend themselves against such punitive power by rebelling, resisting, retaliating, or lying—anything to avoid being coerced, restricted, or controlled.

Research studies have also shown that punishment produces aggression and violence in children—the more frequently punished children, compared to children who receive little or no punishment at home, show more aggression, hyperactivity, and violence toward other children. One study found that nearly 100 percent of punished children had assaulted a brother or sister during the year of the study, while only 20 percent of children whose parents did not use physical punishment had done so (Straus, Gelles, and Steinmetz, 1980).

Understanding the difference between the noun and the verb forms of *discipline* is of utmost importance, in my judgment, for another reason: it clarifies that the discipline controversy is really about *how* we should deal with kids (the *means*) and not about what we want them to do (the ends). Most people would agree that we want kids to be orderly, cooperative, and considerate both at home and in school, but there are intense differences about whether disciplining (the verb) is the best *means* to bring about discipline (the noun), a generally agreed-upon *end*.

TEACHING VERSUS CONTROLLING

Even as a verb, discipline has two very different meanings. The first we have just dealt with—disciplining for the purpose of controlling. The second has to do with the act of instructing, teaching, educating. The dictionary provides this meaning: "to train by instruction and exercise; to drill." My *Rodale Synonym Finder* further provides all these alternative terms for the teaching/educating kind of discipline:

> train, coach, drill, instruct, teach, tutor, give lessons, school, edify, inform, enlighten, inculcate, indoctrinate, ground, prepare, qualify, rear, bring up, guide, familiarize.

Here is another form of discipline that seldom causes arguments. Rarely does anyone question the desirability of adults performing any or all of the above functions with children and youth. In fact, most of us would say it is the *duty* of effective parents and competent teachers to provide this kind of training, coaching, and guidance. Nobody wants to eliminate the teach-train-inform kind of discipline.

However, about the controlling type of disciplining, the controversy is hot and heavy. First, look at the list of all the different synonyms for *this* form of discipline:

> control, correct, direct, govern, supervise, oversee, preside over, manage, keep in line, regulate, regiment, restrain, check, curb, contain, arrest, harness, bridle, rein in, leash, muzzle, restrict, constrain, con-

fine, inhibit, correct, chastise, reprimand, reprove, rebuke, criticize, make an example of, punish, castigate, penalize.

Obviously this suggests something *very* different from the teach-train-inform type of discipline. Blood pressures rise and voices get loud over words like *control, regiment, restrain, harness, bridle, muzzle, castigate, penalize,* and (as we'll see) especially the word *punish.*

While I'm convinced it's not the kind of disciplining that is healthy for my own kids or anybody else's, most parents and teachers stubbornly support this control-restrict-punish kind of discipline. In fact, most books for parents argue that kids not only need it but also want it; that they will feel insecure without it; that they will think you don't love them if you don't use it; that they will become unmanageable little monsters without it. I will question each of these commonly held beliefs in later chapters.

It is important, too, to recognize that the teach-train-inform kind of discipline represents an effort to *influence* children, while the control-restrict-punish kind of discipline is always an effort to control them.

The difference between *controlling* children and *influencing* them isn't widely recognized, yet it is a crucial one. Obviously, most parents and teachers want nothing more strongly than the ability to influence young people and thus have a positive effect on their lives. But in their zeal to influence, most adults unfortunately fall into a trap: rather than use only influence methods, they impose limits, give orders, send commands, punish, or threaten to punish. These control-type methods don't actually influence youngsters; they only coerce or compel them. And when a child is compelled to do something, that child is not really influenced; even if he complies, he usually does it out of fear of punishment.

To have a profound and lasting influence on the lives of young people, adults must forgo using power methods to control children and instead employ certain new methods that will greatly enhance their ability to be a positive influence in the lives of youngsters. These methods, which I'll describe and illustrate in later chapters, serve to reduce the natural tendency of children to resist change, to motivate kids to assume responsibility for modifying their behavior, to influence kids to stick to agreements, and to foster children's consideration of others.

Here is a little-known psychological truth—a paradox, too: *you acquire more influence with young people when you give up using your power to control them!* The opposite is also true, of course: *the more you use power to try to control people, the less real influence you'll have on their lives.* Why? Because power methods create resistance (not doing what the adult wants), rebellion (doing the opposite), or lying (not doing it but saying you did).

OTHER-IMPOSED DISCIPLINE VERSUS SELF-DISCIPLINE

Now let's distinguish between two radically different kinds of control-type discipline. One is externally administered or "other-imposed"; the other is internally administered or self-imposed. Discipline by others versus discipline of oneself; control by others as opposed to self-control.

Everyone is familiar with the term *self-discipline*, but what does it actually mean? Psychologists use the term *locus of control*, which I think is helpful here. Their investigations show that some people tend to have the locus of control *inside* themselves. With self-discipline the locus of control is inside the person, but with discipline enforced by others, the locus of control is outside the person—actually inside the controller.

We don't encounter much controversy about whether self-control is desirable. In fact, almost everyone places a high value on children capable of self-control, self-regulation, self-discipline. There *is* much controversy, however, over what the best way is to foster these desired traits in children and youth—the basic conflict over the means for achieving a particular end.

Most parents and teachers take the position that children eventually will develop inner control automatically, as a direct result of adults applying outer control (discipline). This belief is rooted in a well-known Freudian theory that claims that as children get older they will gradually internalize the early coercive controls of parents and other adults, until eventually those outer controls are transformed into inner controls and self-discipline.

Considerable evidence now exists that refutes this Freudian theory. Everyday observation also tells us that self-discipline isn't formed that way. Remember this adage, "When the cat is away, the mice will play"? Well, when adult controllers turn their backs, youngsters usually show little self-control. Sometimes they rebelliously do exactly what the adult authority has previously prohibited them from doing. Remember too what they used to say about the "preacher's kids": obedient, submissive, good-goody when young, often they turn into rebels and troublemakers during adolescence. Children who meekly submit to parental authority often turn into rebellious teenage delinquents later, reacting aggressively to *all* adult authority, incapable of any self-control or self-discipline.

Self-disciplined youngsters, however, are those who have always been given considerable personal freedom. Why? Because they have been allowed the chance to make many of their own choices and decisions. Children will learn to control or limit behavior that is disturbing to adults only if those adults have shown a similar consideration for them; children will use self-control to follow rules when they have been given the chance to join with adults in deciding what those rules should be. Throughout this book I hope to convince you that *disciplining kids does not produce disciplined kids*, and I'll present the evidence for it. While it is true that obedient, fearful, submissive, and subservient kids are sometimes produced by adult-imposed discipline, truly *self*-disciplined youngsters are not.

A DISAGREEMENT ABOUT LIMITS

Another misunderstanding crops up in most discussions about discipline. It centers on the notion of limits. All parents and teachers recognize the necessity of kids growing up with certain limits, yet few understand that it makes a difference how these limits are established—again, the issue of what *means* are employed.

Dare-to-discipline proponents assert with confident conviction: "Kids need limits and kids want limits." But this is a dangerous half-truth. It *is* necessary that kids feel there are limits on their behaviors, for the sake of others mostly. But what a world of difference there is between the way youngsters react to limits imposed by an adult and the way they react to limits they have a voice in determining! You'll see this clearly in a later chapter when I show how parents and teachers can use the potent "principle of participation" to get kids involved in mutual problem-solving that yields agreements, contracts, rules, and limits that really stick. I think you'll be convinced that kids are much more motivated to keep commitments when adults give them a voice in setting limits on their own behavior.

All families and classrooms need specific rules and clearly understood policies. Given the opportunity, children are quite capable of participating with their parents or teachers to set rules and policies that will govern their behavior. Classrooms and families can govern themselves effectively without adult supremacy, without someone being the boss, the rule maker. You can forget the dire warning of all those dare-to-discipline books that without rules set by adult authority there will be anarchy, chaos, and confusion. It isn't true.

In fact, when children are given the opportunity to participate in setting rules, families often discover they have *more* rules than before and everyone sticks to them. The critical question, then, is not *whether* limits and rules are needed in families and schools, but rather *who* sets them: the adults alone or the adults and kids—together.

SHOULD I BE STRICT OR LENIENT?

I doubt there's a parent who hasn't at one time or another agonized over this. It is just as common for teachers to be uncertain how to come across in the classroom—tough or soft, a strict disciplinarian or a permissivist.

To be strict or not to be strict, that *is* the question—in fact, it's the number-one question among child-rearing authorities, among parents, among education authorities, among teachers.

It is debated in books and articles, at conferences and conventions. (By the way, have you noticed that you seldom hear a parent or a teacher admit, "I'm authoritarian" or "I'm permissive"? These are terms reserved for those with whom you disagree.)

The question of whether to be strict or lenient is what social scientists call a "pseudo problem." It is also a clear case of "either-or thinking." Let me explain.

Seldom do I meet parents or teachers who understand that it's not necessary to make a choice between these two leadership styles. Few adults know it, but there *is* an alternative to being at either end of the strictness-leniency scale. There is the choice of a third style.

The alternative, which may come as a blessing to many of you, is being *neither* authoritarian nor permissive, *neither* strict nor lenient. Does that mean being somewhere near the middle of the scale—moderately strict or moderately lenient? Not at all. The alternative is *not being on the scale at all!* Let me explain.

Authoritarian leadership—whether at home or in the classroom—means that control is in the hands of the adult leader; permissive leadership means that control has been "permitted" to be in the hands of the youngsters.

Authoritarian parents and teachers control and rule, while those who are permissive permit the children to control and rule ("Our children rule the roost"). In schools, as every youngster knows, most of their teachers control and rule and expect strict obedience. Fewer in number are the permissive teachers. They don't control or rule, and as a result, their classrooms are usually noisy, chaotic, unmanageable, and without order, rules or limits.

No parent or teacher really wants to suffer the chaotic consequences of lawless permissiveness. In fact, children themselves don't enjoy permissiveness at home or in classrooms. (I'll never forget the day my daughter came home after her first day in junior high school and complained, "What a horrible semester this is going to be. I have two authoritarian teachers and two permissive teachers!")

It's also true that most youngsters are uncomfortable with the consequences of permissiveness. Children of permissive parents usually feel guilty about always getting their way. They also feel insecure about being loved, because their inconsiderate behaviors make them unlovable.

Central to this book is the idea that there is a much better and easier way to deal with children—a viable and effective alternative to both authoritarian and permissive adult leadership. It lacks a good name (I certainly have not yet been successful in inventing one I like). Nevertheless, I believe I have identified the principal elements or ingredients of this alternative, and I will describe and illustrate the skills and methods required by this new way of dealing with children and youth in the chapters to come.

For now, I want to stress that this new approach to relating to youngsters requires a transformation in the way adults *perceive* children, as well as a shift in the way they *treat* them. But it needn't be difficult to bring about this transformation. Parents need only the willingness to learn a few new methods and skills.

Once parents and teachers fully understand that there is an alternative, and a more effective one at that, to either authoritarianism or permissiveness, they won't be drawn into all the pointless controversies about tough-versus-soft discipline, strict-versus-lenient leadership. Simply by being better informed about the ineffectiveness of maintaining control through power, parents and teachers will not be fooled by the tempting promises of those who call for stricter discipline in families and in our schools. And, by understanding the pitfalls of permissiveness, they can avoid being seduced by the promises of those who advocate giving youngsters unrestricted freedom at home or in the classroom.

THE MULTIPLE MEANINGS OF "AUTHORITY"

Whenever discipline is discussed or debated, you can count on the term "authority" popping up. Unfortunately, the concept invariably adds to the confusion and muddled thinking already surrounding the issue of discipline. The dare-to-discipline advocates constantly urge parents and teachers to "exercise authority" in dealing with children and youth, and they make the claim that children need it, want it, and will be happier for getting it. They also bemoan the "breakdown of authority" in both schools and homes and wish that today's kids would respect authority as they think kids did in the past.

Strict-discipline proponents have grave apprehensions about what would happen in families and schools without adult authority. James Dobson fears that without authority, "There is inevitable chaos and confusion and disorder in human relationships" (Dobson, 1978).

Those who counsel parents or teachers to use power-based authority characteristically caution that it must be "loving" authority or "benevolent" authority. They frequently substitute the term *leadership* for *authority*, and then caution it must be benevolent. Interestingly, you will never hear the authority champions advocate that parents and teachers be "authoritarians." They never use that word, despite the fact that the first definition of the adjective *authoritarian* in my dictionary is "favoring authority," and the first definition of the noun *authoritarian* is "disciplinarian."

To underscore their argument, dare-to-discipline proponents usually claim that children will respect authority, look up to it, yield to it, rely on it. It's puzzling, then, why they worry so much about youngsters rebelling against the authority of their parents or teachers, and they rail against the "breakdown of authority" among today's youth (evidence that adult authority doesn't always bring respect and obedience). None of the dozens of parent-power advocates I've read deal with this critical question: if kids respect, want, need, and yield to adult authority, why then do we see among youngsters such widespread rebellion and resistance to it—such hostility and lack of respect for the adults who use it?

More important, in none of the books, articles, or videotapes produced by the proponents of discipline have I seen any recognition of the fact that all authority is not the same. Indeed, it's very unfortunate that there are at least four, maybe more, different meanings of this one word in our English language, because it makes forming a consensus about the term very difficult. Authority is not a unitary concept. Without recognizing this we can never have an intelligent discussion about authority or a clear understanding of this complex term. Let me explain these four definitions.

1. *Authority based on expertise.* This kind of authority is derived from a person's *expertise*—his or her knowledge, experience, training, skill, wisdom, education. For example, we say, "He is an authority on corporate law"; "It was an authoritative book on the Civil War"; "Let's rely on the authority of the dictionary"; or "She speaks with authority." This often is referred to as *earned authority.* We will call this Authority E, the *E* standing for *expertise.*

In our family, Authority E is in operation frequently. Both my daughter and my wife often influence me to change my shirt or pants (or both) by telling me they don't match. Usually I accept their expertise in such matters. Often (but not always) I can influence my wife to follow my directions when she is driving the car and we are traveling through a strange city, because she usually accepts my expertise in keeping directionally oriented, an ability I learned as a pilot in the Army Air Corps.

On the other hand, because I judge her memory for dates and events to be infinitely better than mine, I usually accept her influence on such matters as what time we said we'd arrive at friends' houses for dinner, or accept her urging me to write letters I promised or to go buy gifts for people's birthdays or anniversaries.

2. *Authority based on position or title.* A second kind of authority is that based upon a person's *position or title* or a mutually understood or agreed-upon *job description*, which defines a person's duties, functions, and responsibilities. An airline captain has been given this kind of authority over his crew and passengers. A committee chairman is given the authority to open and close its meetings; a policeman has the authority to issue a speeding ticket; a teacher has the authority to tell students to take out their spelling books; a boss has the authority to tell his or her secretary to come in and take a letter; a mail carrier has the authority to collect money for an unstamped letter he delivers; the driver of a car has the authority to tell passengers to fasten their seat belts. We will call this Authority J—the *J*

standing for *job*. It's sometimes called designated or legitimated authority.

Note the key concepts of a "mutually understood" and "agreed-upon" job description. For this type of authority to work in human relationships, the people involved must genuinely accept—sanction, endorse, support, approve—the right of the person "in authority" to direct certain of their behaviors (but not all, of course). My secretary, for example, seldom would comply with my saying "Get me a cup of coffee," because that is not a job function listed in her job description. Besides that, I know she opposes the custom of women at work being expected to get coffee for men.

In our family, we have many interactions in which Authority J plays a major part. We have long-term agreements with regard to who does what jobs. On any of my three nights to cook, either my wife or my one daughter still at home may ask me to get up and get them a second glass of milk or bring the mayonnaise to the table. I always comply. And because feeding and bathing our dog is an agreed-upon job of my daughter, it's accepted that I have the right to say, "You haven't fed Katie yet tonight," or "Katie needs a bath." And because we've had an agreement that weekly food shopping is one of my jobs, it's legitimate and certainly acceptable to me for my daughter to write a note that says, "Don't buy the pulpy orange juice for me—I like regular Minute Maid."

All of the duties and responsibilities in the above examples were made legitimate by virtue of their having been arrived at by the involvement of each of us in a group decision-making process that ends up with a decision *acceptable to everyone*. It is from this mutual acceptance of the decision that Authority J derives its amazing potency to influence behavior. Do you see why it is sometimes called "legitimated" authority?

3. Authority based on informal contracts. The third kind of authority in human relationships is derived from the many understandings, agreements, and contracts that people make in their day-to-day interactions. For example, I agree in the morning to drive my daughter to the auto repair shop at 4:00 P.M. that day so she can pick up her car. That promise I made carries a lot of weight (authority, if you will) in influencing me to leave my office and meet my commitment to her. We call this type of authority Authority C with the C standing for *commitments* or *contracts*.

A frequently occurring example of Authority C at work in our own home is the understanding that whenever we say we'll return home (or leave a note to that effect) and later find out we can't make it, we phone home. The purpose of this agreement, obviously, is to avoid causing worry or anxiety.

We also have an unwritten understanding, in existence in our home for years now, that we knock before entering another's bedroom. That understanding has always had a potent influence on each of us, and whenever one of us forgets, the other reinforces the rule by confronting the "intruder" with a strong, "Hey, how about knocking before walking into my room!"

Over the years my wife and I have had an understanding that whoever wakes up and gets out of bed first goes downstairs and makes the coffee, goes out and gets the newspaper, and brings both upstairs to the one still in bed. The one last up makes the bed.

Other understandings and agreements that are in operation in our family:

My wife takes care of the plants.
I usually cook the Sunday breakfast.
My wife uses the couch when we watch TV, I use the big chair.
My daughter has sole responsibility for her homework—to do it or not, and to decide when to do it or where to do it.

Authority C derives its potent influence from the personal commitments it represents.

In a later chapter I'll examine this Authority C in greater depth and give examples of using it to influence youngsters both at home and in school.

4. Authority based on power. The fourth kind of authority is derived from one person having power over another. I shall call this Authority P, the P standing for *power*—power to control, dominate, coerce, bend to one's will, make others do what they don't want to do. This is the type of authority people almost always have in mind when they talk about parents and teachers needing or exercising authority, or when they wish that children would "respect" adult authority, or when they talk about a "breakdown in authority" in families or schools, or when they want children to be "obedient to authority," or when they complain that kids today are "rebelling against authority." Authority P is also the kind of authority we generally mean when we speak of a "hierarchy of authority" in organizations.

In the next chapter, I'll explain in depth how adults use the power of rewards or punishments as the source of authority to try to control children, and why so often it doesn't work. I'll also point out the many damaging effects of Authority P. For now, however, I want to clear up some of the confused thinking caused by the existence of these four different kinds of authority with regard to children.

I'll start with Authority E. Authority based upon expertise is highly valued and quite harmless in human relationships. Most people, including children, respect those who have expertise—they learn from them, seek out their counsel, often follow their advice. When parents and teachers (and authors of dare-to-discipline child-rearing books, too) complain about today's children not respecting authority, they are thinking of Authority P. They really are complaining that children don't *obey* adults— that is, don't do exactly whatever adults tell them to do, just because adults tell them to do it.

My experience with Authority E is that children do have a lot of respect for people who have some sort of expertise. In fact, they often overestimate the Authority E that adults have. This is especially true of younger children. They think their parents know everything there is to know. And they often are awed by the knowledge and skills possessed by doctors, dentists, teachers, coaches, carpenters, and others.

What about children respecting Authority J? I believe that they usually do respect the kind of authority that derives from the generally understood duties, roles, and functions of the jobs that adults hold. When teachers call a classroom to order, most kids honor that request; when teachers give homework assignments children usually consider this function legitimate. When adults are driving a car and tell kids to fasten their seat belts, most youngsters accept this as the driver's legitimate prerogative, a situation not unlike passengers' accepting an airline captain telling them to refasten their seat belts while going through some unexpected turbulence. Kids typically stand when commanded by an adult saying, "Let's stand and sing the National Anthem." As the chief cook in our family, my mother had a lot of Authority J, which we kids (and Dad, too) usually respected. Seldom did we fail to comply with her demands: "Time to come in, dinner's ready"; "Bring the plates in"; "Eat it while it's hot"; "Save some of the meat for your sandwiches tomorrow"; "Clear the dishes off the table"; and so on.

Do children respect Authority P? I don't think they ever do. I can't recall ever respecting a teacher who was bossy and used power to coerce me into doing what I didn't want to do. I've never known a youngster who held in high esteem an adult who consistently used power-based punishment or threats of punishment. Kids, like adults, don't respect power wielders, although they do usually fear them. Otherwise, why do they retaliate against them, resist them, avoid them, lie to them, and grow to dislike them? I think most adults know this from their own experience as youngsters.

I can tell parents are unclear about the word *authority* when they have said to me during the question period after a speech on this subject, "You urge parents and teachers not to use authority. But don't they have a duty to teach children their values and beliefs and share with them their superior judgment and wisdom?" This question illustrates a confusion between two meanings of authority: Authority P and Authority E. My response is to point out that while I am urging parents and teachers *not* to use Authority P, I certainly advocate that they should share their Authority E whenever it seems appropriate to do so. In fact, as I've mentioned, children often seek out the advice, judgment, and opinions of their elders, and they are often curious about what both parents and teachers believe or value.

Stated in a slightly different way: It seldom hurts an adult-child relationship for the adult to be *authoritative*—Authority

E—or to be an *authority* on a subject; but it does harm the relationship to be *authoritarian*—Authority P—as we shall see.

Advocates of discipline have a tendency to be imprecise with their terms (perhaps purposely) when they try to defend their belief that parents have a duty to use power-based discipline. In James Dobson's *The Strong-willed Child* (1978), Dobson makes a case for children to obey parents' Authority P when he quotes the biblical passage, "Children, obey your parents in all things, for this is well-pleasing unto the Lord."

He draws again from the Bible (Ephesians 6:4) in support of disciplining children, but he recommends another kind of authority, Authority E: "Don't keep on scolding and nagging your children, making them angry and resentful. Rather, bring them up with the loving discipline the Lord himself approves, *with suggestions and godly advice* [italics added]."

Suggestions and advice are clearly methods of *influencing* others by sharing one's experience, wisdom, knowledge, and so on—Authority E, distinctly different from *controlling* others with Authority P.

In later chapters I'll explain how and when to use Authority E, Authority J, and Authority C most effectively. For now, let me make it clear that a central, if not *the* central, thesis of this book is that using these three types of adult authority can be extremely effective—and, most important, constructive—ways of *influencing* children, whereas using Authority P is a way of trying to *control* children, and it is often ineffective. This difference between *influence* and *control* is critical, as I shall explain more fully later.

THE MYTH OF "BENEVOLENT AUTHORITY"

The universal tendency of discipline advocates to try to make Authority P sound loving or benevolent generates another significant source of confusion about discipline and authority. Parents and teachers are told that they can safely use punitive discipline provided they do it justly, wisely, lovingly, fairly, or benignly—and always "with the child's best interests in mind." They claim that it's perfectly all right to be "firm but fair," to be tough as long as it's "tough love," to be autocratic as long as they are "benevolent autocrats," to control as long as they are not dictators, to punish as long as the punishment is not too severe.

These ideas are widely believed, no doubt because they are exactly what punitive parents and teachers most *want* to believe. Needing to justify their use of power-based discipline to control children or needing to assuage their guilt, adults desperately want to believe that what they are doing is out of love for the child, for the child's own good. People try to make the *ends* appear benign in order to justify the use of their power-based *means*.

Can power-based authority ever be benevolent? Yes, if by that we mean that the controller *thinks* he or she is acting benevolently and in the best interests of the child. However, if I'm asked, "Is power-based discipline *actually* in the child's best interest—that is, is it *felt by the child* as being in his or her best interest?" my answer is: "Seldom, if ever." In Chapter 5 I will document this conviction by describing the variety of coping methods children employ to fight against Authority P or to escape from it. I maintain that children don't *feel* punitive discipline is ever benevolent or in their best interest.

Nowhere have I found more examples of using words imprecisely or without proper definition than in *Parent Power*, a book written by child psychologist and newspaper columnist John Rosemond. First openly advocating that parents should be "benevolent dictators" who *insist on obedience* from their children, he goes on to explain his position. Now that you understand the critical difference between the four different kinds of authority, see if you can detect the ambiguities and imprecise semantics in the following passage from Rosemond's book:

> Benevolent Dictators are gentle authorities who understand that their power is the cornerstone of their children's sense of safety and security. Benevolent Dictators rule by virtue of natural authority. They know what's best for their children. They don't derive any pleasure out of bossing children around. They

govern because they must. . . . Benevolent Dictators do not need to instill fear in order to communicate their influence. They are authorities, but they are not authoritarian. . . . They restrict their children's freedom, but they are not tryants. . . . We must never, as long as our children are dependent on us, hand complete control of their lives over to them. Children respect their parents by obeying them. Parents, on the other hand, respect their children by insisting that they obey. . . . Learning obedience enhances a child's independence. . . . Children who fear their parents don't obey—they submit. Children who are obedient are not fearful. (Rosemond, 1981)

In this chapter and others to follow I hope to clear up the "authority waters" that have been muddied so badly, and help concerned parents and teachers looking for assistance avoid the obscurantism and mumbo jumbo that have only misled and confused them.

two

The Traditional Reward-and-Punish Approach

Remember the long list of synonyms we found for the verb "to discipline": govern, direct, hold in line, restrain, prohibit, restrict, constrain, and so on. Each identifies some form of control. Each implies the use of power. "Disciplining" children in the minds of most adults is but a euphemism for employing power to control them. Let's see exactly how this power-based control is supposed to work.

The aim of controllers is to place themselves in charge of their controllees, in a position to dominate or coerce them. The controller's wish, of course, is that the controllee will respond by being compliant, submissive, tractable, willing, nonresisting, yielding—euphemisms for *obedient*. Controllers *hope* that their controllees will always be obedient.

This is vividly illustrated in Dobson's book *The Strong-willed Child* (1978):

> A child learns to yield to the authority of God by first learning to submit (rather than bargain) to the leadership of his parents. . . . by learning to yield to the

loving authority (leadership) of his parents, a child learns to submit to other forms of authority which will confront him later in life . . . teachers, school principal, police, *neighbors*, and employers [italics added].

While Dobson uses the terms *submit* and *yield* in this passage, these are clearly his synonyms for *obey*. To Dobson, obedience training is necessary in the home to prepare children *to obey adult authority wherever or whenever they encounter it*. Even obey the neighbors!

Remember, too, that this sort of discipline is employed to bring about specific behaviors judged desirable by the *controller*. The goals or ends are always decided for the controllee by the controller. It is important to keep in mind that controllers may very well choose ends that are seen as beneficial to the child. Their intentions may be good. How many times when you were growing up did you hear: "You'll thank me when you're older," or "I'm only doing it for your own good"? I have observed, in fact, that most controllers—be they parents, teachers, bosses, cult leaders, or dictators—try to justify their use of control by this logic.

Most controllers, I'm certain, feel that they know what's best, because they're older, wiser, more experienced, better trained—whatever. And, for many of the authors of the dare-to-discipline books, their justification derives from their belief in the wisdom of the Bible. "But the Bible teaches it, and I believe it," James Dobson tells his readers.

There is also the possibility that controllers sometimes choose ends beneficial *primarily to themselves* rather than to the controllee, as when a teacher decides to expel from her class a student who is making her feel miserable by interfering with her need to teach her students. Controllers often deceive themselves into thinking they exercise control to help the controllee when actually they do it to meet their own needs. And in my experience, it is a rare youngster who views coercive power as being for his or her "own good."

WHERE DO CONTROLLERS GET THEIR POWER?

Now let's try to understand exactly how controllers acquire their capability. Why are they often successful? Where does their power come from? At some level everyone knows that the power of controllers comes from their use of the carrot and the stick—*rewards* and *punishments*.

Having possession of rewards—the means for satisfying some need of the controllee—is one source of a controller's power. If my small child is very hungry, by exploiting my exclusive access to the food I can use this reward power to make him set the table for me, saying, "Jimmy, if you set the table for me, you can sit down and start eating your dinner." Or if my daughter wants desperately to get a new dress, I can promise, "If you clean up your room every day this week, I'll give you the money for your new dress." This is controlling by promising consequences that will bring need-satisfaction to the child and thus be "rewarding."

The other source of power is possessing the means to inflict pain, deprivation, or discomfort on children. Wanting my son to eat his vegetables, I might threaten him with "Until you eat your vegetables, you stay at the table and no TV program." This is controlling by denying the child something that he or she wants, a consequence that will be felt as "punishing" or "aversive."

Rewards and punishments—these are the ultimate sources of the power of controllers to control, disciplinarians to discipline, dictators to dictate.

The diagram on page 24 illustrates these two sources of power that adult controllers have over children and youth: rewards ($+ +$) and punishments ($- -$), carrots and sticks. P stands for *power*. I've chosen the vastly different-sized circles in the diagram to emphasize that the adult-child relationship is almost always one in which there is a great power differential—that is, the adult possesses far greater means to reward or punish the child than the child has means to reward or punish the adult. This becomes less true when children get to be teenagers, of course.

With *very* young children, adults have in their possession a most impressive storehouse of things children want and need: food, clothes, things to drink, toys, coloring books, records,

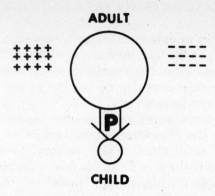

money, candy, gum, plus all sorts of pleasant things like singing or reading to them, playing with them, pushing them in their wagons, piggybacking them, hugging and kissing them.

Similarly, adults possess a mighty arsenal of punishments for young children. In addition to being able to punish by depriving them of any one of the above rewards, adults can inflict physical pain, restrain or restrict, confine children to their rooms, yell and scold, push them away, slap them, spank them, force unwanted food down their throats, instill fears in them ("You won't go to heaven," "God will punish you," "You'll drive me to an early grave"), give them "dirty looks," give them the silent treatment, and hundreds more that most readers can recall from their childhood years.

Clearly, parents and teachers have plenty of potential rewards and punishments. How do they use them?

HOW REWARDS ARE SUPPOSED TO WORK

Three conditions must always be met for rewards to work effectively or work at all:

1. The controllee must want or need something *strongly enough* to submit to the controller's control (to come up with the behavior the controller wants).

2. The reward offered by the controller must be seen by the child as *potentially satisfying some need*.

3. The controllee must be *dependent on the controller* to supply the reward (that is, the controllee is incapable of meeting the need by himself/herself).

Controllers have a choice of using rewards in one of two ways: (1) they may promise the reward contingent on the child's first doing what the controller wants (submitting to the control); (2) they may wait until they observe the child engaging in the desired behavior, at which time they then administer the reward as an unexpected favorable consequence. An example of controlling by promising a reward: you want your child to go to bed, so you say, "If you go to bed right now without a fuss, I'll read you a story." An example of controlling by rewarding after observing a desired behavior: A teacher wants a child to stop getting out of his seat, so when he observes the child staying in his seat the teacher smiles and says, "You're being a good little boy, staying in your seat."

Exercising control over children by using rewards goes by a variety of names, including behavior modification, behavior shaping, operant conditioning, positive reinforcement, behavior engineering, behavior management. (Some terms, such as *behavior modification* or *behavior management*, can also refer to control through punishment.) Whatever name is used, the basic method of control by rewards is to try to obtain some specific behavior by arranging that the consequences of the behavior are felt as positive or rewarding to the child. The principle is sound and quite well documented: *behavior that is rewarded tends to be repeated*.

Rewarding sounds benevolent enough—after all, are not the consequences (or, technically speaking, the *contingencies*) felt by the controllee as desirable, pleasant, satisfying? And, make no mistake about it, the method can work, as proven by countless experiments with children in a wide variety of behavioral settings—schools, hospitals, and various child-care institutions. It has successfully changed certain undesirable behaviors of autistic children, schizophrenic children, physically or mentally handicapped children, and other children confined to institutions.

However, this method of behavior modification has severe limitations and often fails to work, as I will explain more fully in the next chapter. For now, it's enough to stress that modifying and shaping children's behavior by deliberately arranging for the consequences to be positive and rewarding is sound in principle—but not nearly as easy to make work as it appears. In fact, it usually requires a very complex and time-consuming series of prescribed steps to change just *one* discrete behavior, like bed-wetting or hitting. Moreover, it requires that the controller have a very high level of technical knowledge about the reward method and how to apply it consistently and correctly. Finally, control by reward, as I explain later, brings out in children some bad side effects that most parents and teachers find distasteful. Because of all these problems, the method is hazardous and far from dependable, as you will see in Chapter 3.

HOW PUNISHMENT IS SUPPOSED TO WORK

Like rewards, punishment requires certain basic conditions to work effectively in controlling children's behavior:

1. The punishment must be felt by the controllee as depriving, noxious, denying, unwanted, injurious—i.e., it must be *aversive* to the controllee (antagonistic to his or her needs).
2. The punishment must be aversive enough to bring about elimination of the unwanted behavior.
3. The controllee must be unable to escape from the punishing situation or locked in the relationship because of dependency on the controller to provide what the controllee needs.

Punishment also can work in one of two ways. First, the adult can threaten to use punishment if the child does not change his or her behavior: "If you don't stop it this instant, I'll give you a thrashing you'll never forget," Second, the adult can actually administer the punishment as a consequence of some "unacceptable" behavior already performed by the child: "You disobeyed me and rode to the park, so now you can't ride your bike for a week."

Exercising control by using or threatening unpleasant or painful consequences also goes by a variety of names: behavior modification, aversive conditioning, avoidance training, behavior management, disciplining.

The basic principle upon which control by punishment operates is this: *behavior that brings punishment tends to be discontinued.*

However, it isn't nearly as simple and straightforward as that. As I will explain in Chapter 4, there are conditions and complexities that make this method just as difficult to administer as the use of rewards. Some of these factors are the timing of the punishment (it should come immediately after the unacceptable behavior) and the question of intensity (if the punishment isn't strong enough it won't work, yet if it's too severe the child will escape or stop trying altogether). Finally, control by punishment can have very serious side effects, not the least of which is seriously bruising the adult-child relationship and damaging the child either physically or psychologically, or both.

THE CONDITIONS FOR CONTROLLING WITH REWARDS AND PUNISHMENTS

So controlling with rewards or punishments requires that the controller be in possession of the appropriate means to either *meet* the needs of the child or *deprive* the child of meeting those needs. It's a simple matter of *need fulfillment* and *need deprivation*, externally engineered or managed by the controller, with the controller usually holding exclusive title to the means and taking full charge of arranging when they are doled out or dispensed. Thus, the controller has unquestioned mastery in the relationship, clearly the upper hand. *It is always an unequal relationship.*

Even more important, the controller is the one who chooses

the behaviors he or she judges as acceptable or unacceptable. The controller decides which behaviors are to be reinforced by rewards as well as those to be weakened by punishment. There are exceptions to this, as in the case of contracts to reward or punish certain behaviors that are agreed upon by both controller and controllee (for example, in programs that use mild electric shocks to get people to stop smoking). But by far the most frequent use of behavior modification by parents or teachers involves the controller alone deciding which are the desirable (or undesirable) behaviors.

For this kind of control to work, obviously the child must be kept in a continuous state of *dependency* and *fear*—dependent on the controller for the rewards he or she can offer, fearful of the punishments he or she can inflict. The child must also be kept locked in the relationship, unable to get for himself what the controller has to give and unable to escape the controller's feared punishment.

For example, a mother employing candy or food to reinforce a child's doing his chores or homework would lose her power to control if the child had access to all the candy or food he wanted. As children get older, and acquire the ability to earn money and buy their own snacks, parents stand to lose much of their power.

Similarly, a father who has employed physical punishment to try to decrease or eliminate his son's swearing will lose a lot of his power as soon as the youngster gets too big to be hit or spanked. This sequence happens in all families, in all classrooms. As children get older and bigger, as they increasingly find ways to avoid or escape adult punishment, teachers and parents lose their power; they run out of punishments that will be severe enough or aversive enough to control youngsters.

I've heard so many parents say something like, "Jan used to be such a good child but now that she's older we have almost no authority over her." What they mean is they have no more *power to control* her. And because they never learned how to *influence* their children, they now feel impotent. Later, I will offer a more precise and exhaustive explanation of the critical difference between controlling and influencing children. For now I only want to emphasize that parents and teachers generally lose most of their power when kids get older, because the conditions change: *You can't control others unless you keep them dependent on you, afraid of you, and unable to escape from the relationship easily.*

These conditions can be seen in many relationships. They were clearly present in the old master-slave relationship, both before and even a long time after the Emancipation Proclamation legally set the slaves free. They existed in the employer-employee relationships in most industrial organizations during the preunion decades of the Industrial Revolution. And, as everyone knows from experience, schoolchildren have always been dependent on teachers for grades and approval and afraid of their punishments. However, as employees acquired strength from their unions, and as students get older, the power of their controllers dissipates.

So it has been for women in the marriage relationship. Until quite recently, most wives were financially dependent on their husbands, and afraid to be assertive enough to resist their power. And, because it was not easy for women to get divorces, many were locked into the role of a controllee.

Cult leaders, too, exert control over their members, and dictators control the citizens of a country. Both foster extreme dependency and the dread of unpredictable punishment, and both severely restrict opportunities for leaving the group.

However, *relationships based on unequal power are very unstable and transitory, because they foment the very counteractions that will undermine and weaken the power of the controller.* One of the most common counteractions is dissent. Controllers may squelch it for a time, but it merely goes underground to emerge later as outright rebellion. In the words of writer Marilyn French (1985), "The dominator is continually besieged. . . . And although the power seeker may entertain the dream that someday he will be able to rest, that day does not occur until he is ousted from power or dies."

In families, we see teenagers rebelling against parents' use of power to change them or mold them in their image, against adults' coercing them to act according to what the adults think is right or wrong. When this happens the puzzled parents wonder why they have lost their ability to control their kids.

EXTERNAL VERSUS INTERNAL CONTROL

Now let's look deeper into the difference between two types of control in adult-child relationships—*external* control and *inner* control, adult discipline and self-discipline. Parents and teachers who manage and dispense rewards can be said to use *extrinsic* rewards for the external *control* of children. However, those who try to increase their children's capability to find their own pleasant conseqences (called *intrinsic* rewards) are helping them develop *inner* control.

Similarly, parents and teachers who inflict punishment are using external control as opposed to letting children learn inner control from the unpleasant consequences they bring on themselves. As I shall point out many times, ours is a society that is heavily committed to external control of our young people and sadly deficient in promoting inner control. We are avid and chronic disciplinarians with our children but unfortunately do little to promote self-discipline. In Chapter 10 I will offer some reasons why adults hate to give up externally imposed control.

To my knowlege, the P.E.T. and T.E.T. model of dealing with children is alone in renouncing external control by reward and punishment. Without exception, authors of other parenting and teaching books and training programs encourage the employment of rewards, including praise. Regarding control by punishment, many strongly endorse spanking and other forms of physical punishment. Some only caution against its *frequent* use or advise against employing *severe* physical punishment. Another very influential group of authors produces books and training programs that advocate only nonphysical punishment, although they don't call it that; instead they use more humane-sounding euphemisms.

One group, the "behaviorists" or "behavioristic psychologists," uses the terms *aversive conditioning* and *avoidance training*. Another group, much larger in number, teaches parents to employ "natural and logical consequences." This firmly rooted idea in child-rearing books has been promoted by followers of the Adlerian philosophy (of Alfred Adler, the psychoanalyst) or the Dreikurs approach (from Rudolph Dreikurs, author of two well-known books: *Children: The Challenge* [Dreikurs and Soltz, 1964] and *Challenge of Parenthood* [Dreikurs, 1948]).

Considering the wealth of sound principles in the Dreikurs approach to child rearing, it has always puzzled me to find the external-control component of the Dreikurs theory so weak and untenable. Let me explain why I find it so.

A core concept in the theory is that of *consequences* (what we earlier called "contingencies"). Dreikurs tells parents and teachers that children should suffer the consequences of their "misbehaviors." Consequences that will occur automatically, rather than being artificially arranged by adults, he labels "natural consequences." For example: a youngster forgets to tie her shoelaces and as a consequence falls down and skins her knee. Her pain (punishment) is a natural consequence, and Dreikurs wisely warns parents against softening the punishment—by reassurance, for example—for fear that the child might not learn to tie her shoelaces the next time. Suffering such a painful natural consequence as this would be *punishing* to most children and tend to weaken or eliminate that particular behavior (not tying shoelaces). In this case you might say it is nature that doles out the punishment.

Obviously, this is the way all children learn many of their valuable lessons. From such lessons they develop inner controls ("I'd better tie my shoelaces next time so I don't trip and fall"), and there's nothing wrong with that. In addition, even though it mildly hurt the child, this painful consequence certainly won't hurt the parent-child relationship in any way.

But Dreikurs apparently feels he must introduce "logical consequences," which he explains are those purposely designed by, engineered by, and implemented by the adult, as opposed to Mother Nature. Dreikurs's example: a child is late for dinner, so the parent announces that the child must suffer the logical consequences of going to bed without dinner.

Now to me it is perfectly clear that Dreikurs's concept of "logical consequences" is simply another name for the more straightforward term *punishment*. The child misbehaved, so the parent decides to punish him or her for it. But saying that the child has to be made to suffer the *logical* consequences (going to bed without dinner) seems to me no more than an attempt to justify the use of parental punishment by mitigating the guilt most parents feel when they punish their kids. Because Dreikurs somehow won't give up the concept of punishment in his theory of child rearing, he makes it sound "logical."

The concept of adults arranging for (or engineering) aversive consequences is at the heart of most parent-training programs. The most widely known are Positive Parenting, Systematic Training for Effective Parenting (STEP), and the video-based Active Parenting program. While these programs borrowed heavily from the P.E.T. course, including *all* the critical-communications and conflict-resolution skills in P.E.T., their advocacy of punishment makes these programs fundamentally different from P.E.T.

I maintain that it is not at all "logical" that, should my child be late for dinner, the aversive consequences are going to bed without dinner. In our family, the consequences (they seem quite "natural" to me) might be that my daughter might eat a cold dinner, or might heat it up in the microwave oven, or might fix a sandwich, or whatever. But being made to go to bed without dinner! Not only is that illogical, but it's an out-and-out attempt to control with punitive discipline. For this reason, the logical-consequences concept has no place either in the P.E.T. approach to effective parenting or the T.E.T. approach to effective teaching. It's nothing less than a euphemism for external control by punishment; it's another act of punitive discipline.

Let me make a final point. I have come to believe that many parent advisers who defend the use of punishment in their books and try to make it sound as if their ends justify the means, really abhor the idea of punishing children. Proof of their hidden antipathy toward punishment is that all of them warn against making the punishment too severe, against doing it frequently, and against doing it in anger.

Yet psychologists know (and these authors too may know) that to work as a deterrent, punishment must be severe enough to be felt as quite painful to the child. And the researchers who have conducted the very best experiments with punishment tell us it must be frequent as well as severe. In the somewhat academic language of two of the most distinguished researchers:

Punishment, when discontinued, usually results in a recovery of the punished response [behavior] to its previous state. However, when punishment is accomplished by a sufficiently intense stimulus [read: when it is *painful*], this recovery may be delayed for such extended periods that extinction [loss of the conditioned response] apparently fails. (Risley and Baer, 1973)

The bottom line is that today's parents and teachers are getting extremely bad advice from all the authors (and there are scores of them) who don't stand up against the use of punishment in our homes and schools. These authors first insist that their readers need to use punitive discipline, but then *literally insure that it won't work by telling their readers to make it weak, infrequent, and nonaversive.*

Finally, they ask of parents and teachers what is seldom possible: "Don't punish when you are angry." This translates into advising adults to wait a while until their anger subsides before they punish, else it might be too severe. But this idea is counter to the numerous research findings that show that punishment, to be effective at all, must come *immediately* after the unacceptable behavior has occurred, as well as be *severe* enough to be aversive.

Such conditions, I maintain, seldom can be arranged except in a laboratory-like setting managed by experts highly trained in the technology of behavior modification. If you still need to be convinced, I recommend the book *Changing Children's Behavior* (Krumboltz and Krumboltz, 1972).

In Chapter 3, I will be much more specific in explaining why rewards don't work effectively when parents and teachers use them to try to control children. And then in Chapter 4, I'll point out the deficiencies and dangers of punishment.

three

Why We
Can't Count On
Rewards Working

Using rewards to try to control children's behavior is so common that its effectiveness is rarely questioned. In every classroom in every school, teachers use elaborate systems of student control involving rewards—gold stars, grades, good-conduct scores, free-time privileges, preferential seating, jobs that help the teacher, putting kids' papers or artwork on display. Most teachers have a knee-jerk response of praising children to get them to behave or to achieve: "You draw such good flowers," "Your paper is so neat," "You were such good little boys and girls today."

Parents, too, rely heavily on rewards, especially with young children. They employ money to entice them to do their chores, offer them desserts to bribe them to eat their vegetables, stick up gold stars to motivate them to brush their teeth regularly, and promise gifts if they will do their homework. And, like teachers, parents use a lot of praise: "You were a good boy to help Mother set the table," "I'm going to tell Daddy how cooperative you were today," "What a nice job you did on the yard."

Because rewards are used so often with children, one might

assume that it must be an effective method of getting children to do what adults want. But is it? I am inclined to argue the other side: the fact that rewards are used so often and so unsuccessfully by so many teachers and parents proves they *don't* work very well. Otherwise how can we account for the universal problem of poor discipline in our classrooms, and the fact that most parents feel so impotent in dealing with the "misbehavior" of their children? It seems to me that neither teachers nor parents are very successful with their various reward systems. There are many reasons why this is so.

THE TECHNOLOGY OF CONTROLLING WITH REWARDS

The ineffectiveness of using rewards to control children is due in part to the fact that the method requires such a high level of technical competence on the part of the controller—a level few parents or teachers can ever attain. Modifying the behavior of children by arranging that the consequences of desirable behavior are rewarding to them is a science. Only a very small group of scientists understand fully the complex technology of behavior modification. Most of them are Ph.D. psychologists with years of training in the intricacies of conducting rigorous behavior-modification experiments in laboratories on a single specific behavior of either animals or humans.

These learning specialists have proven that rewards won't work unless they are administered immediately after the desired behavior occurs. (Give a dog a biscuit immediately after you get him to roll over, or else he won't do it the next time.) The behavioral engineers also have to follow a systematic schedule of dispensing the rewards—every time the desired behavior occurs at first, intermittently thereafter. In addition, the experimenters must carefully choose only those rewards that will satisfy some felt need of the controllee. Their experiments require keeping careful records of how often the desired behavior occurs so that the controllers can determine if in fact the controllee is changing. And the controllers must make certain they are not inadvertently rewarding some undesirable behavior, as for example when a child who is acting up in the classroom gets the teacher's attention (rewarding to the child). In the hands of even the best-trained practitioner, behavior modification with rewards invariably takes a great deal of time— sometimes as long as several months just to get a child to learn a single behavior pattern, such as going to the toilet instead of soiling his or her pants.

If you have any doubts about how complex and time-consuming behavior modification is, read the following lengthy excerpt from *Parent Power* by Dr. Logan Wright, a strong advocate of controlling children with rewards and punishments. For ten years, Dr. Wright was director of the Division of Pediatric Psychology at the University of Oklahoma Medical School. As we've seen, his book begins with these two sentences:

> The order of the day for any parent who wants to retain some semblance of sanity is to get and maintain control. But the most important reason for seizing control is that *you must be able to control a child before you can really support and love him* [italics in the original]. (Wright, 1980)

Later, Wright describes what he believes is the proper procedure for getting a shy child to greet people who come to the door:

> Begin by asking yourself what it means not to be shy, and set this as your goal. What would you like the child to be able to do without feeling uncomfortable? This is extremely important since it is not possible to reward improvements unless you know what your goal is. Okay, you decide that for his age a child should be able to greet people he does not know at the door, introduce himself and ask their names, and stay with them until the person whom they have come to visit arrives. The next step is to decide what the child already can do without discomfort. Let's say that he can watch from a distance as someone else answers the door. The next step would be to reward

him for getting closer to the door, for viewing the greeting process from a closer point. A common mistake at times like this is to get impatient and yank the child over to the door or even make him participate in the greeting process. Sometimes this gets the job done, though at considerable expense to the child. But sometimes it makes matters worse, so that the child stays even farther away than before. He might, for example, sneak out of the back door when he hears or sees visitors approaching. Be patient and remember that if you reward improvements, further improvements are certain to come. In this way you gradually reward the child for getting closer and closer, never requiring him to move forward, but rewarding him for whatever progress he makes. (Incidentally, it would speed things up if you could arrange to have visitors frequently; if the opportunity to reward improvements occurs only once a month, it would take forever to get the final desired behavior.) After a time, Bernie is quite willing to come to the door with you or some other member of the family to greet visitors. By now, you have the problem practically licked. (Wright, 1980)

My reaction to this method is that if it is this complicated and time-consuming to change only *one* simple behavior, no parent would ever find the time to use this method with the multitude of other desirable behaviors every parent would like to see—such as going to bed on time, taking proper care of toys, cleaning up messes, picking up clothes, not hitting baby brother, eating with mouth closed, brushing teeth daily, feeding the dog every night, getting up in time for school, phoning to let parents know where he or she is, and so on, ad infinitum. Furthermore, can you imagine a teacher having to depend on this complex method to modify the behaviors of thirty kids in her classroom? I can't. I must add that at our house it would have taken over a year before we had the required number of visitors knocking at our door when our daughter was home.

Considering all of the precise conditions that must be met

to make this complex method work and the inordinate amount of time it takes, I am convinced that behavior modification with rewards could *never* be a method of any practical use for either parents or teachers. The experts have achieved unquestionable success with the method in making retarded children learn to walk instead of crawl, autistic children learn to keep their glasses on, schizophrenic children to begin talking, and so on. But to expect parents and teachers to be equally effective with such a complex, specialized, and time-consuming technique seems absurd.

Obviously, there are those who disagree. Like Dr. Wright, some of them have written books in which they try to teach parents the complex technology of behavior modification. Though their books are readable and make the principles understandable, I seriously doubt that many parents or teachers would ever find the time or have the patience to employ the method effectively. Much like surgery, behavioral modification is a high-technology procedure requiring a specially trained person spending many hours with only one (or, at most, several) children in a strictly controlled, laboratory-like situation. Usually it is employed only after other, far simpler methods of modifying the behavior of a child have already been tried and have failed or are considered likely to fail.

DIFFICULTIES PARENTS AND TEACHERS ENCOUNTER WITH REWARDS

When parents and teachers do try to control children with rewards, they run into some very difficult problems. As a result, most of them give up trying, drop the use of rewards, and take up the use of punishment. Readers will recognize most of the following problems inherent in the use of rewards.

When Rewards Lose Their Value
Remember hearing your parents promise that Santa Claus would bring you lots of lovely presents provided you were a good little boy or girl for the several months preceding Christmas? For most youngsters, totally good behavior for several months would

be impossible anyway. And, because the prospect of getting the rewards was so far in the future, it would have little potency. My father promised me, when I was in my early teens, that I would get a gold watch if I didn't smoke until I was twenty-one. It had no power to prevent me from starting to smoke, because at the time a gold watch had little reward value for me, especially if I had to wait for it. Remember: *If getting a reward seems too far removed in time, it will be less potent.*

When Unacceptable Behavior Gets Rewarded

Several of my elementary-school teachers tried all kinds of elaborate reward systems to get me to be a good little boy in class. The problem was that my clowning behaviors brought laughter and amusement (and complete attention) from my classmates, which acted as a reward, reinforcing the very behavior that was unacceptable to the teacher. As a result, I greatly *increased*, rather than decreased, my clownish and disruptive behavior in each subsequent year in school, up through high school. Remember: *Controllers can't always prevent children from getting rewarded by others for the very behavior unacceptable to the controller.*

When Children Can Acquire Their Own Rewards

Rewards don't work if children are getting enough rewards on their own. As children grow older they always find more and more ways of decreasing their dependence on parents or teachers for the satisfaction of their needs. "If you do your chores every day this week, on Saturday I'll take you to see a movie" may be an effective incentive when a child is too young to earn money or have his own bike to get him to the movies. But after children are old enough to earn money, have an allowance, and/or use their own transportation, they can go to plenty of movies without submitting to their parents' control. Recalling my own childhood, before I was nine years old I was earning several dollars a week mowing grass or picking strawberries. Moreover, my friends and I always had our bikes to ride to the nearby theaters. Remember: *For rewards to work effectively for controllers, children must be unable to acquire the rewards on their own—they must be kept dependent, needful, deprived.* Imagine teaching a dog to roll over by using a doggie bone as a reward—right after the dog has eaten a big dinner.

When Rewards Seem Too Hard to Earn

Often behavior modification fails because the price is just too high for the child to earn the offered reward. Take grading as an example. Because of the way most grading systems work, especially when teachers grade "on the curve," approximately 50 percent of students may receive below-average grades. This means, as everyone (including educators) knows, that the reward value of getting A's and B's is very weak, if not nil, for many students: They simply give up trying to get A's because they know they are unlikely to earn the very small percentage of top grades most teachers reserve for the brightest and most gifted in their classes. Remember: *Rewards have to be felt by children as attainable.*

When Acceptable Behavior Goes Unrewarded

It's absurd to expect parents to hover over their children for hours on end waiting for them to do something acceptable so they can dutifully administer a reward. Most of a child's behavior necessarily will never be observed, because Mother and Dad are too busy, or the child is out of sight or not at home. This means that it is often impossible for parents to reward some desired behavior every time it occurs. However, the experts stress that it is absolutely essential for controllers to do that, particularly when first starting the behavior-modification effort. For teachers, who usually have a whole roomful of active kids to whom they must attend, it is impossible to notice each desired behavior as it occurs. Nor is it always possible to be consistent in handing out rewards. Have you ever heard a youngster complain, "You thanked Jimmy for helping carry the groceries in, but I did it yesterday and you didn't even notice"? Remember: *When the desired behavior goes unrewarded, it takes much longer for it to be reinforced and become firmly established.*

When Kids Work Only for the Rewards

"Do you like my picture?"

"Do you think I'm a good speller, teacher?"

"Was I a good boy today?"

"Did you notice how clean my room was?"

"Because I ate all my vegetables, can I have two scoops of ice cream?" These are messages that signal that a child is being taught by parents or teachers that he or she should *always expect to get some sort of payment for good behavior.*

One of the pernicious effects of the grading system in our schools is that some students become far more covetous of the grades they'll get than of increasing their knowledge or improving their skills. This is known as "working for grades"— working for the school's *extrinsic* rewards as opposed to getting enjoyment and satisfaction (*intrinsic* rewards) from the performance of the schoolwork and the learning acquired.

In the extreme, working for grades shows up in cheating, copying, plagiarizing, cramming before exams, padding references, and all the other things students do to "get good grades."

I have seen a small child totally engrossed in building an intricate house out of blocks or Tinkertoys, getting great satisfaction solely from meeting the challenges of the task and clearly getting intrinsic rewards from his or her own performance. If any evaluation of the performance is going on, it's solely within the child.

Now contrast that with another situation, in which the child is shaping an animal out of moist clay, stopping every step of the way to show her parent what she has done, asking such questions as, "Do you like my horse?" "Is the head all right?" "Am I doing it right?" With some children it is clear that the source of evaluation is their parents or teachers. (Psychologists call this an "external locus of evaluation.")

Praise especially acts as an extrinsic reward, and its effect on children is quite predictable. Children who are subjected to frequent praise learn to select only those things they think will please their parents and avoid doing those things that may not. While to some parents this may seem very desirable, we know that such children are much less apt to become innovative, creative, self-directing. They learn to conform rather than innovate, and to follow a pattern known to bring praise rather than to experiment with something new.

Using a lot of rewards with children runs the risk of raising youngsters who derive little or no pleasure from activities and accomplishments *unless* they receive rewards or approval. Such children get little enjoyment from playing a sport unless they get accolades from winning, little pleasure from learning in school unless they get good grades for doing so, little satisfaction from doing things for other people unless they earn some kind of "brownie points" for their behavior. The tragedy is that a failure to win accolades or to get top grades or to earn brownie points for being considerate often causes youngsters to drop those activities out of their lives, thus denying themselves the intrinsic pleasure of just *doing* things, enjoying the activities themselves.

The use of extrinsic rewards to control or motivate children, whether in the form of praise, grades, special privileges, or gold stars, actually tends to undermine intrinsic motivation, thus influencing youngsters to quit an activity. Extrinsic motivators are not only ineffective but corrosive; they eat away at the kind of motivation that *does* produce achievement, competence, and self-esteem.

Alfie Kohn, author of *No Contest: The Case Against Competition* (Kohn, 1986), cites a study that confirms the negative effect of competition. Students were given a puzzle to solve. Some were told to solve it faster than their neighbors, others were not given this instruction. All the students were timed and asked to write how interested they had been in trying to solve the puzzle. The investigator concluded:

> Trying to beat another party is extrinsic in nature and tends to decrease people's intrinsic motivation. . . . It appears that when people are instructed to compete at an activity, they begin to see that activity as an instrument for winning rather than an activity which is mastery-oriented and rewarding in its own right. (Deci et al., 1981)

The late John Holt, a renowned and respected critic of our schools, understood the harmful effect of extrinsic rewards on schoolchildren:

We destroy the . . . love of learning in children, which is so strong when they are small, by encouraging and compelling them to work for petty and contemptible rewards—gold stars, or papers marked 100 and tacked to the wall, or A's on report cards, or honor rolls, or dean's lists, or Phi Beta Kappa Keys—in short, for the ignoble satisfaction of feeling that they are better than someone else. (Holt, 1982)

Remember: *Getting rewards, especially praise, can become addictive and can undermine a child's motivation.*

When the Absence of Reward Feels Like Punishment

You've probably heard the story of the wife with the new hat who says to her husband, "You haven't said anything nice about my new hat, so you must hate it." So it goes with using praise and compliments to control children. If they get accustomed to receiving frequent praise, they worry when they don't get it.

In school, when teachers use a lot of rewards usually reserved for the performance of the best few students, the majority of students will feel the absence of rewards as unpleasant, aversive, punishing. The result: they stop putting forth effort on assignments. This also explains why some children seem always to be fishing for compliments if they are not getting enough from adults.

The weakening of the effect of rewards over time has been experimentally confirmed. It was found that the more praise was used at home, the less effective it was as a reinforcement for learning a laboratory task. Children become "accustomed" or adapted to a given level of praise and pay less attention to it. The interpretation of these findings by Eleanor Maccoby and John Martin in the prestigious *Handbook of Child Psychology* is as follows:

If parental praise is to get an effect, then it must either be used sparingly, or must be escalated in intensity or frequency so as to exceed a gradually rising adaptation level. Similar problems attend the use of rewards. If they are given regularly, they come to be expected, and their absence is experienced as punishment, whereas their presence may no longer stand out as rewarding. (Maccoby and Martin, 1983)

Remember: *Getting no rewards may feel like punishment; getting a lot of rewards may weaken their effect.*

A DEEPER ANALYSIS OF PRAISE

The experts in behavior modification stress the difference between *primary* and *secondary* reinforcers (rewards). Primary rewards are those that meet the basic survival needs of children—for example, food, water, warmth, touching. Most of the authors of behavior-management books for parents readily admit to the severe limitations of using such primary rewards to control children's behavior. Why? Because most older children get all their basic survival needs met and adults can't control them by capitalizing on their deprivation as they can with very young children. Besides, making the child "work" for food or water is simply cruel and exploitative; no normal parent would follow such a path. (Although some exceptions have been reported in the press.)

This is why the power-to-the-parent advocates advise parents whose children have grown beyond infancy or the toddler stage to switch to the strategy of employing *secondary reinforcers*: attention, hugs and kisses, acknowledgments, and principally *praise*. Dr. Logan Wright, author of *Parent Power*, explains this clearly:

> But primary reinforcers have rather severe limitations, especially for older children who live at home rather than in hospitals. For one thing, food isn't reinforcing (has no reward value) unless a child is hungry. . . . Because of these and other limitations, primary reinforcers are ordinarily useful only with very young children. . . . Secondary reinforcers include most of the good things in life: attention, praise, success, hugs, and kisses. (Wright, 1980)

The message of Wright and other behavioral engineers seems loud and clear: when you see that you can no longer manipulate or control children by failing to satisfy their biological (survival) needs, don't give up. You still have plenty of power left through capitalizing on other kinds of deep needs—children's longing for your approval, affection, and attention. But do teachers and parents really "have plenty of power" in the form of such secondary rewards? Let's look deeper—specifically at praise.

I emphasized earlier that controlling another person by rewards requires that the controllee must want or need something strongly enough to submit to the controller's control. Now the question is: Is praise strongly enough needed so that it will work for parents and teachers? Will children readily submit to the wishes of adults out of a need for praise? My experience says, "Don't count on it." Especially with older children.

The mere idea of putting praise to work to control children has an enticing ring to it, doesn't it? It *sounds* quite benevolent, and how could it not be seen as in the best interests of the child? Praising children also *looks* easy. And parents and teachers are not likely to feel the pangs of guilt with praise that they usually feel when they punish. Finally, praise at first blush seems to be something everyone needs, everyone wants. For all these reasons, it is used a lot. And most adults have high hopes that it will get youngsters to do what they want them to do. As my father used to say, "Praise 'em and they'll work their heads off." But will they?

I have come to believe that praise as a method for controlling children is grossly overrated, because it is usually ineffective and is often damaging to the adult-child relationship.* In addition, praise may bring out a number of undesirable and unsociable characteristics in children. To understand why, we must first agree on a definition of praise.

---

* I am indebted to Richard Farson for first pointing out in an article in the *Harvard Business Review* (Farson, 1963) why praise is so often ineffective.

What Is Praise?

Here is my definition of the word *praise*: a verbal message that communicates a positive evaluation of a person, a person's behavior, or a person's accomplishment.

Some examples of praising messages:

"You've been a good boy [or girl]."
"You are getting to be a very good tennis player."
"You did the right thing in refusing to go."
"You have such beautiful hair."
"You paint such beautiful pictures."
"Your game has really improved."
"You're doing much better with your homework."
"You have the intelligence to get top grades."
"You did a very fine job."

Note that all of these messages contain the pronoun *You*, followed by some positive evaluation of something about "you"— your appearance, your behavior, your accomplishments, your characteristics. Later, I'll contrast these "You-messages" with an entirely different kind of positive message, which back in 1964 I labeled "I-messages"—for example: "I appreciated your help tonight because I was so tired." Positive I-messages such as this do not fall into my definition of praise, and they seldom produce the undesirable effects that You-messages do. But for now let's see what problems are inherent in using praise to control children.

The "Hidden Agenda" in Most Praise

Parents, teachers, and other adults, as everyone remembers, often use praise for the primary purpose of trying to change youngsters in some specific way—motivate them to do better, keep up the good work, act nice, make a good appearance, or repeat some other desired behavior. Their intent is to reinforce (reward) some behavior that they value as good, proper, and right. Thus, behind almost every praising message exists the unstated purpose of wanting to change a child. I call it a "hidden agenda," because the purpose of the adult is almost never clearly stated and put out on the table.

When a father says to his twelve-year-old daughter, "You look so pretty tonight with a dress on," his unstated hidden agenda might be, "I wish you'd wear dresses more often rather than those jeans." Or when a teacher says, "Class, you've been very quiet and industrious today," the likely hidden agenda is, "Why can't you be like this every day?"

I recall my father saying to my brother and me, "You boys really did a fine job on the yard today." We knew, however, that Dad was using his tried-and-true principle that I mentioned earlier: "Praise 'em and they'll work their heads off."

Thus, the intention of adults when they use praise is not solely the benevolent one of making the *child* feel good. It's a desire to engineer a behavior change that will make the *adult* feel good—getting a neat yard, seeing a daughter wear what the parent prefers, having a quiet class. Kids usually see through such praise and recognize the adult's hidden agenda.

Praise, then, is often meted out for the convenience, pleasure, or benefit of the praiser. When a parent or teacher praises, the attitude *may* be "I want to make my child feel good," but it can also be "I want to change the child so *I'll* feel good." Parents and teachers who use praise in this way may come to be perceived by youngsters as manipulative, controlling, and not completely honest.

This was precisely the finding of three researchers looking for causes of high achievement in students. In that study, tests of achievement in social studies, science, math, and reading were given to 311 students in the sixth and seventh grades. Their parents filled out a lengthy questionnaire on their child-rearing practices. The findings were most unexpected.

Mothers high in warmth and who permitted the free expression of aggression had children who had scored very high. Mothers who punished often and rarely used reasoning had children who had done poorly on the tests. The surprising finding was that fathers who used a great deal of praise had children who did less well, especially in science and reading. The researchers' explanation: *The parent who praises constantly is certainly doing it for the purpose of pushing the child into further compliance. The praise does not come across as sincere or as really earned.* (Barton, Dielman, and Cattell, 1974)

How Praise Can Communicate Criticism
In the hidden agenda of wanting children to change, which is
part of many praising messages, there is an underlying criticism.
Let's study the following typical dialogue:

> MOTHER: You're driving a lot more carefully today.
> JANIE: What do you mean "more carefully today"? I'm
> always careful.
> MOTHER: I don't think you're always careful.
> JANIE: What do I do that's dangerous? Tell me.

Scenarios such as this are common in families. Parent
praises; child hears criticism and feels the parent's unspoken
desire to change the youngster. It happens a lot, because praise
so often is manipulative—an indirect, unspoken desire to shape
or control a child's behavior by contrasting some acceptable
behavior with the unacceptable behavior. Each experience
youngsters have with praise in which there is an implied criticism
makes them increasingly certain of the parents' real intentions.

Children, like most people, don't like to be manipulated.
They strongly resent disguised attempts to control them, especially with messages that contain subtle, indirect criticisms. In
fact, when they see through the praising message and identify
the hidden criticism, the positive statement such as "You're
driving more carefully today" is often overlooked or ignored.
So instead of feeling good about driving carefully, Janie, in the
above example, feels criticized and is defensive and resentful. She'll probably forget the praise and remember only the
criticism.

Contrary to what most people think, praise often contains
an element of *nonacceptance* of the child. When a teacher says
to a student, "Today you understood the lesson because you
were attentive," the message that most likely comes through to
the student is "Mostly you're *inattentive*, and that's unacceptable
to me."

Praise can also have the effect of defining the relationship
in the eyes of the child as one of superior and inferior, judge
and judged. From my own experience I know that when I
assume the role of judge and evaluator in a relationship, my

underlying attitude is usually a feeling of superiority to the person I am evaluating. In effect, I'm saying that I know better, I have more experience, I'm wiser. If I say to my daughter after our match, "Honey, you played a nice game of tennis today," I am also implying that I think I am highly qualified to judge her tennis—certainly more qualified than she. Better to say, "I sure had to work harder and smarter playing you today."

To understand how praise involves putting oneself above the person praised, imagine yourself just having heard a performance by a famous violinist (and you've never touched a violin in your life). Can you imagine how ridiculous it would sound if you said something like: "Your technique was flawless and your interpretation was brilliant?" If you are like me, you would never send this praising message, because you know you are not qualified to judge someone so far superior to you on the violin. Contrast that message with "I so enjoyed your concert tonight" or "I was in awe of your talent."

There is always the risk, when people praise, that an attitude of superiority will come across, thus reinforcing a feeling of inferiority in the child. Praise so often is an act of one-upmanship. In fact, for praise to have *any* effect, the relationship must be one where one person is clearly superior and the other inferior—one person a "have" and the other a "have-not."

Sometimes adults use praise to soften up a child before they send a critical message, as in these examples:

"Sally, you're doing better than you were before, but you still need a lot of improvement."

"Pete, it was nice of you to wash the dishes, but you didn't put any of them away."

Not infrequently the effect of these double messages is that one fails to hear the positive evaluation (or forgets it) and responds only to the criticism.

A variation of these softening-up messages goes by the name of the "sandwich technique," which, unfortunately, is sometimes recommended as an effective way to deal with youngsters. In this technique, a critical message is "sandwiched" in between two praising messages:

> "Katie, you're obviously trying harder now, but you're still making careless mistakes in arithmetic. I know you're the kind of person who can do anything when you put your mind to it."

> "Mark, your teeth look a lot cleaner than they did a month ago, but you're forgetting to brush at night. You're smart enough to know that food in your teeth all night can cause cavities."

> "You look so nice tonight, Phillip. Of course, you'd look better if you brushed your hair, but you're really showing a lot of improvement in your grooming."

It's not hard for youngsters to see the sandwich technique for what it is—an indirect (and therefore manipulative) attempt at controlling. When they get messages like this from parents or teachers, kids realize that the *real* intent is to criticize and call attention to *unacceptable* behavior—not to praise the acceptable behavior.

For this reason, parents and teachers who make frequent use of praise coupled with critical messages run the risk of being perceived by their children as manipulative, indirect, phony, insincere—sometimes as downright dishonest!

When Praise Doesn't Match a Child's Own Evaluation

It is surprising how often children deny the validity of adults' praise. It doesn't ring true because it doesn't match the child's self-evaluation, as in these examples:

> MOTHER: I think your sand castle is just terrific.
> JIMMY: I don't think it's very good. Sally's is a lot better.

> DAD: You're doing real good, Judy. Before long you'll be hitting that baseball a mile.
> JUDY: Oh, Dad, I'm lousy and you know it. I'll never be a good hitter.

When praise comes across as "simply not true," the chances are good that a child will develop doubts about the adult's integrity. How many times have you heard responses to praise like these?

"It's not *that* good."
"I think it stinks."
"I'm *not* pretty."
"You're only saying that to make me feel good."
"That's all *you* know."
"I *hate* my picture."
"I could have done lots better."

Just as important, we know that when praise doesn't match a child's own self-concept, it may be felt as the adult's denial of the child's feelings, a lack of true understanding of the child. This is especially true at those times when youngsters already have expressed some negative feelings about their performance or progress. At these times, praise can be a strong barrier to further communication between parent and child. When children think their parents or teachers don't genuinely understand how bad they're feeling, they get discouraged about talking further. For this reason, praise can make adults miss countless opportunities to be helpful counselors for children. In the following dialogue, note how Susie's mother's praise causes Susie to become defensive and finally stop talking about the serious problem she's having at school:

SUSIE: I wish I were back in elementary school.
MOTHER: Why do you feel that way, honey?
SUSIE: I don't have any good friends in junior high, except maybe Dawn.
MOTHER: Well, I'll bet there are lots of girls in your class who would be glad to be your friend.
SUSIE: Then how come I haven't made any friends? Tell me that.
MOTHER: It takes a little while going into a new school. You've always succeeded at anything you put your mind to. Just try a little harder to be friendly and more sociable.

SUSIE: Mom, you don't understand! I *have* been trying. I don't want to talk about it anymore.

When someone is sharing a problem, praise acts as a roadblock. Try this experiment: Next time you're with someone who starts sharing a personal problem with you, send some strong, positive evaluations of the person. Then observe how your praise blocked communication. And listen particularly to the defensive responses you'll undoubtedly get. You'll see that praise may stop people in their tracks.

People unhappy or disappointed with themselves or the way things are going in their lives respond to any kind of positive evaluation as a denial of their true feelings of the moment—which, of course, are far from positive. This explains why praise often provokes such responses as:

"You don't really understand."
"You wouldn't say that if you knew how I feel."
"That's easy for you to say."
"I wish I could be as optimistic as you."

Praise Heightens Sibling Rivalries and Competitiveness

Perhaps you can remember how it felt as a child when one of your classmates, or your brother or sister, received praise but you didn't. You may have felt jealous, resentful, or even angry. A failure to get praise or approval can feel like an actual rejection: "You don't like me as much as you do Jimmy!"

In a family in which parents use a lot of praise, competition for the praise is usually very high between the children: "My picture is prettier than yours." Children will sometimes tell lies to build themselves up and tear down their brother or sister: "Barbie won the Monopoly game, but she cheated!"

Because it's next to impossible for parents or teachers to dole out praise equitably all the time, children are going to feel sometimes that their parents are being unfair or they're playing favorites: "How come you told Eric how good he was flying his kite when mine went a whole lot higher?"

On a personal note, I have experienced a lot of sadness recalling how my older brother, John, received so much less praise from our parents than I did. I realize now how hurt he must have felt, hearing both Mother and Dad praise me so much more. He spent most of his adolescence, and later his adult years, desperately trying to find ways to earn their approval, but seldom felt successful. Throughout his life he was convinced that I was the favorite of our parents while he was their big disappointment. He also went through life with low self-esteem. And I know much of his hurt could have been avoided, had my parents been aware of the pitfalls of praise.

How Praise Stunts Decision-Making Ability

As children grow older and have to make important life decisions, strong dependence on parental approval and praise can work against their best interests. Many disastrous career choices have been based on parental desires ("My parents wanted me to be a lawyer, but I would have preferred being an artist"). Most parents sincerely want their children to become self-reliant and to make satisfying long-term choices. Yet they don't realize that praise can stifle the development of self-reliance and independent decision-making ability by teaching children to place too heavy an emphasis on making choices that will win parental approval.

EFFECTIVE ALTERNATIVES TO PRAISE

It's only natural in our relationships with others that something they do or say will on occasion evoke a strong positive feeling within us—appreciation, relief, delight, surprise, pleasure or love. How are we to respond in these situations without using praise and running all the risks I've just described? There are some viable alternatives to praise, and they are far less likely to have negative effects on your relationships.

The Positive I-Message

One alternative to praise is a clear message that expresses to another precisely how his or her behavior made you feel. In all our Effectiveness Training classes, we urge people to use such messages instead of praise. Called *Positive I-messages*, these are accurate, self-disclosing, self-revealing messages that clearly share what is going on *inside you*:

I feel good when . . .
I was pleasantly surprised when . . .
I was relieved when . . .
I enjoyed it so much when . . .
I got excited when . . .

Keep in mind that praise is usually a statement about *others*—how *they* look, what *they* said, what *they* did. As such, praise will logically come out as *You-messages*, followed by judgments or evaluations.

"You did a fine job."
"You are so well coordinated."
"Your speech was excellent."
"You have such beautiful skin."

I-messages, on the other hand, communicate something about yourself, not evaluations of the other person. This difference is crucial, because evaluations are the very parts of praise that cause so many problems. Do you see this important difference illustrated in the following comparisons?

Situation: Your seven-year-old played quietly and happily all the time your friend was in your home visiting this morning:
"You were such a good girl [or boy] while Mrs. Jenkins was here." (PRAISE)
"I really liked being able to talk to Mrs. Jenkins this morning without any interruptions." (POSITIVE I-MESSAGE)

Situation: Your twelve-year-old pitched in without your asking and cleaned up all the mess that remained after his or her birthday party:
"You were thoughtful and considerate to clean up after the party." (PRAISE)
"I felt so relieved when I saw how you cleaned up

everything, because I was so tired after the party, I was dreading the job of cleaning up." (POSITIVE I-MESSAGE)

You might try the brief exercise below to help you sharpen your skill in sending Positive I-messages. In the left column is a list of typical praising messages, all judgmental You-messages. Read each one and then substitute a Positive I-message that would communicate clearly to your child how his or her behavior might make you feel in that situation. Write your I-message in the right column. To help you, here is a simple formula you might use to formulate a good Positive I-message: Express both how your child's behavior makes you feel and why it makes you feel that way—that is, the tangible and concrete effect your child's behavior or achievement has made on your life. Read the example and then go ahead and finish the exercise.

You-message	*I-message*
1. You were such a good boy to put your breakfast dishes in the dishwasher this morning.	1. Not having to put your dishes away this morning made me feel good—it saved me some work.
2. You're being a lot more responsible about taking the garbage out every day.	2.
3. You showed very good judgment not going to that party, where you knew there would be drinking.	3.
4. You behaved like a little lady when the guests arrived and you hung up all their coats.	4.
5. You're getting to be a much better sport when you lose at the family games we play.	5.

Of course, Positive I-messages must be *believable* to your children. Therefore, they must be honest and genuine—messages that accurately represent your real feelings at the time and how strongly you feel them. I-messages will usually meet these requirements if they are spontaneous, genuine, and free from any hidden agendas. By "spontaneous" I mean here-and-now feelings—unplanned and usually unexpected. By "genuine" I mean that the messages closely match your inner feelings. If you say, "I felt so good that you remembered my birthday by buying me a lovely card," be very sure that you're not feeling a little disappointed because the youngster didn't buy you a present! Finally, when I say "free of hidden agendas," I mean that your I-message is not motivated by an intent to educate, preach, evaluate, or bring about some behavior modification in your child—as is apparent in these double messages:

> "I like the way you have fixed your hair tonight much better than the way you usually pin it up."

> "It pleases me to see you finally taking responsibility for doing your jobs around the house."

> "I really like it when you take the time to finish something you start for a change."

> "Now those are the kind of grades that really make me feel proud of you."

The Active Listening Response
Another effective alternative to praise is a verbal response that expresses nothing more than empathic understanding and acceptance of what a child is expressing or experiencing. It involves first listening with your ears and then proving with your mouth that you've understood. Here is a dialogue that illustrates a mother Active-Listening to a child who is in effect asking for praise:

TOMMY: Do you think I've made any improvement in keeping my room clean?
MOTHER: It sounds like maybe *you* think you have, Tommy, is that right?
TOMMY: Yeah, it's a little better than it used to be.
MOTHER: You can see a *few* improvements?

TOMMY: Yeah, but I still forget to empty my wastebasket.

MOTHER: That particular job is hard for you to remember to do.

TOMMY: Right. I guess I need something to remind me. Maybe I'll make a sign and hang it on my door.

In this exchange, Tommy's mother took a very special posture: she didn't evaluate, she didn't praise, she didn't involve herself at all in the content of the problem, which happened to be the condition of her son's room. Instead, she became a mirror to Tommy's feelings, reflecting back to him what she thought she heard him say: "*You* think you've made some progress," "*You* can see a few changes yourself," "That job is hard for *you* to remember to do."

In contrast, she could have chosen to praise with, "Yes, I see real progress, Tommy, and I'm proud." Instead she chose to listen and acknowledge Tommy's feelings. She also learned more about what was in her son's thoughts; praising probably would have ended the conversation at the start. Her responses to Tommy are very special responses called Active Listening: listening with your ears, then "feeding back" in your own words what you heard. Note how the Active Listening led Tommy into solving the wastebasket problem.

Why might a parent choose Active Listening instead of sending a Positive I-message? Because there are some important benefits when parents use Active Listening. One of these was illustrated in the interchange with Tommy. Did you notice how Tommy shifted from asking for his *mother's* evaluation to offering his *own* evaluations of his progress? With her Active Listening, Tommy's mother effectively threw the ball back into her son's lap, keeping the locus of evaluation with the real owner of the problem, Tommy.

What does that do? Why keep the locus of evaluation with the child? Two important benefits result from doing this: (1) productive problem-solving often begins to occur, as with Tommy's coming up with a solution to forgetting the wastebasket; and (2) the parent provides an opportunity for a small increment of growth for the child—growth toward self-responsibility, growth toward less dependence on the parent, growth toward becoming the active solver of his own problems.

To summarize our analysis of using either tangible rewards or praise to control children, my counsel is that there are real risks. You're not an expert behavioral engineer; the method is too complex and time-consuming; your kids will detect your intent and see you as devious and indirect (which most people are when they use praise to control); you'll be fostering some behaviors you won't like in your children, such as dependency, jealousy, and sibling rivalry; you'll be seen as judgmental and evaluative, which will inhibit open and honest communication from your children; and you'll miss countless opportunities to help your child become a self-evaluative, self-directing, self-controlling problem solver.

But also remember, it will always feel good to your children, on those rare occasions (quite rare, in my experience) when you witness them doing something or saying something special that makes you feel unusually warm, appreciative or loving inside, if you tell them clearly how *you* feel—without judging *them*, without intending to change *them*. Obviously you won't be intending to control your children at those moments, but what you say will certainly *influence* them! This kind of message, as you know, can't be planned; it will just pop out spontaneously. And don't worry too much if it's not always a perfect I-message.

"Wow! You look absolutely radiant in that dress."
"I love to look at that picture you painted."
"You did the dishes while I shopped. How very nice."
"I'm amazed sometimes at your sensitivity."
"What a cute hairdo!"

We need another term besides *praise* for these rare, un-planned, noncontrolling messages.

The
Deficiencies and
Dangers of Punishment

In the landmark book *Beyond Closed Doors: Violence in the American Family* (Straus, Gelles, Steinmetz, 1980) the authors report that 84 to 97 percent of all parents surveyed said they used physical punishment at some time in their children's lives; mothers who beat up their children do it more than once every other month. Hitting, spanking, or beating children undoubtedly occurs frequently in American families.

Such a high incidence of physical punishment confirms the ineffectiveness of rewards. In most homes, when parents learn that rewarding *desirable* behaviors doesn't work, they drop that and start punishing *undesirable* behaviors.

We can only guess at how many parents employ other kinds of punishment besides physical—confinement to one's room, being sent to bed without dinner, making the child atone for "being bad" by doing extra work, "grounding," the "silent treatment," deprivation of a favorite toy or a bike, forced feeding, having the child remain at the dinner table until a distasteful food has been finished, calling the child derogatory names, humiliation in front of friends, yelling, ignoring. No doubt in my mind, close to 100 percent of parents use some form of punishment as a primary method for controlling children. I've asked audiences of parents how many were never punished as a child. Seldom have I seen a hand raised.

In schools it is no different, although reports show that the frequency of paddling students in the United States has decreased from 1.5 million in 1976 to 792,556 in 1982, with the national average about 3.5 percent of students paddled in a year (Maurer, 1984). However, we must add other forms of assault on schoolchildren that go unreported: slapping, cuffing, grabbing, yanking, shaking, dragging, shoving, kicking, banging a child against the wall, washing a child's mouth with noxious substances, not allowing a child to go to the bathroom, allowing or encouraging bullies to torment a child, deliberately provoking a child to violence, taping a child's mouth shut, tying a child to the desk, forcing a child to do push-ups or run laps, denying a child adequate free time for recess and lunch, making a child stand in a corner for an hour.

In schools other nonphysical forms of punishment are employed. For example: using racial slurs, cursing or screaming at a child, insulting a child about appearance or a disability, deliberately ignoring a child who needs help, using sarcasm or put-downs, punishing the whole class for the behavior of an individual, setting up a child to be scapegoated, meddling in a child's friendships, and so on.

Obviously there are innumerable ways for parents and teachers to punish children. The evidence is clear that they are used frequently. What is the evidence for its effectiveness?

Punishment has a lot of what psychologists call "face validity"—that is, it looks like it works on the face of it. Everyone has seen a child stop some disruptive or troublesome behavior in the supermarket immediately after being given a smack by an upset parent. Children's disruptive behavior in the classroom, too, is sometimes inhibited—at least temporarily—by the teacher's threat of punishments. So, both punishments and threats to punish at times do change children's behavior. However, as we found with rewards, certain specific conditions must be met before punishment can be made to work effectively *and* retain its effectiveness over a period of time. And these conditions are very difficult for parents and teachers to meet.

IT TAKES EXPERTISE
TO MAKE PUNISHMENT WORK

Like rewards, punishment must be administered with considerable expertise to be effective in controlling children; yet most parents or teachers obviously have not received the extensive training needed to make them competent in this highly technical methodology. Because of this, they stand little chance of making punishment work effectively. It is true that psychologists have been successful in using painful electric shocks to help people quit smoking, and they have employed the same method successfully in modifying troublesome behavior by mentally retarded, handicapped, and emotionally disturbed children. Yet it requires a controlled, laboratory-like environment, and the controllers must follow certain prescribed procedures to achieve results, such as the following:

1. A behavior once punished should always be punished.
2. The punishment should be administered immediately after the disapproved behavior has occurred.
3. Punishment should not be done in the presence of other children; otherwise, the child may be embarrassed and become aggressive toward the controller.
4. The punisher should take care that the behavior is *never* rewarded.
5. Children should not be punished too severely or too often, or they may withdraw (stop trying, leave the scene, quit school, run away from home, quit the team, escape with alcohol and drugs).

These are not the easiest principles to follow, for either parents in the home or teachers in the classroom.

Take the first principle: *Once punished, always punished.* Most teachers violate this principle every day. And understandably so. How can a teacher possibly punish *every* child who whispers, *every* time it happens? She wouldn't have any time left to teach! Then, too, most teachers I've known ignore certain disruptive behaviors on days they feel good while punishing the same behavior on days they feel like climbing the wall. That's being inconsistent, but that's the way most teachers are—they're human.

Consider the second principle: *Punish quickly*. Psychologists who are considered experts in the field of behavior modification are in agreement that the most effective use of punishment calls for applying it almost simultaneously with the occurrence of the undesired behavior. Any delay in punishment results in a reduction in its effectiveness (Azrin and Holz, 1966). In a systematic review of over sixty research studies on punishment, psychologist Anthony Bongiovanni has this to say about the practice of punishing students in schools:

> School personnel would need to be minutemen, ready to jump at the detection of undesirable behavior. One may wonder how such an ability would affect the classroom process. . . . The available research on punishment, when applied to corporal punishment in the schools, suggests that it is ineffective in producing durable behavior change, is potentially harmful to students and personnel, and is highly impractical in light of the controls necessary for maximal effectiveness. . . . Corporal punishment appears to be impractical, time consuming, and contrary to the goal of education. (Bongiovanni, 1977)

What is a teacher to do when, looking out of his classroom window, he sees a child hitting another child on the playground? By the time he walks outside to punish, it's too late, according to the experts. But even if the teacher were a champion sprinter and able to get to the child in seconds, he'd be administering the punishment in front of the transgressor's buddies—thus violating principle number 3: *Don't punish in the presence of others*.

Consider the fourth principle: *Never reward the behavior*. I've already touched on the difficulty of being consistent in using punishment. It is also difficult to avoid inconsistency between two controllers. Take this situation: Mother punishes seven-year-old Larry for skateboarding in the street. Three days later Dad and Larry are in the front yard alone, whereupon Larry proceeds to show Dad some tricks on the skateboard in the street. His proud father says, "Wow! Those are tough tricks for a kid of your age." Larry gets rewarded. Violation of principle number 4.

At school, similar inconsistencies between the child's various teachers are commonplace. Every schoolchild learns early that there are strict teachers and lenient ones. What gets punished in one class, in fact, can even be rewarded in another—for example, helping kids with class assignments, telling a funny joke, making classmates laugh. This seriously weakens the effect of punishment in the long run.

Consider the fifth principle: *Punishment that comes too often or is too severe may cause the child to withdraw.* Psychologists, as everyone knows, often use white rats as subjects in their learning experiments. In one procedure they observe how rats go about learning to find their way through a complicated maze. Invariably the rats learn how to get through the maze if they are consistently rewarded with food when they get to the end. Some years back, a curious psychologist figured he might speed up the rats' learning time by throwing in a few punishments to supplement the reward. So he built in some electric grids at the entrance to each of the blind alleys in his maze, giving the rats a mild electric shock whenever they took these incorrect turns. Sure enough, under these new conditions the rats learned to find their way through the maze much more quickly than rats that had only been rewarded. This led the pleased experimenter to reason that he might reduce the learning time even more by increasing the strength of the electric shocks—making the punishment quite painful.

But it didn't work that way. Instead, *the rats gave up trying.* They would lie down at various spots along the maze, unwilling to subject themselves to any more of the painful punishment. Dogs do this, too, when they're punished severely—they hide under the bed, crawl under the porch, or run away.

So it is with youngsters. If they get punished severely or too often for unacceptable or incorrect behavior, they look for ways to escape. Severely punished children often become runaways as soon as they are old enough. School dropouts are almost always students who have given up trying, either because they have been physically or psychologically punished by the teacher or because they want to escape the daily punishment of getting failing grades, of being rebuked by their teachers and ridiculed by their classmates. Severely punished kids often turn to alcohol or drugs as an escape from such painful experiences.

"PUNISHMENT IS ACCEPTABLE IF IT'S MILD"

Advocates of punishing children never fail to rationalize that *their* punishment is mild, benign, loving. Severe punishment, they maintain, would be cruel and inhuman (and nonloving). This advice certainly gives the pro-punishment people the appearance of being benevolent in their autocracy, yet there is good reason to question the wisdom of such advice.

In the first place, researchers consistently have found that mild punishment fails as a deterrent. Every parent or teacher has had the experience of administering a mild punishment to a child, only to watch in exasperation as the child repeats the unacceptable behavior as if nothing had happened. Consider this example: When Laurie grabs her brother's truck out of his hands, Mother responds by slapping her on the wrist and recovering the truck for her brother. Laurie looks startled, but then proceeds to snatch the truck away once more, giving her mother a guilty little grin in passing.

In this case, the potency of the slap was too weak to have an aversive effect on Laurie, too weak to compete with her stronger need to commandeer the truck. This puts Mother in a quandary: either she must increase the severity of the punishment, which parents are often loath to do, or she can give up and supply baby brother with another toy. The latter strategy may pacify baby brother, but it teaches Laurie that she can get by with stealing another's toy (a rewarding consequence) by paying a very small price.

Laurie's mother could use two nonpunitive alternatives here, both to be described and illustrated in subsequent chapters: confronting Laurie with an I-message ("I can almost feel myself how unhappy Jimmy is when his truck is snatched away"); and getting Laurie and Jimmy started in a problem-solving process (the No-Lose Method described in Chapter 7).

In fact, psychologists tell us that Laurie's stealing will probably be *reinforced* in this mild-punishment situation—because she also was rewarded with her parent's attention. Teachers encounter this dilemma daily in their classrooms. This incident with Steve is a good illustration:

Steve stands at the pencil sharpener and noisily grinds away until his new pencil is shorter than his little finger, all the while distracting his amused classroom audience and exasperating his teacher. The teacher sharply commands him to return to his seat unless he prefers to stay after school. With a straight face Steve informs teacher that he has just one more pencil to sharpen and proceeds to grind at that one, causing the class to snicker more.

Even if the teacher carries out her threat to keep him after school, it's doubtful that the punishment will be as aversive for Steve as his classmates' enjoyment was rewarding. Probably what Steve learns here is that it's quite satisfying to capture the attention and appreciation of his classmates with his clowning, without having to suffer more than a mild and temporary deprivation. For Steve, the punishment is well worth the crime—a common reaction of children to weak punishments.

Evidence for the failure of weak punishment was reported in a 1986 study by psychologist Thomas Power and graduate student M. Lynn Chapieski (1986). They made observations of sixteen fourteen-month-old infants at play with their mothers, noting every object the infants grasped and their mothers' attempts to restrain them. In both the long and the short term, neither using physical descipline immediately (a light slap on the hand) nor using physical discipline after attempting to distract the child proved successful. Punished babies were more likely to grasp breakable objects and less likely to obey restrictions. On a test measuring infant development seven months later, the punished babies scored lower than did those who received no (or low) discipline! In the researchers' words, they showed "less exploration, which leads to a limited channel to improve their visual/spatial skills and problem-solving ability."

THE RISKS OF MAKING PUNISHMENT SEVERE

Every parent and teacher has been tempted to make the next punishment more severe when the first mild one doesn't work. Responding, usually angrily, to what looks like "disobedience" or "stubbornness," adults are tempted to pull out their "bigger guns." If those don't work, chances are they'll try even more severe measures. Now the risk of serious injury gets high; now the "zone of child abuse" is closer.

In the name of making discipline "stick," parents and school personnel may inflict injurious physical punishment. This happens more frequently than most people think. According to the study described by the authors of *Behind Closed Doors*, almost four children out of one hundred are at risk of *serious* injury *each year* from parents using at least one of the following dangerous forms of punishment: kicks, bites, punches, burns, beatings, and threats with, or use of, guns or knives (Straus, Gelles, Steinmetz, 1980).

This translates into a shocking statistic: between 1.4 million and 1.9 million children were vulnerable to *serious* physical injury from their parents during the year of that study. Worse yet, these severe forms of violence are seldom one-shot events, according to the investigators. They found violence occurring regularly.

Statistics published by the Chicago-based National Committee for Prevention of Child Abuse also reveal how widespread child abuse is in the United States:

- An estimated 2.25 million cases of child abuse and neglect were reported in 1987. Since many cases of abuse go unreported, the numbers may be much higher.
- At least 1,200 deaths from child abuse were reported in 1986.
- Every two minutes a child is attacked by one or both parents.

In their perturbing pamphlet, *Think Twice: The Medical Effects of Physical Punishment*, Lesli Taylor, M.D., and Adah Maurer, Ph.D., document the injuries that can be caused by physical punishment:

From blows to the head: hematomas that require surgery to prevent possible death, concussions, cerebral contusions, the "punch drunk syndrome," skull fractures, cauliflower ear, retinal hemorrhage, brain atrophy.

From shaking: whiplash injuries to the brain, compression fractures to the vertebrae.

From blows to the chest and abdomen: lung contusion, lung collapse, multiple rib fractures, hemorrhagic shock that can lead to death in a matter of minutes, tears to the liver, burst spleen, ruptured stomach or bowel, duodenal hematoma, pancreatitis, bladder hematoma.

From beatings and spankings: broken bones, bruised muscles, radial head dislocation (pulled elbow), bruising of the tailbone, fracture of the sacrum, sciatic nerve damage, paralysis of legs, damage to the genitals, deranged sexuality in adulthood. (Taylor and Maurer, 1985)

Although I have found no study that confirms it, I suspect that in most instances where severe and damaging punishment was used, parents had first tried mild forms of punishment. When parents find that the mild punishment seldom brings the obedience they want, they then get so frustrated and angry that they impulsively reach deeper into their arsenals for stronger ones—for some form of violent physical punishment that is painful enough to inflict serious injury. I've heard parents rationalize the use of violence with statements like these:

"I had to show the kid who's boss."
"We didn't want him to think he could get away with it."
"We were determined not to let him win the battle."
"We wanted to start early making our discipline stick."

This tragic sequence of events often leads to serious child abuse. It conjures up visions in my mind of cowboys breaking in colts or dog owners jerking on choke chains—where the goal of the controller always is to break the will of the animals and bring about total obedience to their masters. With children, these violent and inhumane acts of punishment are usually done in the name of discipline, justified by the belief that "parental authority" must be respected, that children must obey their parents, that parents must not "lose."

One of the most complete and scholarly analyses of child abuse is contained in a book by A. Kadushin and J. Martin, *Child Abuse: An Interactional Event.* It summarizes the characteristics and behavior of physically abusive parents:

> It is suggested that abusive parents are strict disciplinarians who have rigid expectations regarding child behavior without empathic regard for a child's feelings or particular individuality. The parent is seen as "owning" the child, as being solely responsible for molding the child, and as having a sense of righteousness in making autonomous decisions as to what is best for the child. . . . Abusive parents tend to regard the behavior of even very young children as willful, deliberately disobedient. Strict discipline is then perceived as justified, since the child is consciously disobeying the parent. (Kadushin and Martin, 1981)

In schools the pattern is no different. When mild punishment fails to deter disruptive behaviors of students (as it usually does), teachers sentence kids to corporal punishment (it's still allowed in most U.S. schools). As many studies have shown, corporal punishment sometimes results in serious physical injury to students, including contusions, broken bones, blistering welts, head injuries, black eyes, torsion of the testes, and kidney damage. Hundreds of cases were reported in the *Newsletter of the Committee to End Violence Against the Next Generation*, in Berkeley, California. Some typical examples:

> In a shop class in Pittsburgh in one of the "best" elementary schools, a seventh-grade student allegedly mumbled something under his breath. Whatever it was, the teacher became enraged, grabbed the student by the throat, and slammed him against the wall.

In Vermont, a sixth-grade student was seriously beaten by the principal for striking another student. The principal struck the child repeatedly, knocking him from his seat and onto the floor. He then kicked him in the abdomen, back, and legs and pulled his hair. The child suffered severe body bruises.

In Missouri, three boys caught with cigarettes were given the choice of paddling or eating their cigarettes. Two of the boys chose to eat the cigarettes, which resulted in a three-day hospitalization for both boys. One boy suffered an aggravation of a pre-existing ulcer because of the tobacco.

Even the common practice of punishing students by suspension from school for various lengths of time can be potentially damaging. Suspension often brings kids physical punishment by their parents. In addition, they may suffer loss of self-esteem and self-confidence, fall hopelessly behind in their schoolwork, or become permanently alienated from school itself—all severe punishments, too, and ultimately self-defeating.

WHEN THE CAT'S AWAY . . .

Punishment (or the threat of it) on occasion may deter some unacceptable or disruptive behavior by children. However, this works *only as long as the controller is present.* As soon as the punishing parent or teacher leaves the scene, the behavior often recurs, sometimes with even more frequency or disruptiveness than before. This phenomenon is rampant in our classrooms, as every teacher—and substitute teacher—will testify; it goes on in every family, as every parent can recall; and it has been clearly demonstrated in experimental research studies with children.

One such study, the classic research of Ronald Lippitt and Robert White at the University of Iowa, demonstrated that children in a boys' club that had controlling, authoritarian leaders consistently showed more hostile, aggressive, and disruptive behavior when the leader left the room than did children in another club that had noncontrolling, democratic leaders. The latter youngsters were much more apt to continue doing the tasks or activities initiated before the leader left the room. The youngsters with controlling, authoritarian leaders, on the other hand, stopped working at their activities as soon as their adult leaders left the room, and they promptly engaged in previously prohibited disruptive and aggressive behaviors (Lippitt and White, 1943). I have seen the films of these experiments and I recall being impressed with the sharp differences between the two groups of children.

As we saw earlier, *externally applied control* by adults is not the best way to teach children internally generated self-control; *punitive adult discipline* does not produce self-disciplined children.

HOW PUNISHMENT FOSTERS AGGRESSION AND VIOLENCE

In direct contrast to the conventional, "commonsense" belief that punishment will prevent aggressive behavior by children, the evidence indicates that harsh, punitive, power-based punishment actually *causes* aggression in children.

Here is how it happens. Punishing a child always brings about some sort of deprivation of his or her needs. When children (adults, too, for that matter) can't get their needs satisfied, they feel frustrated—and one common reaction to frustration is aggression. Psychologists discovered this relationship many years ago. Using first animals, then children, and still later adults, they designed laboratory experiments in which it was impossible for their subjects to get what they strongly wanted or needed (such as food, water, toys, and other rewards). Obviously frustrated, these subjects very frequently—but not always—responded by exhibiting various kinds of physically aggressive, often violent, behavior toward others. From these experiments psychologists proposed the "frustration-aggression theory" (Dollard et al., 1939), now almost universally accepted by social scientists as one valid explanation for some acts of aggression.

In everyday life we see ample evidence of the frustration-aggression theory at work: the losing tennis player throwing his racquet; the child hitting a playmate who takes his toy; the father smacking a child who disturbs his rest; the adolescent slamming the door behind a parent who has denied her use of the car; the husband or wife throwing dishes against the wall during an argument.

When, as a form of punishment meted out by their parents or teachers, youngsters are thwarted from getting something they want, they also may react aggressively and sometimes violently—slamming doors, breaking toys, throwing things, pounding a fist through the door, punching someone smaller than they, hitting the teacher.

Families in which parents frequently use punishment often produce hyperaggressive, hyperactive children. *Clearly, punishment doesn't prevent aggressive behavior by children; it promotes it.* It's a vicious cycle: aggressive behavior brings on punishment, which then causes more aggressive behavior, bringing on more punishment, and so on.

Punishment promotes aggression in children not only by depriving and frustrating the child but also by a process called *modeling.* As we know, children are great imitators—they learn from watching what adults do, especially their parents. Thus, if parents rely heavily on violent actions to control and discipline their children, they are teaching some powerful lessons their children are not likely to forget—such as:

Physical force and violence are suitable and accepted behaviors in human relationships.

Might makes right.

It is legitimate to use violence on those we love.

If you don't get what you want, fight for it.

Conflicts are won by those who are bigger and stronger.

Physical punishment actually teaches youngsters to use violence themselves, both in and outside their families. It serves as a vivid learning experience, inculcating in its victims that the use of force is sanctioned in relationships with people. Thus the members of each generation learn to be violent through modeling what they have observed and experienced in their violent families.

Consider these stark findings from a national survey conducted by the authors of *Behind Closed Doors: Violence in the American Family* (Straus, Gelles, and Steinmetz, 1980).

People who received the most punishment as teenagers have a rate of spouse-beating that is four times greater than those whose parents did not hit them.

Husbands who experienced severe violence at home as a child have a 600 percent greater rate of wife-beating than husbands who came from nonviolent homes.

Over one out of four parents who had grown up in a violent household were violent enough to risk seriously injuring their child.

While only 20 percent of children whose parents *did not* use physical punishment had severely assaulted a brother or sister, nearly 100 percent of children whose parents *did* use a lot of physical punishment had severely assaulted a brother or sister.

The absurdity of using physical punishment, itself an act of aggression, to deter aggression is perhaps nowhere more clearly portrayed than in a cartoon I saw in *The New Yorker* magazine some years ago: A father in the act of spanking his young son, who was bottom-up over his father's knees, was depicted saying, "I hope this will teach you not to hit your baby brother."

ADULTS INEVITABLY RUN OUT OF PUNISHMENTS

In much the same way that they run out of effective rewards when children grow older, adults also gradually and inevitably lose their power to control with punishment as youngsters move into adolescence. When teenagers get to be as big and strong as their parents, using any kind of punishment becomes a somewhat foolhardy adventure for parents because they risk suffering violence in return. In schools, it is the same for high school teachers, so they are left rather empty-handed, without effective punishments.

Despite the obvious possibility of counterviolence, many parents continue trying to make punishment work even after their children are almost fully grown. About one-third of children between the ages of fifteen and seventeen are hit by their parents. I suspect a double standard is operating in most of these families—parents feel free to hit their kids, but they count on their kids following the unwritten law that offspring should never hit their parents.

Even nonviolent kinds of punishment lose their effectiveness when children enter their teens. As punishment for some unacceptable behavior, you deny your daughter the use of the family car, but she bums rides with her friends or hitchhikes with strangers. Punish a son by declaring him "grounded" for a week, and you might discover him sneaking out of his room at night. Threaten some sort of punishment if your daughter goes with a boy you don't like, and she'll most likely arrange to see him secretly—perhaps even more often than before.

To understand why this so often happens, you need only recall the conditions required for punishment to work. The first was that the punishment must be strong enough to be felt as depriving or painful by the youngster. But with teenagers, parents don't have many painful punishments left in their arsenal. The second condition was that the child cannot easily escape from the punisher in order to avoid the punishment. But teenagers can easily escape the scene. I recall one mother in a P.E.T. class admitting, "The only way I might stop my sixteen-year-old from smoking pot would be to chain him to the bedpost. And of course that is ridiculous." She was finally facing a reality that many parents ignore, which is that by the time children are old enough to get out of the house and away from constant parental surveillance, their parents have lost most of the power they have relied on.

The failure to understand this fact can lead to some tragic consequences for parents and their children. I firmly believe that the single most important cause of the severe stress and strain in families during the adolescent years is that parents keep trying to use their power-based authority *when in reality they no longer have any power.* Then they ask, "What's gone wrong? Why doesn't discipline work anymore?" Most parents don't wake up to the fact that their powerlessness has left them without *influence.* The inevitable result of consistently employing power to control their kids when they are young is that parents never learn how to *influence.* When they reach adolescence, the kids can do whatever they wish—no controls, no restrictions. This is when parents are wrongly accused of being permissive. But they are *not* permissive parents; they are authoritarian parents who have lost their power. They are impotent parents who wish they weren't.

In schools, too, teachers run out of power. Beginning with junior high, youngsters resist or ignore power-based discipline because teachers are either reluctant to administer painful punishment or prohibited from doing so. They're left with only nonaversive, ineffective punishments such as making kids stay after school, go to the principal's office, or be briefly suspended from school.

TO THE CONTROLLER, POWER COMES AT A PRICE

It is not just the controllee who is crippled by power; the controller, too, pays a stiff price. As Lord Acton wrote, "Power tends to corrupt and absolute power corrupts absolutely," by which, of course, he meant the corruption of the power wielder.

The controllers of the world feel continually threatened by those whom they control. Dissent and rebellion are inevitable whenever rule by coercion is the norm, as the history of all authoritarian regimes shows. If dissent is put down, it may subside for a time, but it usually goes underground and erupts later as rebellion. Thus all power is inherently unstable. As Marilyn French states in her book *Beyond Power*:

> The dominators of the world never have a day off.
> . . . Thus the dominator is continually besieged. . . .
> To keep a slave in a ditch, one must stay there oneself,
> or appoint an overseer to guarantee the slave's obe-

dience. But then it is necessary to appoint a supervisor who will make sure that the slave and the overseer do not collude; then a governor who will make sure that all three do not collude . . . and so on. There is no place of safety for a dominator, ever; there is no security, peace, or ease. The urge to control others backfires; it cannot be satisfied and it entraps the controller. . . . (French, 1985)

Exercising power to control others is terribly time-consuming, often expensive, and usually requires tedious activities to ensure that it works. While coercion may not appear to be time-consuming in a family or in a classroom, in reality it usually is. Parents and teachers often encounter stubborn resistance—passive or otherwise—to their demands and commands. They also find it necessary to monitor the activities of their charges to make sure they are complying and then deal with those who don't comply. While the act of making unilateral decisions or laying down rules for controllees may take less time than involving group members in these processes, autocratic leaders often require inordinate amounts of time to get group members to accept and implement their decisions and commandments. This was pointed out by the president of a company to which I served as a consultant for many years:

When I was using [power] to resolve conflicts, I prided myself on being a person who could make decisions quickly. The trouble was, it often took ten times as long to overcome all the resistance to my decisions as it did to make them. I had to spend too much time "selling" my decisions—getting other people to buy them.

Because controllees have low motivation to carry out decisions imposed on them, as scores of research studies have documented, enforcement is both difficult and time-consuming. Nowhere is this more evident than in schools, where studies have shown that teachers spend as much as 75 percent of classroom time "playing policeman"—enforcing their rules or their administrator's rules.

Becoming alienated from their group members is another hidden cost for leaders who rely heavily on power. Two factors work to deteriorate these relationships. First, people don't feel warm and kindly toward those they fear and whose coercion makes them feel hostile. Second, coercive leaders typically avoid developing close relationships with subordinates in order to escape being accused of playing favorites. No wonder most authoritarian leaders feel alone at the top and have few close relationships with the people who work for them. I see no reason to believe this is not true for coercive parents and teachers as well.

That authoritarian leaders find their jobs stressful—often damaging to their physical and mental health—is widely accepted. The price of being a controller can often include high blood pressure, coronary problems, ulcers, insomnia, and/or alcoholism. Could it be that power makes its users "sick"?

A strong case can be made for an affirmative answer to that question. Not only must controllers be vigilant, as I pointed out before, but they experience anxiety about losing their power, they develop suspicions, they grow to distrust others. Even more important, winning at the expense of others, as controllers frequently do, can produce a lot of guilt. My many years as a consultant and counselor to organization managers, school administrators, and teachers convinced me that those who rely on power create their own psychological hell of distrust, anxiety, vigilance, tension, suspicion, and paranoia.

One additional cost to controllers is often overlooked but equally important: their subordinates develop a variety of behaviors that are nonproductive and deleterious to the effectiveness of the group; the subordinates' behavior in turn undermines the job security of the controller. One of the most damaging aspects of such behavior is a marked reduction of communication with the controller. Autocratic leaders are heard to complain, "Nobody tells me anything" or "I'm the last person to know." Subordinates of power-oriented leaders are reluctant to reveal their problems for fear of punishment or having the boss impose some distasteful solution. "What the boss doesn't know won't hurt me" is the attitude of many controllees. Or "Tell the boss only what he wants to hear." Such self-protective behaviors eventually can reduce the effectiveness of a group, whether a work group, a classroom, or a family.

Flattery and apple-polishing flourish in groups with auto-cratic leaders. The business and industry people who always side with their boss are called "yes-men." Such ingratiating behaviors have the effect of seriously limiting the leader's awareness of what goes on or what people think, thus reducing the leader's ability to identify problems.

Another fairly predictable reaction to coercive power is heightened rivalry and competitiveness between group members. It occurs in work groups, in classrooms, and with children in families (sibling rivalry). In business particularly, we find intense power struggles, backbiting, and gossiping. These competitive and combative behaviors are the antithesis of the co-operation and team play needed in effective and productive groups, and explains why "team building" is simply an empty, unattainable abstraction for groups whose leader controls with power.

Group members sometimes cope with coercive leadership by finding ways to remove themselves from the environment—either psychologically or physically. In group meetings some members deliberately refrain from speaking out; students take pains to avoid being called on; teenagers seek escape from parental control by isolating themselves in their rooms. Some kids drop out of school under the same impulse.

It is high time we stop to assess the high costs of the widespread use of power by the leaders in our society—from the family on up to our government leaders. We have too long worshiped power, too long had illusions about its effectiveness. We have paid far too little attention to its harmful effects, its severe limitations, its destructiveness. Power suppresses creativity and productivity; it is hazardous to the health and well-being of both the controller and the controllee. Power generates the forces that will inevitably destroy or replace it; power bites its own tail; it stifles creative dissent; it extinguishes trust, fellowship, intimacy, and love; power entraps the controller as it enslaves the controllee.

five

How
Children *Really*
React to Control

hen one person tries to control another, you can always expect some kind of reaction or response from the controllee.

The use of power involves two people in a special kind of relationship—one wielding power, the other reacting to it.

This seemingly obvious fact usually is not dealt with in the writings of the dare-to-discipline advocates. Invariably they leave the child out of the formula, omitting any reference to how the youngster reacts to the control of his or her parents or teachers.

They insist, "Parents must set limits," but seldom say anything about how children respond to having their needs denied in this way.

"Parents should not be afraid to exercise their authority," they counsel, but rarely mention how youngsters react to authority-based coercion. By omitting the child from the interaction, the discipline advocates leave the impression that the child submits willingly and consistently to adults' power and does precisely what is demanded.

"Be firm but fair," "Insist that your children obey," "Don't be afraid to express disapproval by spanking," "There are times when you have to say 'no'," "Discipline with love," "Demonstrate your parental right to lead," "The toddler should be taught to obey and yield to parental leadership." These are actual quotes from the many power-to-the-parent books I've collected along the way. What these books have in common is advocacy of the use of power-based discipline with no mention of how children react to it. In other words, the dare-to-discipline advocates never present power-based discipline in full, as a cause-*and*-effect phenomenon, an action-*and*-reaction event.

This omission is important, for it implies that all children passively submit to adult demands, perfectly content and secure in an obedient role, first in relationships with their parents and teachers and, eventually, with all adult power-wielders they might encounter.

However, I've found not a shred of evidence to support this view. In fact, as most of us remember only too well from our childhood, we did almost anything we could to defend against power-based control. We tried to avoid it, postpone it, weaken it, avert it, escape from it. We lied, put the blame on someone else, tattled, hid, pleaded, begged for mercy, or promised we would never do it again.

We also experienced punitive discipline as embarrassing, demeaning, humiliating, frightening, and painful. To be coerced into doing something against our will was a personal insult and an affront to our dignity, an act that devalued the importance of our needs.

Punitive discipline is by definition *need-depriving* as opposed to *need-satisfying*. Recall that punishment will be effective only if it is felt by the child as aversive, painful, unpleasant. When controllers employ punishment they always *intend* for it to cause pain or deprivation.

It seems so obvious, then, that children don't ever *want* punitive discipline, contrary to what its advocates would have us believe. No child "asks for it," "feels a need for it," or is "grateful for it." And it's probably true, too, that no child ever forgets or forgives a punitive parent or teacher. This is why I find it incredible that the authors of power-to-the-parent books try to justify power-based discipline with such statements as:

"Kids not only need punishment, they want it."

"Children basically want what is coming to them, good or bad, because justice is security."

"Punishment will prove to kids that their parents love them."

"The youngster who knows he deserves a spanking appears almost relieved when it finally comes."

"Rather than be insulted by the discipline, [the child] understands its purpose and appreciates the control it gives him over his impulses."

"Corporal punishment in the hands of a loving parent is altogether different in purpose and practice [from child abuse]. . . . One is an act of love; the other is an act of hostility."

"Some strong-willed children demand to be spanked, and their wishes should be granted."

"Punishment will make children feel more secure in their relationship."

"Discipline makes for happy families, healthy children."

Could these be rationalizations intended to relieve the guilt controllers feel after coercing or committing acts of physical violence against their youngsters? It seems possible in view of the repeated insistence that the punishing adult is really a loving adult, doing it only "for the child's own good," or as a dutiful act of "benevolent leadership." It appears that being firm with children has to be justified by saying, "Be firm but fair"; being tough is acceptable as long as it is "tough love"; being an autocrat is justifiable as long as you're a "benevolent autocrat"; coercing children is okay as long as you're not a "dictator"; and physically abusing children is not abuse as long as you "do it lovingly."

Disciplinarians' insistence that punishment is benign and constructive might be explained by their desire that children eventually become subservient to a supreme being or higher authority. This can only be achieved, they believe, if children first learn to obey their parents and other adults. James Dobson (1978) stresses this point time and time again:

> While yielding to the loving leadership of their parents, children are also learning to yield to the benevolent leadership of God Himself.
>
> With regard to specific discipline of the strong-willed toddler, mild spankings can begin between 15 and 18 months of age. . . . To repeat, the toddler should be taught to obey and yield to parent leadership, but that end will not be accomplished overnight.

It's the familiar story of believing that the ends justify the means. Obedience to parental authority first, and then later to some higher authority, is so strongly valued by some advocates of punitive discipline that the *means* they utilize to achieve that end are distorted to appear beneficial to children rather than harmful.

The hope that children eventually will submit to all authority, I think, is wishful thinking. Not all children submit when adults try to control them. In fact, children respond with a wide variety of reactions, an assortment of behaviors. Psychologists call these reactions *coping behaviors* or *coping mechanisms*.

THE COPING MECHANISMS CHILDREN USE

Over the years I have compiled a long list of the various coping mechanisms youngsters use when adults try to control them. This list comes primarily out of our P.E.T. and T.E.T. classes, where we employ a simple but revealing classroom exercise. Participants are asked to recall the specific ways they themselves coped with power-based discipline when they were youngsters. The question yields nearly identical lists in every class, which confirms how universal children's coping mechanisms are. The complete list is reproduced below, in no particular order. Note how varied these recurring themes are. (Can you pick out the particular coping methods *you* employed as a youngster?)

1. Resisting, defying, being negative
2. Rebelling, disobeying, being insubordinate, sassing
3. Retaliating, striking back, counterattacking, vandalizing
4. Hitting, being belligerent, combative
5. Breaking rules and laws
6. Throwing temper tantrums, getting angry
7. Lying, deceiving, hiding the truth
8. Blaming others, tattling, telling on others
9. Bossing or bullying others
10. Banding together, forming alliances, organizing against the adult
11. Apple-polishing, buttering up, soft-soaping, bootlicking, currying favor with adults
12. Withdrawing, fantasizing, daydreaming
13. Competing, needing to win, hating to lose, needing to look good, making others look bad
14. Giving up, feeling defeated, loafing, goofing off
15. Leaving, escaping, staying away from home, running away, quitting school, cutting classes
16. Not talking, ignoring, using the silent treatment, writing the adult off, keeping one's distance
17. Crying, weeping; feeling depressed or hopeless
18. Becoming fearful, shy, timid, afraid to speak up, hesitant to try anything new
19. Needing reassurance, seeking constant approval, feeling insecure.
20. Getting sick, developing psychosomatic ailments
21. Overeating, excessive dieting
22. Being submissive, conforming, complying; being dutiful, docile; apple-polishing, being a goody-goody, teacher's pet
23. Drinking heavily, using drugs
24. Cheating in school, plagiarizing

As you might expect, after parents and teachers in the class generate *their* list, and realize it was created out of their own experiences, they invariably make comments such as:

"Why would anyone want to use power, if these are the behaviors it produces?"

"All of these coping mechanisms are behaviors that I wouldn't want to see in my children [or my students]."

"I don't see in the list any *good* effects or positive behaviors."

"If we reacted to power in those ways when *we* were kids, our own children certainly will, too."

After this exercise, some parents and teachers undergo a 180-degree shift in their thinking. They see much more clearly that power creates the very behavior patterns they *most dislike in children*. They begin to understand that as parents and teachers they are paying a terrible price for using power: they are causing their children or students to develop habits, traits, and characteristics considered both unacceptable by most adults and unhealthy by mental health professionals.

You may have observed as you read down the list of coping mechanisms that some were "fighting" responses, some were "escaping" responses, and some "giving in" responses. It's useful to think of coping mechanisms falling into the three categories of *Fight, Flight*, or *Submit*.

Most kids tend to use more of one type of response than the other two. Boys are more apt to *fight* adult authority, while girls can be expected more often to *submit* to it. Also, some children *submit* when they are young and then *fight* more often when they become teenagers. As for *flight* responses, they seem to be adopted by children at any age when the punishment they receive is very severe or the rewards seem too difficult for them to earn. Runaway youngsters tend to come from homes where the punishment was severe. School dropouts tend to be those who find it too difficult to get passing grades.

Each of these coping mechanisms, of course, will provoke some sort of a follow-up response from the controller. For example, the fight coping mechanisms have a high probability of causing adults to invoke even stronger punitive discipline. This is the case with resisting and defying, rebelling and disobeying, retaliating, hitting others, breaking rules, getting angry. These fighting coping mechanisms often start the vicious cycle we see in both families and schools—where kids' fighting responses cause adults to pull out even stronger punishments, which then provoke more severe fight responses, which bring on even stronger punishments, and so on and so on. The fight responses are typically found in juvenile delinquents and criminals.

The submit responses are less apt to provoke adults into more severe discipline but they do play havoc with youngsters' peer relationships. Most kids don't like other kids who apple-polish, need to look good, make others look bad, are afraid to try anything new, are complying and dutiful, or are goody-goodies or teacher's pets. Such coping mechanisms provoke ridicule, teasing, derision, rejection.

The flight responses have a high probability of being permanently damaging to adult-child relationships, making the lives of both parent and child even more miserable, as when children totally withdraw from meaningful communication or contact with parents and other children, run away from home, or quit school. Some flight responses obviously are even damaging to the health of youngsters—for example, overeating, using drugs, drinking heavily, fantasizing, being shy.

RETALIATORY VIOLENCE AGAINST CONTROLLERS

If youngsters cannot escape from the pain and humiliation of punitive power and choose not to submit to it, they often take out their anger and hostility by acts of aggression and violence against their parents or teachers. Today, as almost everyone knows, the increasing incidence of student violence against teachers is a serious problem in many schools.

Retaliatory violence is not confined to the classroom. It happens in a surprisingly large number of families, too. The survey done by the authors of *Behind Closed Doors* found that *one out of three children between the ages of three and seventeen hit their parents each year*. The retaliatory nature of child-to-parent violence is apparent in these additional findings from the same study:

> Less than 1 out of every 400 children whose parents did *not* hit them were violent to the parent we interviewed. This is in striking contrast to the children

who had been hit the most by their parents. About *half of these children had hit their parents* in the year we asked them about it. (Straus, Gelles, and Steinmetz, 1980)

In view of abundant evidence showing how and why youngsters retaliate against those who try to control them, I find it hard to understand how authors of the dare-to-discipline and parent-power books try to sell parents on the idea that punitive discipline makes for happy family relationships. In fact, punishment of children undermines and weakens adult-child relationships, and punishment that is either *frequent* or *severe* provokes counterviolence.

WHEN YOUNGSTERS "DIVORCE" THEIR PARENTS

The most tragic consequence to adult-child relationships occurs when disciplinarians end up losing their children. Teenagers in great numbers "divorce" their parents psychologically—they withdraw from the relationship while physically remaining at home. Defeated in their efforts to gain freedom from the punitive control of their parents and weary of losing the neverending conflicts and power struggles at home, these youngsters withdraw into sullen isolation and detachment, and cease all meaningful communication with their parents. Such youngsters arrange to stay away from home as much as possible, returning only to eat and sleep. Their parents know next to nothing about their activities, their beliefs, their values or feelings, because these kids make sure they divulge nothing about themselves to their parents. They've learned from daily experience that one way to avoid being controlled, deprived, and punished is to avoid being present in the relationship, or, if that's not possible, to avoid any open and honest communication.

The more intrepid of these teenagers may eventually pack up and run away from home, preferring to risk the insecurities and dangers of the outside world rather than suffer the oppression of punitive and controlling parents. Studies of runaway children have shown that a very high percentage leave home in order to shake off the yoke of their parents' punitive power. In a related method of "escaping," many teenage girls get pregnant out of wedlock in order to use marriage as a way out of a tyrannical relationship with their parents.

It has become clear recently that a surprising number of runaway teenagers don't run away from home at all—they are actually kicked out of their home by the parents! The most frequent reason given by the parents is that the youngster was "incorrigible," "unmanageable," "rebellious," "uncontrollable." It is sad but true: some parents are willing to discard their children when they realize that they have lost the power to make them obey. Obedience becomes a higher value to these parents than their relationship with their offspring.

Usually in these cases, parents have made one grievous mistake that they rue immediately. Finding that they've run out of almost all other means to control these now grown-up children, they threaten them with some version of "As long as you're in my house, you'll obey my rules. If you can't, then you'll just have to get out." This is precisely the treatment advocated by the "Toughlove" organization. These parents usually end up carrying out their threat, and paying the terrible price of ejecting the youngster from home and family.

The analogous scenario in our schools is the nearly universal practice of threatening suspension or expulsion as a means of controlling disruptive students. When the threats don't work and the students resist being controlled, as is so often the case, school administrators are hoist with their own petard: to avoid losing face they now have to suspend or expel the youngster. But that, of course, alienates the student still more and causes him to get even further behind in his course work. Too often, the student is permanently lost.

SOWING THE SEEDS OF CRIMINAL BEHAVIOR

Ask parents to name the worst thing that could happen to their children and they're likely to say, "Getting into trouble with the law." It's this very fear that lures many parents into the trap of using punitive discipline as the primary means for teaching kids right and wrong and demanding respect for adult authority. Their hope is that punitive discipline will instill in their children the moral virtues that are required to produce law-abiding citizens. Unfortunately, it turns out to be a false hope.

To prevent what they so deeply fear, most parents put their faith in strict discipline: They control, confine, restrain, set limits, prohibit, forbid, and command. And if these methods don't produce obedience, they turn to punishment. The rules for the youngsters are usually set unilaterally by the parents, and infractions of those rules carry punishments. Disobedience is not tolerated.

But as we've seen before, strict discipline does not produce disciplined kids. Punitive discipline actually *causes* delinquent or criminal behavior rather than prevents it. The facts prove it:

- Studies of the family backgrounds of both male and female juvenile delinquents consistently show a pattern of harsh, punitive, power-assertive parental punishment, in contrast to nondelinquent children (Martin, 1975).
- A study of violent inmates in San Quentin prison found that 100 percent of them had experienced extreme violence at home between the ages of one and ten (Maurer, 1976).
- Murderers were found to have received more frequent and more severe physical punishment as children than their brothers who did not go on to commit a homicide (Palmer, 1962).
- In a follow-up study of young boys judged at high risk to become criminals, only 32 percent of those with two loving parents had been convicted of crimes; 36 percent of those with a loving mother and a punitive, rejecting father had been convicted; 46 percent of those with a punitive, rejecting mother and a loving father had been convicted. *But 70 percent of those with a punitive and rejecting mother and a punitive and rejecting father had been convicted of crimes* (McCord and McCord, 1958).
- Brian Gilmartin, author of the *Gilmartin Report*, states: "Virtually every study into the backgrounds of violent

criminals has shown that they are far more likely than law-abiding citizens to have been subjected to a great many beatings and other forms of physical punishment by their parents and other adult guardians." (Gilmartin, 1979)

• A study conducted in Oregon demonstrated a positive correlation between school vandalism and corporal punishment. Schools using more physical punishment had more vandalism. Those using less punishment had less vandalism (Hyman, McDowell, and Raines, 1975).

Precisely how physical punishment of children sows the seeds for later delinquent or criminal behavior is still not entirely clear. Probably, one or more of the following factors are at work: (1) modeling, (2) the frustration-aggression reaction explained earlier, (3) reactive hostility projected toward all authority figures (school administrators, bosses, police), (4) a need to retaliate or get revenge, and (5) feelings of hopelessness and helplessness (lack of fate control). Whatever the precise dynamics, physical punishment of children predisposes them to a possible life of lawbreaking, counteraggression, and violence—first toward siblings and parents, then toward teachers and principals, and, later, toward all authorities they encounter.

THE FAILURE OF JUVENILE COURTS

There is another institution besides the family in which punitive control of youth has failed. I refer to the juvenile courts, established around the turn of the century and considered at the time a triumph of progressive reform. The goal of these courts, it was hoped, would be "not so much to punish as to reform, not to degrade but to uplift, not to crush but to develop, not to make . . . a criminal but a worthy citizen" (Mack, 1909).

In the past two decades, however, the underlying concept of the juvenile courts and the way most of them operate have come under harsh attack. How did this come to be? In a bold and profound attempt to analyze our system of juvenile justice, Charles Silberman's 1978 book *Criminal Violence, Criminal Justice* documents why he feels our juvenile justice system delivers much more punishment than treatment. Silberman believes that it is more myth than reality that juvenile courts are run "in the best interests of the child," and a myth that they are for rehabilitation and treatment rather than for punishment. A striking statistic: In 1974 at least 460,000 juveniles were incarcerated in detention centers (the juvenile equivalent of the adult jail), with an average stay of around eleven days. According to the LEAA Jail Censuses, another 250,000 were placed in adult jails. Yet of this number, fully 75 percent of girls detained and 25 percent of boys were charged only with minor-status offenses (those for which only juveniles are arrested—e.g., truancy, sexual promiscuity, etc.). No more than 10 percent were accused of robbery or other violent crimes. Silberman infers from these statistics that judges, policemen, and probation officers seem to be locking up a large number of youths (a severe form of coercive and punitive treatment) to "teach them a lesson" or to "put a little fear in them" *before* they have committed a more serious act of criminal violence.

Even more shocking is the 1974 finding (again from an LEAA Jail Census) that perhaps as many as 680,000 boys and girls were detained *before* trial—locked up while awaiting court action or transfer to another jurisdiction. In Arizona, for example, less than 10 percent of juveniles held in pretrial detention are considered dangerous enough to be removed from the community after trial (Silberman, 1978).

While there are exceptions, most detention centers and, even more so, adult jails, are terribly oppressive, coercive, and punishing to youngsters. There is the trauma of being separated from one's family, the degrading effect of being stripped of personal possessions, the anxiety of being confined for an unpredictable amount of time, and the fear of being physically attacked, even sodomized.

Like parents and teachers, juvenile courts have pinned their hopes on coercive and punitive measures to deter children from delinquent or criminal behavior—a system of deterrent-based penalties. And yet there is no evidence that such methods work in juvenile courts any better than they do in families or in schools. In fact, the experience of such detention probably makes many youngsters feel more angry and combative, more resentful and retaliatory, and more prone to violence than ever. I have no doubt that it damages youngsters' self-esteem and their feelings of self-worth.

It appears that youngsters sent to juvenile detention centers and training schools are more likely to be brutalized than rehabilitated. Silberman quotes the warning of Austin Mac-Cormick, one of the deans of correctional professionals, who declared to the members of the National Council of Juvenile Court Judges, "There are things going on, methods of discipline being used, in the state training schools of this country that would cause a warden of Alcatraz to lose his job if he used them on his prisoners" (Silberman, 1978).

WARNING: DISCIPLINE IS HAZARDOUS TO CHILDREN'S HEALTH AND WELL-BEING

Those who support the "spare the rod, spoil the child" philosophy of child rearing usually invoke the argument that discipline is "for the good of the child" and will make children healthier and happier persons—they'll feel "more secure," they'll know better where they stand with people, they'll become more socialized, they'll have happier relationships. In short, discipline is thought to sustain mental health and wellness. James Dobson, you'll recall, theorizes that submission to authority is *"necessary to healthy human relationships."*

But how does this belief square with findings from research studies? It doesn't. There is abundant evidence that strict, punitive discipline actually makes kids sick—it's hazardous to their psychological health.

- A study by noted experimental psychologist Robert Sears revealed that twelve-year-old boys whose parents were high in restrictiveness and punishment showed strong tendencies toward self-punishment, accident proneness, and suicidal tendencies (Sears, 1961).
- In three independent studies it was shown that inhibited, neurotic children are those who had more constraint and

excessive control in their family backgrounds than other children (Becker, 1964).

- Mothers of children with low self-esteem were found to have used less reasoning and discussion and more arbitrary, punitive discipline. They also used fewer rewards and more punishment in training their children (Coopersmith, 1967).

- Columbia psychologist Goodwin Watson did intensive interviews with 230 graduate students who had rated how often and severely their parents had punished them as children. Those who had been subjected to the *most* punishment, compared with those who had received the *least* punishment, reported more hatred toward their parents, more rejection of their teachers, poorer relationships with classmates, more quarrels, more shyness, more unsatisfactory love affairs, more worry, more anxiety, more guilt, more unhappiness and crying, more dependence on their parents (Watson, 1943).

In a 1971 study, Diana Baumrind identified several clusters of parental behavior, one of which she labeled "authoritarian" parenting. Parents in this category had relatively high scores on several or all of the following characteristics: (1) attempting to shape, control, and evaluate the behavior and attitudes of their children in accordance with an absolute set of standards; (2) valuing obedience, respect for authority, work, tradition, and preservation of order; (3) discouraging verbal give-and-take between parent and child; (4) discouraging the child's independence and individuality. At preschool ages, the children of the authoritarian parents showed relatively little independence and scored only fair on a measure of "social responsibility."

In another study it was found that children of authoritarian parents tend to lack social competence with peers—they tend to withdraw, to not take social initiative, to lack spontaneity (Baldwin, 1948). According to psychologists E. Maccoby and J. Martin (1983), they also show lesser evidence of "conscience" and display an external locus of control—their source of control is outside, not inside, giving them poor self-control.

The mass of experimental evidence we have accumulated

proves it: *Punishing children will be hazardous to their mental health.*
To think otherwise is absurd.

Because discipline with punishment is emotionally damaging to children, it follows that it is ultimately damaging to our society: sick children grow up to be emotionally crippled, unproductive, antisocial, and often violent citizens.

GETTING HIGH AND TUNING OUT

As frightening to parents as delinquency in their children is the threat of alcoholism or drug abuse. While for many generations some kids have turned to alcohol and drugs, today it seems that drinking and drug taking have become much more widespread forms of escape than ever before.

Drug use is now as much a scandal in professional athletics as it has been for many years among professional entertainers. Joining such stars as Janis Joplin, Elvis Presley, Judy Garland, and John Belushi, all of whom died from drug overdoses, are star athletes Len Bias and Don Rogers. Ben Johnson, the world record holder in the 100 meters, had his Olympic gold medal taken away because of the presence of drugs in his body, found when he was tested after his victory. Alcohol-induced public rowdiness is rampant in stadiums in both the United States and Europe, often resulting in serious injuries and death. Accidents involving drunk driving are the second most frequent cause of death among teenagers.

Restricting the supply or the sale of these dangerous substances has not worked to curb abuse because over the years something new always comes along that's easy to get—LSD, marijuana, heroin, PCP, cocaine, crack.

The causes of alcohol or drug abuse appear to be numerous and complex, but using these substances as a means of escaping anxiety, pain, loneliness, hopelessness, rejection, or some other form of need deprivation must rank among the top causes.

Responding to peer pressure, the fear that saying no will lose the friendship or acceptance of one's peers, is yet another principal antecedent of drinking and drug taking. Self-control and self-discipline seem to be absent in those who can't refuse drugs or can't limit their intake of alcohol to reasonable and safe amounts. It's important to remember that of all the youngsters who start drinking and who try drugs, only about 5 to 10 percent, according to some studies, actually become problem drinkers or drug addicts. What differentiates the 5 to 10 percent from the larger group who do control their intake?

A reasonable hypothesis is that those who have acquired the *self-discipline* to keep from excessive or inappropriate use of alcohol or drugs are those whose lives have been so rewarding, satisfying, and fulfilled that they don't need to risk losing what they have or what lies ahead for them—friends, success in some aspect of their lives, a good relationship with a girlfriend or boyfriend, a good marriage, the prospect of learning a profession, feelings of self-confidence and self-esteem. They also have the feeling that they can control their own lives, the critical "fate-control factor" I've mentioned a number of times.

In contrast, the 5 to 10 percent who do get into serious trouble are more likely to live lives that are unrewarding and unsatisfying. They already feel like losers. They feel deprived and disappointed, have low self-esteem, and feel helpless to control their destiny. For these have-nots, both alcohol and drugs provide a quick, easy escape from their despair, a temporary surge of euphoria and self-assurance.

While recognizing that economic, social, and environmental factors contribute heavily to how one feels about oneself or about life, I believe that the *strongest* influence on one's outlook is how the person was treated at home and in school. I've presented only a small sample of the growing body of research findings that show that power-based punitive discipline in school and in the home can make children's lives so miserable that they want to retaliate against those who try to control them or want to escape from the environment that feels so painful to them.

Punitive and controlling teachers and parents can make children's lives wretched. I believe the so-called war on drugs, "Say no" slogans, and programs that try to scare kids into abstinence will never succeed until parents and teachers learn new ways of dealing with children and youth that make any need for such escape obsolete.

THE CONTROLLER'S LOSS OF INFLUENCE

Most parents and teachers want, above all, to have a strong positive influence on children. They want to teach children right from wrong, to convince them of the value of a good education, to influence them to live a healthful life, to help them learn to get along with others, to get them to drop behaviors that interfere with others—to raise them to be happy and productive citizens. By choosing to use punitive discipline, however, adults *greatly reduce* their chances of exerting positive or constructive influence on youngsters.

It's a paradox: Use power, lose influence.

Several factors operate in concert to cause this. First, power creates the very responses that eventually will weaken it, among which are resistance, rebellion, retaliation, avoidance, withdrawal, deception, organizing alliances to balance the controller's power, law breaking, and so on.

Second, adult Authority E, which is one of the principal sources of influence, won't work with youngsters unless they have warm, positive feelings toward the influencer. I said it somewhat differently before: in order for children or students to accept an adult's experience, wisdom, or values, they must like, look up to, and respect the adult. Conversely, we know that kids grow to dislike, hold a low opinion of, and treat with contempt those who would try to coerce them, bridle them, or deny their right to get their needs met.

On the other hand, we also know that kids will seek out, listen to, believe, and model themselves after those whom they like and admire, who treat them with respect, who trust them, who refrain from bossing them around, who are easy to talk to. So our paradox has its analogue: *Give up using power, gain more influence.*

DO WE WANT OBEDIENT YOUNGSTERS?

One coping reaction to power-based discipline requires our special attention. Everyone knows that some youngsters respond to adult authority by giving in, submitting, obeying. As I have repeatedly pointed out, obedience to adult authority is precisely what the dare-to-discipline and power-to-the-parent champions want more than anything else. Having a child learn to obey is their highly valued goal, and defiance their greatest fear.

Throughout history, in fact, obedience to authority has been a deeply ingrained and greatly valued behavior in many societies. Submission to authority is considered a necessary source of social control within institutions and nations, the cement that holds people together in organizations, and a critical requirement for all communal living. As such, it has been elevated to the status of a noble or moral virtue in military organizations and religious cults, as well as in families and schools. This is particularly so in families in which some higher authority or ideology dictates a hierarchy of authority, with the husband and father as "head of the household," occupying the top of the hierarchy, the wife next, and the kids at the bottom.

Some philosophers have warned us that the fabric of any society will be rent by disobedience. And, as I pointed out earlier, some contemporary authors similarly warn parents that without respect for parental authority there can be only "anarchy, chaos, and confusion" (Dobson, 1978).

Rather recently, however, a handful of social scientists and historians have begun to question this traditional view. The brilliant historian C. P. Snow, citing the Nazi extermination of European Jews as an extreme instance of a hideous and immoral crime carried out by thousands of German soldiers in the name of obedience to their superiors, concludes:

> When you think of the long and gloomy history of man, you will find more hideous crimes have been committed in the name of obedience than have ever been committed in the name of rebellion. (Snow, 1961)

Other writers have documented the many horrible actions of American soldiers against Vietnamese citizens, done in the name of obedience to their officers. More recently, the tragic murders and suicides of nearly one thousand members of the Reverend Jim Jones's religious cult provided another shocking example of using "duty to obey orders." In this tragic event, blind obedience to their leader caused members to kill their own children and, finally, themselves.

Instead of viewing obedience to authority as a virtue, I believe we should see it as a malady that has become commonplace in our society. We are creating future citizens who believe they should unquestioningly do what they are told to do. This approach begins in the family and is continually reinforced in our schools, in the military, in many churches and religious cults, and in many business and industrial organizations. There is much evidence, however, that people conditioned to obey others come to view themselves as *instruments for carrying out another person's wishes, and as no longer responsible for their own actions.*

Nowhere has this been more dramatically demonstrated than in the award-winning, pioneering experiments of psychologist Stanley Milgram and his associates at Yale University in the 1960s.

Under the guise of engaging in a study of how people learn, Milgram's subjects were told to administer electric shocks to a strapped-in "learner" (the victim) whenever he gave a wrong response in the learning task. The subjects, however, didn't know the victim was actually an actor. He didn't really receive the shocks but only acted as if he did—first protesting only verbally, then, as the apparent strength of the shocks increased, groaning and shrieking as if in agony, finally begging to be released from the experiment because of his intense pain.

The experimenter (the authority in the white lab coat) demanded that the subjects increase the strength of the shock each time the learner gave a wrong answer—which, of course, he was programmed to do on occasion.

The real purpose of the experiment, known only to the experimenter, was to study how the subjects (those administering the shock) resolved the conflict between either obeying the orders of the authority figure to administer increasingly stronger shocks or refusing to obey the authority after observing the victim's apparent pain and his pleas to be released from the situation—a conflict between an "obedience" response and a "disobedience" response.

Milgram (1974) himself found the study results "surprising and dismaying." These were some of the findings:

- Almost two-thirds of the subjects fell into the category of "obedient" subjects.
- Many subjects experienced a lot of personal stress in the situation and made frequent verbal protests to the experimenter ("The man seems to be getting hurt in there" or "I won't go on with the guy screaming like that"). Nevertheless, a substantial proportion *continued shocking the victim* up through the strongest voltage on the indicator.
- Later, some subjects acknowledged being convinced that what they were doing was wrong, but admitted that they could not bring themselves to disobey authority.

The most common thought adjustment these obedient subjects made, Milgram concluded from interviews with them, was to see themselves as not responsible for their own actions. Each saw himself not as a person choosing to act in a morally unacceptable way but rather as the agent of external authority; they were "just doing their duty." Milgram concluded: "The disappearance of a sense of responsibility is the most far-reaching consequence of submission to authority." The findings from this carefully designed and creative experiment clearly contradict the argument that teaching children to obey external authority will foster self-control and a sense of responsibility. Milgram's study supports the opposite argument: obedience to authority brings about the *disappearance* of self-control and responsibility.

Obedience to authority recently has been seen as playing an important role in child sexual abuse. Repeatedly it has been found that the majority of child victims have been molested by a family member or an adult *known to the child.* Generally, the child has been taught *to respect the authority of such adults and obey them*, and thus may have readily submitted to the parent or adult authority figure. In such cases, the child is unclear or confused about whether the sexual act is wrong or unusual. Children's inherent reluctance to challenge adult authority and the very real possibility of retaliation may also contribute to the sexually abused child's ambivalence about reporting what has happened. In short, the imbalance of power in these adult-child relationships and the abused child's resulting helplessness explains why so many children fail to resist the abusing adult, as Roland Summit has described:

> Children often describe their first experience as waking up to find their father (or stepfather, or mother's live-in companion), exploring their bodies with hands or mouth. Less frequently, they may find a penis filling their mouth or probing between their legs. . . . Like the adult victim of rape, the child victim (of abuse) is expected to forcibly resist, to cry for help, and to attempt to escape the intrusion. By that standard, almost every child fails. The normal reaction is to "play possum," that is, to feign sleep, to shift position and to pull up the covers. Small children do not call on force to deal with overwhelming threats. When there is no place to run, they have no choice but to try to hide. Children generally learn to cope silently with terrors in the night. Bed covers take on magical powers against monsters, but they are no match for human intruders.

To conclude, I offer my own prescription for parents and teachers—in fact, for all persons:

As a society we must urgently adopt the goal of finding and teaching effective alternatives to authority and power in dealing with other persons—children or adults—alternatives that will produce human beings with sufficient courage, autonomy, and self-discipline to resist being controlled by authority when obedience to that authority would contradict their own sense of what is right and what is wrong.

In the following chapters I will offer many such alternatives, showing both parents and teachers a number of specific non-power, noncoercive skills and methods they can use to deal effectively with children and youths. I believe it will be clear to most readers that these alternatives will help youngsters become autonomous, responsible, self-directing, self-controlled, and self-disciplined—characteristics I believe are needed by citizens of a truly healthy, democratic society.

PART

TWO

ALTERNATIVES TO DISCIPLINING CHILDREN

SIX

Noncontrolling Methods to Get Children to Change Behavior

Why has the control-by-discipline model of dealing with children persisted for centuries with only minor modifications? Why do both parents and teachers keep on trying punitive power when there is so little evidence that it changes children's behavior? Why do adults persist in thinking that they are limited to the use of power-based discipline when they certainly must recognize that most children fight it or escape from it by trying all the coping mechanisms they can muster? And why do parents and teachers keep trying to control and coerce teenage youngsters when by that time they don't have power anymore?

Three decades of professional experience working with parents and schoolteachers have given me some answers to these questions. One simple answer is that people persist in playing the role of disciplinarian because they think the only alternative is to be permissive, and nobody likes that role in relationships with children, or in *any* relationship, for that matter. I called attention to this either-or thinking in an earlier chapter. Of the two choices, being authoritarian seems much better to most adults than being permissive; having and using power, better than power in the hands of children; controlling children, better than the chaos they think would result from giving up the control.

I am in complete sympathy with those who are leery of permissiveness, because I've seen what happens when parents and teachers let children do whatever they want with no rules or limits. It makes the adults' lives miserable, and it produces children who are inconsiderate, thoughtless, selfish, unmanageable, and unlikable.

It is unfortunate indeed that so few parents and teachers understand that there are many alternatives to control by discipline, many methods that are effective in *influencing* children to change behavior that is unacceptable—methods that ensure that both persons in the relationship get their needs met.

Creating, developing, and teaching these nonpower ways of influencing others has been my work—in fact, a kind of professional mission—since 1950. That was the year in which I designed and tested out a brief leadership-training program for educational and religious leaders at the University of Chicago, where I was a member of the faculty.

For that workshop I drew heavily on my past experience as a counselor and therapist, convinced that the communication skills I had learned in my counseling training were the very skills that were needed by leaders (managers, administrators, supervisors) for developing productive groups and motivated and satisfied group members. For me, that marked the beginning of a decade of consulting with business, industrial, and government organizations, primarily doing leadership training that stressed methods of influencing workers rather than trying to control them with rewards and punishments.

In 1962, after realizing that parent-child relationships were very similar to boss-subordinate relationships, I designed a leadership-training course for parents. It was immediately successful, first attracting parents throughout Los Angeles County, then in the San Francisco Bay area and in San Diego County. Carrying the name Parent Effectiveness Training (P.E.T.), the course eventually attracted persons who wanted to become P.E.T. instructors themselves. Training and authorizing many hundreds of these people accelerated the rapid spread of P.E.T. into many additional states within a period of five years.

Now over a million parents have completed this course in classes taught by several thousand authorized instructors. Our cadre of instructors includes people in every state and twenty-five foreign countries. The year 1987 marked the twenty-fifth anniversary of the P.E.T. course—a quarter of a century of providing education and skill training to parents. That experience has provided me with impressive evidence that most parents can learn, and later apply in the home, new methods and new skills that will dramatically transform the job of parenthood, improve the quality of family life, and produce *self*-disciplined youngsters.

Several years after I introduced the P.E.T. course, requests came from a number of school administrators to teach their teachers the same skills we were teaching parents. This encouraged me to design Teacher Effectiveness Training (T.E.T.). Since then, our T.E.T. instructors have taught over 100,000 participants (including school administrators, counselors, and school psychologists, as well as teachers) throughout the United States and in a dozen foreign countries. T.E.T. has shown that most teachers can learn these new alternatives to their traditional classroom disciplining methods and that these nonpower skills and procedures will reduce disruptive behaviors in the classroom, as well as improve the scholastic performance and emotional health of their students.

I will present these alternative methods and skills in this chapter, starting with those that are appropriate during the child's earliest years, before language and communication skills have fully developed. Then I will present additional methods and procedures that call for two-way verbal communication.

But first, some explanation is needed about the P.E.T. and T.E.T. courses. Until recently, I always thought of these training programs only as increasing people's effectiveness, giving them new interpersonal skills, new communication skills, new problem-solving procedures. However, I've come to view such descriptions as inadequate and somewhat misleading. They make the training sound mechanistic and technique-oriented; they also fail to represent fully what this training actually does for parents and teachers—and, of course, for children.

More than providing training in specific skills and tools, the P.E.T. and T.E.T. courses give participants an entirely different *model*, a different *role*, a different *style of leadership*, a different *way of being* in relationships with children and youth.

To make such a complete transformation, as many course graduates have done, for some may require a profound shift in their attitudes and in their posture toward discipline, power, and authority. After taking the course, people find themselves speaking a new nonpower language, discarding the traditional language of power universally used in adult-child relationships. I refer to words such as *authority, obey, demand, permit, allow, set limits, deprivations, discipline, restrict, punish, prohibit, enforce rules, respect for authority*. Course graduates take on a completely new role as a parent or teacher, a nonpower role that can be described by such terms as *facilitator, consultant, friend, listener, problem solver, participant, negotiator, helper, resource person*.

This transformation is evident in the following personal experience reported by an elementary-school teacher who had recently taken T.E.T.:

> I used to try to control students by asking my class leading questions in such a way that the children were forced into ritual answers that I wanted. For example, "Are we quiet when we walk to the library, class?" Then the students would answer like good little boys and girls, "Yes." "And do we run?" They would answer, "No, we don't run." I used to rehearse my classes before we would go on trips, or fire drills, or have visitors. Well, the kids always agreed with me. "No, we never run." But then they always ran, and they pushed and yelled. When I got them back in the room, I asked a different question: "Do we keep our promises, class?" And the usual answer, "Yes, we keep our promises."
>
> When the T.E.T. instructor played a tape in class and I heard how stupid that teacher on the tape sounded and how much I sounded like her, I decided to try something else. I decided to try Method III [problem solving] with a problem I'd been lecturing the class about for weeks—getting in on time after recess. In the past I handled it my usual way—they

were always late lining up and I'd have to go out and yell at them to line up. By the time they all got there and lined up and walked to the room, we'd wasted at least ten minutes. When we got in the room, I'd say, "When the bell rings do we continue to play, class?" And they'd say, "No." Then I'd say, "What do we do when the bell rings, class?" And they'd chant, "Line up." Then I'd say, "From now on I won't have to yell at you to line up, right?" And they'd say, "Right!" And the next day there I'd be, yelling at them to line up.

Can you believe that? Well, this week I sent an I-message instead of asking my usual questions. I told them how tired I was of yelling at them to line up and how afraid I was that the principal was going to give me a poor rating because of all the time we wasted. Then I listened to them. I couldn't believe my ears. They said they were sick of standing out there in the hot sun waiting for me and asked why they had to line up anyway. They couldn't understand why they couldn't come to the room when the bell rang. I said that we'd always lined up, and they asked, "Why?" I thought about it for a while and then I said I couldn't think of any reason why students had to line up except that it was just the way things were done.

Well, they didn't buy that. We then decided to define our needs. Mine was to have them get from the playground to the classroom in an orderly, disciplined manner in as short a time as possible. Theirs was to avoid standing in a line for five or more minutes in the hot sun waiting for me to arrive to escort them to the classroom, and then having to march like soldiers. We decided on a solution suggested by one of the kids—namely, when the bell rang, they were to walk to the room from the playground. I was to walk from the teacher's lounge, and we'd go in.

We've been trying it for three days now, and it's

working beautifully. We save ten minutes a day in
the roundup, as well as a lot of time that I used to
spend lecturing them on lining up and marching
quietly. And I don't have to walk clear out to the
playground anymore. But the biggest difference is
how we feel about each other when we get to the
room. Everybody used to be mad by the time we'd
lined up and marched quietly to the room. Now we
go into the room feeling good, or at least not mad at
each other. That sometimes saves a whole afternoon.
The hardest part of this problem was for the kids to
convince me that I didn't have a need for them to
line up, that lining up was only my solution to a need,
and, in our case, a very bad one.

CHILDREN DON'T REALLY MISBEHAVE

The P.E.T. and T.E.T. courses bring about a radical transformation in how parents and teachers look at children's behavior. Most parents and teachers think of children as either
"behaving" or "misbehaving." This labeling of behavior as good
and bad begins when the child is quite young. In our training
programs we try to help parents see that children don't really
misbehave.

Interestingly enough, the term is almost exclusively applied
to *children*—seldom to adults. We never hear people say:

"My husband misbehaved yesterday."
"One of our guests misbehaved at the party last night."
"I got so angry when my friend misbehaved during lunch."
"My employees have been misbehaving lately."

Apparently, it's only children who are seen as misbehaving—no
one else. Misbehavior is exclusively *parent and teacher language*,
tied up somehow with how adults traditionally have viewed
children. It is also used in almost every book on parenting I've
read, and I've read quite a few.

I think adults say a child misbehaves whenever some specific
action is judged as contrary to how the adult *thinks* the child

should behave. The verdict of misbehavior, then, is clearly a value judgment made by the adult—a label placed on some particular behavior, a negative judgment of what the child is doing. Misbehavior thus is actually a specific action of the child that is seen by the adult as producing an undesirable consequence for the *adult*. What makes a child's behavior *mis*behavior (bad behavior) is the perception that the behavior is, or might be, bad behavior *for the adult*. The "badness" of the behavior actually resides in the adult's mind, not the child's; the child in fact is doing what he or she chooses or needs to do to satisfy some need.

Put another way, the *adult* experiences the badness, not the child. Even more accurate, it is the consequences of the child's behavior for the adult that are felt to be bad (or potentially bad), not the behavior itself.

When parents and teachers grasp this critical distinction, they experience a marked shift in attitude toward their children or students. They begin to see all actions of youngsters simply as behaviors, engaged in solely for the purpose of getting needs met. When adults begin to see children as persons like themselves, engaging in various behaviors to satisfy normal human needs, they are much less inclined to evaluate the behaviors as good or bad.

Accepting that children don't really misbehave doesn't mean, however, that adults will always feel *accepting* of what they do. Nor should they be expected to, for children are bound to do things that adults don't like, things that interfere with their own "pursuit of happiness." But even then, the child is not a misbehaving or bad child, not trying to do something *to the adult*, but rather is only trying to do something *for himself*.

Only when parents or teachers make this important shift—changing the locus of the problem from the child to the adult—can they begin to appreciate the logic of some of the nonpower alternatives for dealing with behaviors they don't accept.

WHO "OWNS" THE PROBLEM?

To help people make this transformation, we utilize the concept of "problem ownership." Let me explain. Whenever a child is doing something that prevents you from getting some need satisfied, think of that behavior as unacceptable since it is causing *you* a problem. It is you who "owns" the problem.

However, should it be the child who is experiencing some type of need deprivation, think of that situation as one in which the child has a problem—that's when the child "owns" the problem.

In our classes we ask parents and teachers to visualize a rectangular window through which they will see each and every possible behavior of a child. Then we explain that some behaviors will be acceptable and some unacceptable. Behaviors that are unacceptable are to be seen through the bottom of the window, where the adult owns the problem.

THE BEHAVIOR WINDOW

ACCEPTABLE BEHAVIOR ⎬ CHILD OWNS PROBLEM	Child's behaviors causing problem for child
NO-PROBLEM AREA	Child's behaviors not causing a problem for either child or adult
UNACCEPTABLE BEHAVIOR ⎬ ADULT OWNS PROBLEM	Child's behaviors causing problem for adult

Here are some examples of children's behaviors that would cause a problem for most parents: child is being noisy when parent is talking on the phone, child is dawdling when parent is in a hurry, child is walking through the living room with dirty shoes, child is hitting his baby brother with one of his blocks, child is driving the family car too fast.

In the top panel of the rectangle, we put those behaviors of the child that signal that the child owns a problem. Examples: child is upset at not having anyone to play with, child says she was rejected by one of her friends, teenager acts unhappy about being overweight. These are problems they are experiencing in their own lives, independent of the adult.

The middle panel of the rectangle is for behaviors of the child that are not causing a problem either to the child or to the adult. These are the delightful times in adult-child relationships when children are happily doing their thing independently, or when adults and children are doing something together in a problem-free relationship. We call this the No-Problem area of the behavior window.

In this chapter I'll be presenting alternatives to discipline that parents and teachers can use to modify the behavior causing them a problem. In a later chapter, I'll describe another set of methods that help children solve their problems.

Alternative #1: Find Out What the Child Needs

Barbara, six months old, starts to cry loudly in the middle of the night. Her parents are awakened from the sleep they need and naturally find this behavior unpleasant and unacceptable. But how can they get Barbara to stop crying? They have to start guessing. Finding the need behind an infant's crying in order to remedy the parents' problem is like trying to solve a puzzle:

> Maybe she's wet and cold. I'll check on that. No, she's still dry. Well, could it be we didn't burp her enough and she's feeling uncomfortable with gas? Let's try picking her up and start the burping process. Bad guess again; she won't burp. Wonder if she's hungry. Her bottle still has some milk in it, but it got pushed down to the end of the crib. I'll act on that guess next. Success! She is sucking and drinking.

> Good. She's getting sleepy. Maybe I can put her back into her crib now. Great! She's falling asleep. Now we can go back to bed and get our sleep.

Parents often have to use the guessing approach with infants—when they whine incessantly, when they are restless and pestering, when they can't get to sleep, when they throw their food on the floor, when they dawdle. Remember: when infants do things that are unacceptable to their parents, there's always some reason for it—some need they're trying to satisfy. When parents focus on discovering what the child needs instead of seeing the behavior as "misbehavior" to be punished, they usually can remove whatever it is that is causing the unacceptable behavior or supply whatever it is the child needs and can't supply for himself.

As infants and toddlers grow older and start to talk, the guessing game gets much easier. Now parents need only listen accurately to the child's communication, as for example, these messages:

> "My tummy hurts."
> "Bobby took my ball."
> "Why do I have to go to bed?"

Of course, at times parents may have to ask simple questions, like:

> "Why are you crying?"
> "What do you want?"
> "Why did you hit your baby brother?"
> "Why are you not getting ready?"

The answers will give you clues as to what might be done to change the particular behavior that is at that moment unacceptable to you.

Alternative #2: Let's Make a Trade
Another effective nonpower method for changing unacceptable behaviors of infants and toddlers involves trading:

substituting for the *unacceptable* behavior some other behavior that would be *acceptable* to you.

Laura, your curious one-year-old, has found a pair of your new nylons, which she finds enjoyable to touch and tug. You find this unacceptable because you're afraid she'll snag or destroy them. So you go to your drawer and pull out an old pair that is already snagged and beyond repair. You place this pair in her hands and gently take away the new pair. Laura, not knowing the difference, finds the damaged pair equally as enjoyable to touch and tug. Her needs are met, but so are yours.

When adults start thinking in terms of trading, they're not as apt to rush in with power and authority and start punishing the "misbehavior."

Alternative #3: Modify the Environment

Most parents and teachers intuitively know that they can stop a lot of unacceptable behavior by altering the child's *environment*, as opposed to making coercive efforts to change the *child*. Who has not watched a whiny, pestering, bored youngster get totally (and quietly) involved once he is provided with some materials that capture his interest—clay, finger paints, puzzles, picture books, some other activity. This is called "enriching the environment" and is something that effective nursery school or kindergarten teachers practice every day.

At other times kids need just the opposite. For example, when kids are keyed up and hyperactive just before bedtime, the wise parent knows it's time to "impoverish the environment." Overstimulated children will often calm down if you read them a fairy tale, tell a story, or ask them to share their day's events with you. Much of the fighting and hassling of bedtime could be avoided if parents made an effort to reduce the stimulation of their children's environment at that particular time.

Then, too, a lot of unacceptable—and dangerous—behavior by toddlers can be avoided by serious efforts on the part of parents to "childproof" the environment, as with:

Buying unbreakable cups and glasses
Putting matches, knives, razor blades out of reach
Locking up medicines and sharp tools

Keeping the basement door locked
Fastening down slippery throw rugs

Again, the principle here is to limit the *environment* instead of the *child*.

Preschool teachers are old hands at modifying the classroom environment to prevent or change disruptive and unacceptable behaviors. This is why children in the typical preschool are generally busy, nondisruptive, occupied, quiet. Teachers of very young children usually have had training in how to enrich the classroom environment to prevent boredom (which is usually what produces unacceptable behavior). Good preschool teachers make a multitude of stimulating alternatives and choices available to their charges. They also make effective use of individualized activities—students doing different things at the same time.

Good preschool teachers also know when to impoverish the environment—reduce the amount of stimulation for their children. They darken the room, schedule quiet times, or use some "focusing technique" such as painting, films, video, stories.

With very young children, restricting or limiting the environment can prevent a lot of disruptive or unacceptable behavior—designating areas for certain activities (e.g., finger painting only in the kitchen or garage), limiting the number of children who may be in one place at one time, assigning quiet corners.

Undesirable behaviors sometimes occur when the environment of young children is too confining. Sensitive teachers extend the environment into the outside world—study trips, use of gymnasium or library, combining classes, field trips and so on.

Sometimes the classroom or home environment can be unnecessarily complex and difficult for children to manage. This is especially true for toddlers who have to function in an environment built for six-foot-tall adults. Unacceptable behavior can arise when there are too many adult rules, regulations, procedures that children find hard to follow. Teachers and parents can simplify the environment by such procedures as putting things children use where they can reach them; posting rules where kids can see them; making a small step-stool available; labeling drawers, cabinets, files, and storage areas.

Alternative #4: The Confrontive I-Message

A confrontive I-message is a nonblameful, nonevaluative message that tells the youngster what the adult is experiencing in response to some unacceptable behavior of the child, as in the following examples:

> "When the TV is on so loud, I can't carry on a conversation with your mother."

> "I'm afraid I won't be able to enjoy the flowers I planted if they're trampled on."

> "When there is this much noise in the classroom, I can't hear what anyone is saying."

> "When I have to wait so long for you to get ready for school, it makes me late for work and my boss gets mad at me."

One of the principal educational objectives of our Effectiveness Training courses is to encourage the use of such *I-language* as an alternative to traditional, blameful, and often coercive *You-language*. You-messages contain heavy loads of blame, judgment, evaluation, criticism, and coercion. They are the verbal expressions of adults who see children as "misbehaving," as in these examples:

> "You ought to know better than to do that."
> "You stop that noise or I'll send you outside."
> "You ought to be ashamed of yourself."
> "You are driving me crazy."
> "If you don't put your clothes away, you'll get a spanking."
> "You are eating like a pig."
> "Now you've given me a headache."

I-messages keep the responsibility with the adult (because it's the adult who "owns" the problem), and they are more likely to make children *want* to modify their behavior out of consideration for others. If kids are not put down or blamed for their behavior, they are much more willing to respond helpfully, more willing to modify their behavior themselves after hearing that someone has a problem with it.

Not so with You-messages. Children get defensive and resist change when they are blamed and put down. And You-messages are damaging to children's self-esteem. No wonder youngsters retaliate by sending back You-messages of their own, thus escalating the situation into a verbal battle that brings hurt feelings, tears, slammed doors, or threats of punishment.

For many people, it comes as a shock to discover for the first time how much of their normal conversation is filled with You-messages. They have always been under the impression they were honestly saying what was on their minds. "The last thing I would ever want to do," they insist, "is make my child feel guilty. I've had enough of that done to me." Then why are You-messages so common?

It seems easier to express ourselves in You-messages. Requiring no self-awareness, they roll readily off the tongue, shifting responsibility for our feelings from ourselves to others. They are also an easy, impulsive way to get back at people for causing us a problem. However, they usually don't accomplish your purpose; in fact, You-messages cause resistance and defensiveness in children. In addition, You-messages:

- Provoke destructive arguments or mutual name-calling.
- Cause children to feel guilty, put down, criticized, hurt.
- May cause the child to feel like getting back at you, put *you* down.
- Communicate a lack of respect for the needs of the other person.

Dropping You-messages and learning to use I-messages, however, is more than acquiring a new skill. Parents and teachers undergo a major perceptual transformation when they accept that *they* own the problem when some behavior of a child is unacceptable to them.

With children too young to understand verbal I-messages,

parents must send *nonverbal* messages, as in the following examples:

> While Dad is carrying little Tony in the supermarket, he starts to kick Dad in the stomach, laughing with each kick. Dad immediately puts Tony down on his feet, rubs his tummy where it hurts, and continues walking. (Nonverbal message: "It hurts me when I get kicked in the stomach, so I don't like to carry you.")

> Judy stalls and pokes getting into the car when Mother is in a terrible hurry. Mother puts her hand on Judy's rear and gently guides her onto the front seat. (Nonverbal message: "I need you to get in right now because I'm in a hurry.")

In addition to influencing kids to change, I-messages let children know that their parents or teachers are human: they too have feelings, needs, wants, and limits. I-messages imply that a certain equality exists between adult and child. We also know that the remarkable effectiveness of I-messages derives from the fact that they come across as *appeals* to children— asking for their help. The underlying message is "I have a problem with your behavior, and I need your help." As you may remember from your own experience as a child, when you heard such appeals for help, you were ten times more willing to modify your behavior than when you were chastised, reprimanded, scolded, blamed, threatened, or ordered around by such put-downs as these:

> "You're being a bad boy."
> "You go to your room."
> "You're acting like a baby."
> "You stop it or you'll get the hairbrush!"
> "Don't you ever do that again."
> "You've ruined my day."
> "You'll be the death of me yet."

I-messages could also be called "responsibility messages," for two reasons: (1) an adult who sends an I-message is taking responsibility for his own inner condition (listening to what he is feeling) and is assuming responsibility by openly sharing this assessment of himself with a child; (2) I-messages leave the responsibility for changing the unacceptable behavior with the child—as opposed to the child feeling coerced by the adult. At the same time, I-messages avoid the negative judgment that accompanies You-messages, thus making the student more willing to be considerate and helpful instead of resentful, angry, and retaliative.

I-messages meet three important criteria for effective confrontation:

1. They are likely to promote a willingness to change.
2. They contain minimal negative evaluation of the child or student.
3. They do not injure the relationship.

One teacher, after her first use of I-messages in her classroom, reported this incident:

> I was reluctant to try an I-message with the kids I have. They are so hard to manage. Finally I screwed up my courage and sent a strong I-message to a group of children who were making a mess with water paints in the back of the room by the sink. I said, "When you mix paints and spill them all over the sink and table, I have to scrub up later or get yelled at by the custodian. I'm sick of cleaning up after you, and I feel helpless to prevent it from happening." I just stopped then and waited to see what they would do. I really expected them to laugh at me and take that "I don't care" attitude they've had all year. But they didn't. They stood there looking at me for a minute like they were amazed to find out I was upset. And then one of them said, "Come on, let's clean it up." I was floored. You know, they haven't turned into models of perfection, but they

now clean up the sink and tables every day whether
they've spilled paint on them or not. (Gordon, 1974)

This teacher's experience is not unique. Most teachers really
have to screw up their courage to confront their kids directly
and openly—it means revealing themselves. Yet, almost without
exception, once having taken the risk, teachers find that students
they had seen as "bad" or "inconsiderate" show more consideration for their teacher's feelings than expected.

Another teacher pointed out how difficult it was for him to
shift from the blaming, guilt-producing You-messages to I-
messages:

It was really hard for me to send I-messages, even
though I could understand what my You-messages
were doing to the students and our relationships. I
kept having trouble changing. For one thing, I had
been taught that it was rude to use the pronoun *I*.
Teachers used to mark my papers all up with red
pencil when I wrote about myself in the first person.
Another thing, probably worse, was that as a child I
had been taught not to expose my feelings, that it
was unmanly and a sign of weakness to let people
know how I was feeling. Even though I've been
working on it, I still have trouble knowing how I am
feeling. It seems like I'm upset all the time, and I
know I've got to get past the upset and find out what's
really bugging me. (Gordon, 1974)

Students will begin to look at this teacher as a real person,
because he is developing the inner security to expose his feelings,
first to himself and then to others—to show himself as a person
capable of feeling disappointment, hurt, anger, or fear. He will
be seen by students as genuine, someone with weaknesses, with
feelings of inadequacy—someone very much like the students
themselves.

Good I-messages do not include giving solutions—"You
must do such and such," "You should do this," "Here's what I
think you should do." Rather, they permit youngsters to come

up with their own solutions for helping solve the adult's problem. And those solutions are often surprisingly creative and ingenious, some that adults would never have thought of. Even two- and three-year-olds are capable of unusually creative solutions, as shown in this incident with a mother and three-year-old Mark, whose many fears kept him from going to sleep. He'd often come into his parents' bedroom and wake them up. His mother submitted this summary:

> He had expressed fears of certain objects in his room. He loves monsters in the daytime but at night gets frightened. He used to come in and get in our bed. We said, "Mark, you know, we'd appreciate it if you could stay in bed because we really need our sleep; when you come in and wake us up, then we're very tired the next day and get crabby." The first ten times he didn't respond, but eventually he did. He'd get up and play his record player. Then we told him his record player also woke us up. He was so cute—he just turned the machine on so he could hear that hum. And that was enough to comfort him. Most of the time we couldn't even hear the hum.

A father told us about another ingenious solution that emerged when his son trampled his newly planted grass:

> I came home and found Gary's street-hockey net sitting just off the edge of the driveway, right in the middle of some new grass I had planted. There were numerous footprints in the grass, which had just sprouted. I sent him a strong I-message about how sick I was to see the new grass messed up because I didn't want to take the time and trouble to replant it. He grunted an acknowledgment and went on about his business—watching TV. A few days later I came home to find a hockey game in process with four or five neighborhood boys and my son. The net was on the driveway this time and I noticed the boys were leaping across the new grass rather than stepping on

it. I commented on this and one of the boys popped up with, "It's a penalty shot for every footprint." I never did find out how this solution came about, but it worked great, and it was one I never would have thought of myself.

Kids really want to come up with solutions, because they hate to have their needs blocked. You can almost see their little heads working to find a solution that will take care of the parent's needs and still not stop them from doing their thing. Perhaps this is what motivated the youngster in this incident:

A young mother in our P.E.T. class had polished the stereo cabinet in preparation for company. Her two little boys (ages seven and four) wanted to play their records that afternoon, but she was worried about fingerprints. She resisted saying, "Ask me to put the records on." Instead she sent an I-message: "When you open up the lid, I'm concerned there'll be fingerprints and I'll have to clean it again before company comes." Her seven-year-old came up with his own creative solution: he carefully stretched his pullover sleeves down over his hands and opened the stereo without leaving fingerprints.

It warrants repeating: *we tend to underestimate kids' capacity to change until they're given a chance to show it.*

Alternative #5: The Preventive I-Message

When parents or teachers disclose a need whose fulfillment will require future support, cooperation, or direct action from children or students, we call that a *preventive I-message.*

As opposed to confrontive I-messages, whose purpose is to influence children to modify unacceptable behaviors that have already occurred, preventive I-messages are for influencing kids to take a particular action *in the future* in order to *avoid* the adult's displeasure (nonacceptance). It is a message, then, that lets others know ahead of time what you might need or want.

Informing others of your needs helps them stay closely

involved with what you are planning to do. It keeps them from being surprised later on and prepares them for possible changes you might want them to make. Here are some examples of clear preventive I-messages:

"I'd like you to tell me when you plan not to come home right after school, so I won't get worried when you don't."

"I'd like us to figure out now what needs to be done before we leave for the weekend, so we make sure we have time to get it all done."

"We are going on a field trip to the museum next week, so I'd like us to decide what special rules we'll need to prevent any problems."

"Grandma is coming for a week with us, so I want us to figure out what we need to do to make her stay pleasant for all of us. Grandma has to be in a wheelchair most of the time, so I want us to give special thought to changes we might have to make in the house so she can get around easily."

We find again and again that parents and teachers are astonished—and delighted—to find cooperation when they send such assertive messages. Children commonly respond:

"We didn't know."
"You never asked."
"I'm glad you told me."

How many unmet needs and unrealized goals of parents and teachers can be traced to the fact that they "never asked" or that they made aggressive-sounding demands that turned kids off or created resistance?

To avoid sounding aggressive, demanding, or authoritarian, it's important to include the *reasons* for your need, as in this preventive I-message:

"I've decided to go back to work because I'd like to help with the increasing expenses we have now. Also, I need to have a job that gives me a chance to use my special training. I'll need some help from you kids with some of the household chores I've been doing myself."

You'll find that preventive I-messages bring many benefits, not only for you but also for your children or your students:

- You maintain awareness, responsibility, and control of your needs and feelings.
- Others learn what your needs are and the strength of your feelings about them.
- You model openness, directness, and honesty, thereby fostering similar behavior by others.
- You reduce the chances of future conflicts and tensions from unknown or uncommunicated needs, thus decreasing the element of surprise that often jolts even the closest relationships.
- You take full responsibility for the plans you've made, and you prepare for future needs.
- Your relationships stay healthy, because they're based on openness, honesty, and mutual need-satisfaction.

A less obvious effect of the preventive I-message is that kids learn that their parents are human: they have their own needs, wants, preferences, and wishes like everyone else. And, of course, these I-need messages give kids a chance, without being *told* what to do, to come up with something that will please their parents.

A mother, raising her three teenage sons by herself, described how she sent a preventive I-message to her son Don about a PTA meeting:

I feel Don has been closer to me—I can tell him what I feel. The other night I went to this PTA thing where he was going to play the guitar and sing. He wanted me to go, but I'd never been before, and I was feeling like I didn't want to be dumped in there and left alone, not knowing anyone. So I said, "Don, I've never been to your school meeting before and I'm feeling just a little scared, you know. I'd like you to take care of me in there and not just leave me." And he did! He took me in and introduced me to a bunch of people I didn't know, and he brought me a cup of tea. He just really looked after me! (Gordon, 1976)

Alternative #6: Shifting Gears to Reduce Resistance

Although you'll be surprised how often youngsters respond constructively and helpfully after hearing your I-messages, you should expect occasionally to hear resistance, defensiveness, guilt, denial, discomfort, or hurt feelings. It's understandable that I-messages sometimes provoke these responses. They confront kids with the prospect of having to change habitual behavior. The kids are often surprised or shocked to hear how you feel, and certainly don't like to be told their behavior is unacceptable or that it caused you a problem, even if by chance you've sent a perfect I-message.

So, when you hear these not-so-uncommon responses to your I-messages, it is useless to keep hammering at children with repeated assertive messages—the strategy usually recommended in assertiveness training programs. What children hear if you keep repeating your message is: "I need or want such and such and it's not important to me what *you* need."

When you hear resistance or some other feeling reaction to your I-message, you'll need to make a quick shift from your sending/assertive posture to a listening/understanding posture. Such a shift will communicate, "I want to be sensitive to the feelings my assertiveness brought out in you," "I will delay trying to get what I want and listen to what you're feeling now." This shifting gears (think of it as shifting from a going-forward gear to a backing-up gear) lets others know you are not out to get your need met at their expense. Although you're not ready to abandon your needs, you want to empathize and understand the nature of the problem your assertive I-message caused the person to whom it was directed. This can lead to seeking a compromise solution.

Shifting gears often causes an immediate dissolution of the recipient's resistant feelings. Having feelings acknowledged seems to help kids decide on their own to modify their behavior. *Children find it easier to change if they feel the adult understands how hard it might be.* Here is an interaction between a father and daughter that illustrates shifting gears and the immediate effects it has:

> FATHER: I'm upset about the supper dishes being left in the sink. Didn't we agree that you would get them done right after dinner?
>
> JAN: I felt so tired after dinner because I stayed up until three A.M. doing that term paper.
>
> FATHER: You just didn't feel like doing the dishes right after dinner.
>
> JAN: No. So I took a nap until ten-thirty. I plan to do them before I go to bed. Okay?
>
> FATHER: Okay by me.

Here is another illustration of shifting gears, this time after a teacher confronts a student who is often late to class:

> TEACHER: Allan, your being late to class is causing me a problem. When you come in late I have to stop whatever I'm doing. It's distracting to me, and I'm frustrated.
>
> STUDENT: Yeah, well, I've had a lot to do lately and sometimes I just can't get here on time.
>
> TEACHER [shifting gears to listening]: I see. You're having some new problems of your own lately.
>
> STUDENT: Right. Mr. Sellers asked me to help in the chem lab after third period—you know, setting up for fourth period. It's a good deal.
>
> TEACHER [still listening]: You're really pleased he asked you.
>
> STUDENT: Right! I can probably get to be the lab assistant next year and I could sure use the job.
>
> TEACHER [still listening]: There may be a good payoff for you and that's pretty important.
>
> STUDENT: Yeah. I know you're upset about me being late.

I didn't think it would be such a problem. You know, I've tried to sort of slip in quietly.

TEACHER [still listening]: You're a little surprised that it's such a problem to me even when you try to be quiet.

STUDENT: Well, not really. I can see your point. You do have to stop and change the attendance record and stuff. Mostly I'm late because Mr. Sellers and I get to talking too long. I'll tell him it's a problem for you and I'll just leave a few minutes earlier, okay?

TEACHER: That would sure help me. Thanks, Allan.

STUDENT: No problem!

In this incident, the teacher laid out his problem with his initial I-message, but then he shifted to a listening posture to enable Allan to work through his own problem to the point where he was able to come up with an acceptable way to help the teacher with his problem.

Alternative #7: Problem Solving

Sometimes neither I-messages nor shifting gears will influence children to modify their behavior right away. Such messages may only set up a conciliatory atmosphere that opens the door to some kind of problem solving.

Although an I-message tells the youngster precisely why his behavior is unacceptable to you, he still may have some strong need to continue the behavior for reasons unknown to you at the time. So when he does not immediately modify his behavior, you both now own the problem—you don't like his behavior, and he does! Even if you send a stronger I-message the second time he still might not want to change.

This certainly doesn't call for giving up (permissiveness). Your needs are still unmet, so you still have a problem. Your job is to start mutual problem solving, which usually involves at least these four steps:

1. Defining the problem. (What are your needs? What are the child's needs?)
2. Generating possible solutions.
3. Evaluating each solution suggested.

4. Getting agreement (making a mutual decision) on some solution acceptable to both of you.

How this works is reported by an Arizona P.E.T. graduate and a trained P.E.T. instructor:

We had a really neat play yard, so all the kids in the neighborhood would come to our house and play. My problem was that I didn't want them to come on Sunday morning because that was the time I wanted to be free from watching the kids—to have some quiet time and sit and drink my coffee and read my paper. So I said, "I would really appreciate it if you wouldn't come to the door until noon because I want time to be alone and drink my coffee and read the paper!"

But that didn't work, because they came and rang the doorbell every fifteen minutes asking me if it was noon yet. So my I-message didn't work. So I decided we'd problem-solve it and see what we could come up with, because I really liked the kids and wanted them to feel comfortable about being there, but I needed some time to myself.

We came up with the solution that when it was noon, I'd put a flag out in front, because we had a flag holder on our porch. When they saw the flag, that was their signal that they could come to the yard. But until they saw the flag they weren't even to come to the door.

The first Sunday we did this I went outside to put the flag in the flag holder, and there, lined up on the sidewalk in front of the house, were all these little kids just waiting, with their eyes glued to the house to see when the flag was coming out. It really did solve the problem. I don't even remember who came up with the decision—it just evolved, and it worked.

In the next chapter, this problem-solving method will be examined more fully. My point here is: When I-messages don't work initially, you may have to move into problem solving to find a solution that will meet *your* needs as well as the child's.

Alternative #8: When Angry, Find the "Primary Feeling"

Some parents and teachers, when first introduced to I-messages, feel they now can vent their pent-up emotions like a human volcano. One mother returned to class and announced that she had spent the entire week being angry at her two children. The only problem was that her children were scared out of their wits by her new behavior.

Why is anger so frightening and damaging to children? How can parents and teachers be helped to avoid getting angry? What is anger anyway?

Unlike most other feelings, anger is almost invariably directed at another person. Anger usually gets delivered as a message that translates into "I am angry at *you*" or "*You* made me angry." So it's really a You-message, not an I-message. And you can't disguise this You-message by saying, "I feel angry." Consequently, anger feels like a blameful You-message to children. They hear that they are bad because they have caused the adult's anger. The predictable effect, then, is that they feel put down, blamed, and guilty, just as they have been by other You-messages they've heard.

I am convinced now that anger is something we generate *after* we have experienced some other feeling. We "manufacture" the angry feeling as a consequence of having experienced a *primary* feeling. Here are two illustrations of how that happens:

I am driving along on a freeway and another driver cuts in front of me, precariously close to my right front fender. My primary feeling is fear; it really scared me. As a response to my fear, some seconds later I honk my horn and "act angry," perhaps even shouting something like "You jerk, why don't you learn how to drive!"—a message that no one could deny is a pure You-message. The function of my acting angry is to punish the other driver or to make him feel guilty for scaring me, so that he might learn a lesson and not do it again. (Gordon, 1970)

A mother loses her child in a department store. Her primary feeling is fear—she is afraid that something unpleasant may have happened to him. If someone asked her how she was feeling while she was searching for him, this mother would say, "I'm scared to death" or "I feel terribly worried." When she finally finds the child, she experiences great relief. To herself she says, "Thank God, you're okay." Out loud, however, she says something quite different. Acting angry, she will send some message such as "You were a naughty boy" or "I'm really mad at you! How can you be so stupid to get separated from me?" or "Didn't I tell you to stay close to me?" In this situation, I believe the mother is putting on an angry act to teach the child a lesson or to punish him for causing her to be so afraid.

As a secondary feeling, anger almost always becomes a You-message—one that communicates negative evaluation and blame to the child. I am convinced that most anger is a kind of posture deliberately and consciously assumed for the express purpose of blaming, punishing, or teaching a lesson to a child—showing him that his behavior caused some unpleasant feeling (the primary feeling). When we get angry at others, we could be purposefully playing a role to influence them—to show them what they have done, teach them a lesson, persuade them not to do it again, get back at them. I'm not suggesting that the anger isn't real. It is very real, and it can raise one's blood pressure, speed up the heart rate, and make you boil inside and shake outside. But these reactions usually come after you have *acted angry*. It's the acting angry that brings on the physiological changes. What I am proposing here is that people make themselves boil and shake with anger because they were first made to feel afraid, hurt, embarrassed, jealous, lonely, or what have you. Here are some other examples:

A child acts up in a restaurant. The parents' primary feeling is embarrassment. Their secondary feeling is anger: "Stop acting like a two-year-old. I wish I hadn't brought you with me today."

A child brings home her report card with C's and D's. The mother's primary feeling is disappointment. Her secondary feeling is anger: "I know you were goofing off all semester. I hope you feel very proud of yourself."

In the same way, teachers may make themselves angry as a result of experiencing an unpleasant primary feeling. Some examples:

A student almost falls through a window while hanging display materials. The teacher's primary feeling is fear. The teacher then acts angry and says, "Get down right now; I can see you can't be careful."

The teacher has gone out of her way to prepare an interesting demonstration, but her students are restless and bored, passing notes to their neighbors. Her primary feeling is disappointment. Angrily she says, "I feel like I will never again try to make this subject interesting for this class. Look how ungrateful you are!"

A student cannot grasp the concept of adding fractions. The primary feeling of the teacher is frustration. The teacher angrily shouts, "You're not even trying. It's so simple a third-grader would get it before you do!"

Teachers readily admit that angry messages don't help kids learn. If they did, no student would ever fail.

How can parents and teachers learn to stop sending angry You-messages to children? The experience in our classes has been rather encouraging. First we help the adults comprehend the difference between primary and secondary feelings. As a result, they become more focused on their primary feelings and more in control of their secondary angry feelings. This helps them become more aware of what is really going on inside them when they feel like acting angry. It helps them identify the primary feeling, as in these situations:

A conscientious mother told her P.E.T. class how she discovered that her frequent angry outbursts at her twelve-year-old daughter were secondary reactions to her disappointment that the girl was not turning out to be as studious and scholarly as her mother had been. Mrs. C. began to realize how much her daughter's success in school meant to her, and how, whenever her daughter disappointed her academically, she had been blasting her with angry You-messages.

Mr. Jones, a professional counselor, admitted in class that he now understood why he got so angry at his eleven-year-old daughter when they were out in public. His daughter was shy, unlike her socially outgoing father. Whenever he introduced her to his friends, his daughter would not shake hands or say the accepted amenities. Her muffled, almost inaudible little "Hello" embarrassed her father. He admitted that he was afraid his friends would judge him as a harsh, restrictive parent who had produced a submissive and fearful child. Once he recognized this, he found himself not having angry feelings at such times. He could now begin to accept the fact that his daughter simply did not have the same outgoing personality as he. And when he stopped getting angry, his daughter felt much less self-conscious.

One T.E.T. class participant talked about his experience with a particular student and the angry feelings he had about their relationship:

> I was always mad at Charles, even though I couldn't ever put my finger on exactly what he was doing to make me angry. I just wrote it off as "one of those things." Charles was just one of those people who rubbed me the wrong way. Yet I was constantly upset. When we began looking at anger in this class, I thought, "What's my primary feeling about Charles?" I almost hate to admit what I found out, because it makes me look like I'm a lot more insecure than I

feel I really am, but my primary feeling was fear. I was afraid that Charles with his brilliance and sharp tongue was going to make me look stupid in front of the other students. Last week I asked him to stay after class and I just told him how threatened I get when he pins me down on some minor point or when he asks me technical questions that I have no way of knowing answers for. He was kind of stunned, and said he wasn't trying to make me look bad, that he was really trying to score "brownie points" with me. We ended up laughing about it and I'm not threatened by him anymore. When he forgets and pins me down now, I just laugh and say, "Hey, that's another brownie point for you."

Parents and teachers learn that if they find themselves frequently venting angry You-messages, they had better hold a mirror up to themselves and ask, "What is going on inside me? What needs of mine are being threatened by the child's behavior? What are the primary feelings I don't like?"

HOW I-MESSAGES CHANGE THE SENDER

When parents and teachers begin to send I-messages, not only do they notice changes in the children but they experience a significant change in themselves. The different words I've heard describing this change all add up to a feeling of greater honesty, genuineness, and openness:

"I don't have to pretend anymore when I'm not in the mood for playing with my preschooler."

"I'm not wishy-washy anymore."

"I'm much more congruent—my words match my feelings."

"I'm up-front; I level with people now."

"I-messages allow me to be open and honest with others."

Apparently, the old maxim, "You become what you do," applies here too. By using a new form of honest communication, adults begin to feel inside themselves the very honesty their I-messages communicate to others. The I-message skill provides them with the vehicle for getting in touch with their real selves. You-messages don't do this because they're entirely other-oriented.

Our interviews with P.E.T. graduates have given us clear evidence that the course does provide a kind of honesty training, as this mother reports:

> It seems to me that before P.E.T., I had to play certain roles—be a certain way. I don't think I have to be that way anymore. I'm free to be me. And free to risk that I'll still be loved and accepted, and if not, well, that's all right. . . . And it's freed my husband to be more open, more willing to talk about things and not hold feelings in. . . . The whole thing about sending an honest I-message about how you feel . . . [is that] now I feel it's okay for me to say, "I don't have time for it," or "I can't do it right now."

Another parent, a father, tells how he has changed:

> It's been a lot better, because I feel both of us have gotten away from making parental promises we can't keep. And that's been a real relief. If it's no, we'll tell them: "No, maybe tomorrow, but right now I have something that's more pressing for me."

One mother talked about how she and her husband were brought up to repress their real feelings:

> It's been one of our biggest difficulties—accepting negative feelings, which were not accepted in either of our families. I mean, we were all supposed to be happy and interested in things, and doing things. Feeling bored or feeling depressed was just a bad way to be. I think it was really great that through the

P.E.T. course I became more aware that it's okay to feel that way.

Another parent felt liberated by the I-message concept:

> I think it's liberating . . . for me to be able to express myself and not feel guilty for being self-centered or something like that. I think it helps to have the freedom to convey those messages to my children. I never used to say, "You know I feel like such and such."

I-messages also have a definite cathartic effect—they help parents get their feelings out instead of keeping them bottled up inside, as this parent told us:

> With an I-message you don't bottle up your feelings. You've expressed what you feel and you know someone else has heard you. Whether they do anything about it or not, things don't seem to be as big anymore.

The principal of a continuation school (a special school for troublesome high school students) gave this dramatic account of leveling with a few of his students:

> For weeks I had been resentfully tolerating the behavior of a group of boys who were continually ignoring some of the school regulations. One morning I looked out my office window and saw them casually walking across the lawn carrying Coke bottles, which is against school regulations. That did it. Having just attended the session in the T.E.T. course that explained I-messages, I ran out and started sending some of my feelings: "I feel so darned discouraged with you guys! I've tried everything I can to help you get through school. I've put my heart and soul into this job. And all you guys do is break the rules. I fought for a reasonable rule about hair length, but you guys won't even stick to that. Now, here you've

got Coke bottles and that's against the rules too. I feel like just quitting this job and going back to the regular high school, where I can feel I'm accomplishing something. I feel like an absolute failure in this job."

That afternoon I was surprised by a visit from the group. "Hey, Mr. G., we've been thinking about what happened this morning. We didn't know you could get mad. You never did before. We don't want another principal down here; he won't be as good as you've been. So we all agreed to let you take the electric clippers and cut our hair. We're also going to stick to the other rules." (Gordon, 1974)

After recovering from his shock, he told us he went into another room with the boys, and each submitted to his barbering until their hair was short enough to conform to the regulation. He told our class that the most significant thing about this incident was how much fun they all had during the voluntary haircutting session. "We all had a ball," he reported. The boys got close to him and to each other. They left the room as friends, with warm feelings and the kind of closeness that is rare between adults and students in schools.

This story illustrates how kids can be responsive and responsible if adults would only level with them. I think it flatters kids to know that they alone can give adults what they need in the situation. What a pity that teachers and administrators fail to bring out students' willingness to accommodate the needs of adults; what a pity they order, command, and put down students rather than tell them openly how they feel.

By sending I-messages, parents and teachers are also modeling a behavior: they are showing that it is legitimate to tell other persons that you want or need something from them. And they are also modeling that there is a way of communicating their feelings that is not blameful of the other, not threatening, not a put-down.

Children exposed to this modeling have shown us that they learn to use I-messages themselves in order to get what they need in their own relationships. Because parents and teachers have leveled with them, these kids start to come across to others as being open, honest, direct, real. They get to be seen as authentic and trustworthy, and others know where they stand with them.

I-messages obviously are not a method by which adults can *control* children but rather one that leaves the responsibility with the child for *self-control.* I-messages foster self-responsibility and self-discipline. Confirmation of this important principle comes from a classic experiment with nursery school children done by Diana Baumrind at the University of California at Berkeley. Baumrind (1967) found that nursery school children who rated high in self-control and self-discipline had parents who refrained from punitive messages or punishments and instead made extensive use of reasoning and what she termed "cognitive structuring." This academic-sounding term turns out to be our I-message—telling children the negative effects of their behavior on others. Baumrind explains that these messages help children internalize the consequences of their behavior *and develop conscience or inner control*—what I've been calling *self-discipline,* as opposed to externally imposed discipline.

Such messages, according to Baumrind's study, are far more effective when parents are *generally* accepting (in P.E.T. terms, when parents see most of their children's behavior in the top two panes of their behavior window). The child of a parent who is ordinarily quite accepting obviously will pay more attention to an occasional I-message that tells him some particular behavior is *not* acceptable. The message gets his attention. But the child of a parent who is unaccepting most of the time may fail to notice or respond to "just another" unaccepting message.

The effects of using I-messages to change students' disruptive behaviors was reported in an experiment involving a fifth-grade and a sixth-grade teacher. In the experiment, the two teachers were taught the concept of I-messages, shown when they might be used, and given practice in role-playing situations. The fifth-grade teacher subsequently reduced disruptive behaviors by 50 percent and increased students' work time by 25 percent. However, she soon reverted to using You-messages, and as a result the gains were lost. The sixth-grade teacher maintained the use of I-messages with eight targeted students, six of whom reduced the frequency of disruptive behavior and four of whom increased time spent in study (Peterson et al., 1979).

Another study contrasted the relative effectiveness of punishment and I-messages in getting children to refrain from playing with some attractive toys in the playroom. Look at the message sent to these children in the experiment, and you'll see a good I-message (it wasn't called that in the experiment):

> Some of these toys you should not touch or play with because I don't have any others like them, and if they were to get broken or worn out I wouldn't be able to use them anymore. For that reason I don't want you to touch or play with these toys.

This message (also called a "cognitive message") was more influential than punishment in preventing children from playing with the prohibited toys *in the absence of the researcher*. In the words of the investigator, "The internal thought processes of the child, what the child may be telling himself or herself when faced with temptation, act to control the child's behavior more than the externally located punishment." Another finding from the same study: The effects of the I-message in controlling the temptation to deviate continued over time, whereas the effects of physical punishment began to wear off (Parke, 1969). This study provides one of the most valid arguments *against* punitive discipline and *for* nonpower I-messages.

The concept of self-esteem also tells us a lot about the value of I-messages. Self-esteem—or the lack of it—is critical in people's lives. Positive self-esteem has been found to be related to high motivation or drive for achievement—in sports, in work, in school. Studies also show that youngsters with high self-esteem have more friends, are more apt to resist harmful peer pressure, are less sensitive to criticism or to what people think, have higher IQs, are better informed, more physically coordinated, less shy and subject to stage fright, and are more apt to be assertive and get their needs met. High self-esteem is considered by some to be the essential core, the basic foundation, of positive mental health.

In a well-known study, psychologist Stanley Coopersmith (1967) set out to identify the antecedents of high self-esteem—what actually produces it. He found that mothers of boys with high self-esteem had used "verbal reasoning [like our I-message] and discussion," whereas mothers of boys with low self-esteem had used more arbitrary, punitive discipline. This study obviously gives strong support to the position I've repeatedly taken against punitive discipline. And it confirms the advocacy of the nonpower methods we've been teaching in our courses—sending I-messages when the child's behavior is unacceptable. Coopersmith also provides experimental verification of the harmful effects of sending blameful You-messages, which we know are so often belittling, critical, deprecating, and berating put-downs—the kinds of messages that inevitably chip away at a child's self-esteem and self-respect.

Later, I'll describe a study that revealed that the largest effect of the P.E.T. course was an increase in children's self-esteem.

seven

New Ways
of Governing
Families
and Classrooms

In the previous chapter we looked at ways a parent or a teacher can more effectively *influence* a child to assume responsibility for changing a behavior that is unacceptable to the adult rather than use *authority* or blaming You-messages. In this chapter, I will offer yet another alternative to power-based discipline—a new and better way to govern a family or a classroom of children.

This new style of leadership and management, as I will document, is less a method for *changing* unacceptable and disruptive behaviors of children than it is a method for *preventing* the occurrence of such behaviors. This new management style already has proven itself in many business and industrial organizations, and it can be equally effective in managing families and classrooms.

PARTICIPATIVE MANAGEMENT

A quiet revolution has been taking place in corporate America as a result of a new leadership style, called *participative management.* (It is sometimes referred to as the "Japanese model of organizational leadership," although this terminology may be misleading.) The new approach increases employee involvement in making decisions about the workplace environment, production methods, quality control, design of products and services, and rules and policies.

More than six thousand U.S. corporations—among them many Fortune 500 companies such as AT&T, General Motors, Ford, and Honeywell—have adopted this philosophy of management and trained their managers and supervisors in the skills needed to implement this more democratic style of leadership. My own organization, Effectiveness Training, is among the firms providing this special training. Our course, called "Leader Effectiveness Training," is described in my book of the same name (Gordon, 1977).

In a pioneering book, *Working Together* (1983), John Simmons and William Mares summarize the findings from their study of fifty companies—both in the United States and in Europe—that have launched projects to increase employee participation in decision making and problem solving. They found the benefits of participation quite impressive:

> Productivity increases of 10 percent and more are not unusual and continue for several years. Early in the programs, productivity per employee may jump 100 percent. Grievances have fallen from 3,000 to 15, and stayed at that level. Absenteeism and turnover can be cut in half. . . . For some people who have led the way in introducing participation, the more important benefit has been human development. The material benefits are secondary. People feel better about themselves. They like to go to work. They have more self-esteem and self-confidence. They have gained control over their lives, if only a little, and lost some of their sense of powerlessness. (Simmons and Mares, 1983)

This democratic style of leadership, or "workplace democracy," should not be confused with "political democracy." Workplace democracy gives people direct, face-to-face participation in decisions that affect their jobs, while political democracy generally gives them the right to vote for a representative to deal with problems—a person several steps removed from their daily concerns.

Participative management involves a radical redistribution and sharing of power within an organization. In sharp contrast to the old-style management philosophy that puts a wall between those who manage and those who are managed, workers have more control over their jobs and working conditions, and together with their managers make decisions about rules and regulations of the business. James F. Lincoln, a pioneer participative company president, described it provocatively: "Let every worker manage; let every manager work."

Among teachers, school administrators, and teacher educators, there is a small but growing recognition that student participation in decision making is a key element in schools with good discipline (i.e., strong student self-discipline).

More than anyone I know, William Glasser, a renowned psychiatrist and consultant to schools, has clearly seen the analogy between the traditional manager-worker relationship and the teacher-student relationship. In his 1986 book, *Control Theory in the Classroom*, he writes:

> Teachers are also considered managers, at least to the extent that they direct their students and use their power to reward or punish them to try to get them to follow their direction. As managers, they rarely go beyond this traditional managerial role of direct reward or punish. Most teachers have given little thought to what managers might do that goes beyond this traditional concept, because they perceive themselves much more as workers than managers, and workers don't spend much time thinking about what managers can do. Until they begin to see themselves solely as managers and their students, not they, as workers, there will be little change in the amount of effort that most students now make in school. (Glasser, 1986)

Glasser points out that teachers who become *modern managers* would be willing to share power, while a *traditional manager* is never willing to give up any power and is generally looking for more. The traditional American teacher sets up her class her way, directs all the work, makes all the assignments, develops all the standards of student performance, sets all the goals, grades all the work, identifies the poor students whom she either tries to help or fails in order to get rid of them.

Glasser prescribes a challenging remedy for our schools: *the cooperative learning team*, which would also promote teachers' functioning as *participative managers*. And he warns us that "we will not improve our schools unless we try to offer what we want to teach in a recognizably different form from the way we are presently teaching." Here is Glasser's comparison of the learning-team model and the traditional teaching model (the traditional model is printed in italics):

1. Students can gain a sense of belonging by working together in learning teams of two to five students. The teams should be selected by the teacher so that they are made up of a range of low, middle and high achievers. *Students work as individuals.*

2. Belonging provides the initial motivation for students to work, and as they achieve academic success, students who had not worked previously begin to sense that knowledge is power and then want to work harder. *Unless they succeed as individuals, there is no motivation to work and no ability to gain the sense that knowledge is power.*

3. The stronger students find it need fulfilling to help the weaker ones because they want the power and friendship that go with a high-performing team. *Stronger students hardly even know the weaker ones.*

4. The weaker students find it is need fulfilling to contribute as much as they can to the team effort because now whatever they can contribute helps. When they worked alone, a little effort got them nowhere. *Weaker students contribute little to the class initially and less as they go along.*

5. Students need not depend only on the teacher.

They can (and are urged to) depend a great deal on themselves, their own creativity and other members of their team. All this frees them from dependence on the teacher and, in doing so, gives them both power and freedom. *Almost all students, except for a few very capable ones, depend completely on the teacher. They almost never depend on each other and there is little incentive to help each other. Helping each other now is called cheating.*

6. Learning teams can provide the structure that will help students to get past the superficiality [sterile facts, shallow thinking] that plagues our schools today. Without this structure, there is little chance for any but a few students to learn enough in depth to make the vital knowledge-is-power connection. *The students' complaint that they are bored is valid. Bored students will not work.*

7. The teams are free to figure out how to convince the teacher and other students (and parents) that they have learned the material. Teachers will encourage teams to offer evidence (other than tests) that the material has been learned. *The teacher (or the school system) decides how the students are to be evaluated and they are rarely encouraged to do any more than to study for the teacher-designed tests.*

8. Teams will be changed by the teacher on a regular basis so that all students will have a chance to be on a high-scoring team. On some assignments, but not all, each student on the team will get the team score. High-achieving students who might complain that their grade suffered when they took a team score will still tend consistently to be on high-scoring teams so as individuals they will not suffer in the long run. This will also create incentive regardless of the strength of any team. *Students compete only as individuals, and who wins and who loses is apparent in most classes, except some honors classes, after only a few weeks of school.*

It doesn't take much imagination to see how very different classrooms would be in a school that incorporated Glasser's model of learning teams.

The superiority of cooperative effort over competition was conclusively established by an unusually comprehensive review of 122 studies published from 1924 to 1980. The results were remarkable: 65 studies found that cooperation promotes higher achievement than does competition, only 8 found the reverse, and 36 found no statistically significant difference. Cooperation promoted higher achievement than independent work in 108 studies, while 6 found the reverse and 42 found no difference. The superiority of cooperation held for all subject areas and all age groups (Johnson et al., 1981).

In addition to promoting higher achievement, cooperative learning has been shown to build bridges and produce closer relationships between people of different colors and backgrounds, whereas competition creates an atmosphere of hostility, envy, and rivalry. Simply desegregating our schools doesn't improve cross-ethnic relationships; it's what happens to students with different backgrounds once they are in the same classroom that counts (Johnson et al., 1984). Once cooperative learning brings children together, they continue to spend time with each other after their lessons are over.

A small but growing number of schools are incorporating new practices and procedures that give students an opportunity to have a greater voice in determining what happens to them both in and out of the classroom.

Some schools have even allowed students to monitor their own academic progress and to identify subject areas in which they need improvement. In one of these schools they found such students made significant gains in their study habits and in measures of their scholastic achievement (McLaughlin, 1984). Still others have given students the responsibility of setting their own personal academic goals and then designing tailor-made high school courses to help them reach their goals (Burrows, 1973).

I found reports of schools that gave their students the responsibility of correcting behaviors of their peers that they judged as unproductive (Duke, 1980); and there are schools that have sought out the opinions and evaluations of students on the quality of their teachers' instructional skills and their suggestions for improving teacher-student relationships (Jones and Jones, 1981).

Even more pioneering are schools that allow active student participation with teachers and administrators in schoolwide issues, such as textbook adoptions, absenteeism, tardiness, new courses to be added in the curriculum, budget cutting, energy saving, and school discipline (Aschuler, 1980; Urich and Batchelder, 1979).

Such applications of participative management and student involvement are not common, particularly in the traditional public schools in this country. Let's hope, however, that a trend is developing. It is encouraging to find more and more prominent leaders in the field of education who recognize the potential of this new management and leadership philosophy for developing self-disciplined students. An example is Arthur Combs (1985), a noted educational psychologist and frequent consultant to school systems, who writes:

> Self-disciplined responsibility requires participation in decision-making, so that students can feel they matter and are in control of their existence. It is learned from confronting problems, finding solutions, and living with the consequences. Any teacher can find ways of giving students responsibility in any classroom.

An outstanding application of the principle of participation is the Cluster School, established in 1974 by the late Lawrence Kohlberg of Harvard. Called a "just community," the school incorporated self-governance, mutual caring, group solidarity, moral development, a democratic community, and the use of naturally occurring classroom and school problems as a basis for moral discussions and moral decisions. Discipline problems were dealt with by a formal "judicial" body called the Fairness Committee, made up of students, teachers, and administrators (Kohlberg, 1980).

A four-year longitudinal evaluation of the effects of the Cluster School (Power, 1979) found that the maturity of students' moral reasoning increased over time toward a more advanced, mature, humanistic level of moral reasoning, and that students complied more completely to rules they had established. Another study found very significant gains in moral reasoning maturity of those students who had been in serious difficulty in previous schools (Wasserman, 1976).

In a study of eighteen "schools within schools," or "alternative high schools," in California, the investigators found that both teachers and students reported fewer and less serious behavior problems than in conventional high schools. Personalized teacher-student relations, student participation in school governance, and a nonauthoritarian rule structure contributed to the low rate of disciplinary problems. In contrast, the conventional high schools studied often had a large number of minutely defined rules and rigid ways of dealing with infractions (Duke and Perry, 1978).

Both the Cluster School as a "just community" and the nonauthoritarian alternative high schools are very promising new models of *how to get students to discipline themselves*—by developing their own standards of what is right and wrong and behaving in accordance with those standards.

Psychologist Raymond Corsini has developed a new model of schooling, first called Individual Education and now called the Corsini Four-R system (C4R). In a 1988 article in the journal *Holistic Education Review*, he and a colleague, D. Lombardi, describe their model school as follows:

> C4R is a learning environment based on mutual respect in which children are treated as equals with adults (parents and faculty), with rights and obligations established by a "constitution" which governs the school's functioning based essentially on the American ideal of democracy. The C4R system advances four goals for student development: *responsibility* (to be built by involving children in decisions about their own education, under close realistic guidance), *respect* (to be nurtured by treating students with respect and by requiring respect), *resourcefulness* (encouraged by opportunities to prepare for three main life tasks: occupation and leisure, family life, and membership in society), and *responsiveness* (encouraged by striving for a school environment in which

people demonstrate trust in others and caring for others).

Here are some of the more unusual aspects of C4R: (1) children have considerable options on where to be and what to do during the school day; (2) children have five different modes for learning academic subjects: (a) in class (b) studying in the library (c) studying with peers (d) working with teacher/tutors (e) studying in their home; (3) every child has a self-selected faculty member as his/her teacher/advisor; (4) there are no grades; (5) the kind and degree of learning is based on objective tests given weekly in terms of specific units of instruction; (6) faculty are not to communicate with parents unless the child is present; (7) children "nominate" faculty members as advisors but once a faculty member accepts a child as a counselee, only the child can make changes to another teacher/advisor; (8) there are no report cards, only weekly progress reports to *students* who are advised to show them to their parents; (9) children set their own pace of learning and can be simultaneously studying subjects at different levels; (10) no rewards, honors, or special attention given to children for academic performance.

The democratic, relaxed ambience of the school comes from two sources: a philosophy of freedom and responsibility and a simple disciplinary system based on three rules and logical, predictable, pre-accepted consequences for breaking rules by all (parents and children).

The C4R school rules are the following: (1) Do nothing that could be dangerous or damaging; (2) Always be in a supervised place or en route from one supervised place to another; (3) If a teacher signals you to leave a classroom, do so immediately and in silence.

The C4R disciplinary process is an exact analog of our legal system: all students know the school's three rules and consequences for breaking the rules.

There is due process, and students have the right to counsel since in C4R the child's teacher/advisor becomes his/her lawyer in front of the principal for disciplinary infractions. Every child has a clear understanding of the exact consequences of a series of violations. For example: After a sixth violation there will be a conference with the principal, the child's teacher/advisor, and the child's parents.

What I've said before bears repeating here: the only effective discipline in schools, as well as in families, is self-discipline; and you don't produce self-disciplined kids by adult-imposed and power-based discipline. We need to scrap traditional discipline and design new and more effective ways of managing both families and schools.

GROUPS NEED RULES

Defenders of "good old-fashioned discipline" and strict adult authority over children often try to buttress their position by arguing that without such external control and adult discipline, chaotic anarchy would result: no rules, no limits—license for children to do anything they want.

Those who sound this dire warning apparently don't see that families and schools could scrap punitive and power-based discipline and still have rules and policies governing the behavior of their members. No rules or ineffective rules are not the only alternatives to completely adult-made rules. Let me explain.

All groups, of whatever size or nature, need laws, regulations, rules, policies, and standard operating procedures. My argument is pointedly *not* to deny they are needed, or to eliminate them. Without them, groups may very well fall into confusion, chaos, and conflict. The functions that rules and policies can serve are indispensable. They can prevent misunderstandings and conflicts between people; define rights and privileges; legislate what is considered appropriate, fair, and equitable in human relationships; and provide guidelines to help people know what limits they must set on their own behavior.

The critical issue is not *whether* groups need rules—they do need them—but rather how to motivate all group members to comply with them.

At some time in our lives we all have felt unmotivated to comply with some rule or policy that we had no voice in making. Denied the opportunity to participate in establishing a rule, most people feel imposed upon and resentful of the new rule. But when people actively participate in formulating a rule that will affect them, they are more highly motivated to comply with it—and usually strongly committed to honor it. Psychologists call this the *principle of participation*, and have proven its potency in numerous research studies.

Note that this commitment is the source of our Authority C, the authority that derives its influence from people's *commitment* to a decision they've had a hand in making or an agreement they have voluntarily entered into. A major objective of our P.E.T. and T.E.T. courses is to influence parents and teachers to involve children in the process of determining the rules they will be expected to follow, as opposed to adults making the rules themselves.

When children are given the opportunity to participate in determining policies and in setting rules, several good things happen. Children feel better about themselves, have higher self-esteem and self-confidence. Most important, they feel they have gained more "fate control"—more personal control over their own lives. They also feel they are equal members of the family, classroom, or school, with an equal voice in making decisions and establishing rules—they're part of a team, not second-class citizens. This means that families and classrooms that function collaboratively and democratically will have closer and warmer relationships than those in which the adults act as bosses or authorities expecting the children to obey the rules made for them.

Another important reason for encouraging the full participation of children in decision making, both in the family and in the classroom, is that it often produces higher-quality solutions to problems. Two heads (or three, or four) are better than one; shared decisions will be based not only on the knowledge and experience of the adults but also on the knowledge and experience of the children. In my first book, *Group-Centered Leadership* (1955), I pointed out that most arguments about who can make the wisest or best decisions always pit the leader against the members, with the leader winning out. I stressed that this is not the right way to pose the question. Rather, the question should be: Who can make the wiser decisions—a group leader *without the resources of the group members* or the total group, *including the leader?*

In my judgment the answer is the total group, including the leader. Thus the admonition "Father knows best," which implies that father knows better than son or daughter, should be challenged with the more reasonable, "Yes, but does father know better than father and children?"

To conclude, enlisting the participation of children in rule setting results in important benefits: (1) a higher motivation on the part of the children to implement or comply with the rules; (2) decisions of higher quality; (3) closer, warmer relationships between children and adults; (4) higher self-esteem, self-confidence, and sense of control over fate on the part of the children; and (5) more personal responsibility and self-discipline.

Parents who've taken P.E.T. have supplied us with hundreds of examples of using the participation principle for the task of making decisions and setting family rules. We've found a way to make this task easier and more systematic. It involves what we call the Six-Step Problem-Solving Process, which I'll describe in a moment. I borrowed these steps from the psychologist, educator, and philosopher John Dewey, who thought following them would help people arrive at creative solutions to all kinds of problems they encounter in their lives. We use this process not only as a guide for individuals solving problems, but also for groups (families, classrooms, work groups) or for helping two or more persons resolve their conflicts (a special kind of problem).

THE SIX-STEP PROBLEM-SOLVING PROCESS

Now we're ready to examine the actual process of group problem solving—the steps usually involved in tackling a problem, finding a good solution to it, and implementing the decision. To illustrate, I will use a real-life problem my own family faced some years ago. It's a problem common to most families and one that usually causes a lot of arguments and bad feelings: Who does the chores? How do you divide up the work that any family needs to do?

Traditionally in families, parents lay down the rules concerning chores, with little or no participation from the children in the decision-making process. And, as one would expect, children resent being asked or told to do chores, so consequently are not very responsible about doing them well or on time without a lot of parental nagging and goading. In fact, most children see doing the chores as solely their parents' responsibility. How could it be otherwise when their parents ask them to "help Mommy with the dishes," or "help Daddy wash the car," as if these jobs belonged to Mommy and Daddy in the first place?

How chores will be distributed can be solved more effectively by including all members of the family in the problem-solving process and by beginning with a list of all the jobs that have to be done to maintain the household, then deciding who is to do each one, how often, and up to what standards.

I can still recall in great detail the meeting in which our family tackled this complex problem. It was initiated by my wife, Linda, because she found herself doing a disproportionate share of the housework after she started working full-time outside the home.

As I describe the problem solving, I'll also point out the specific steps our family went through, the same six steps parents and teachers learn in our classes. We recommend using these steps as a guide for the persons involved to follow, no matter what kind of problem they are trying to solve, be it a personal problem (What do I really want to do in life?), a family problem (What should be our rules for watching TV?), or a parent-child conflict (your son wants to buy a motorcycle but you're strongly opposed because of the danger).

Linda started the meeting by stating her problem with appropriate I-messages. **Step I: Identifying and Defining the Problem.** "I don't feel it's fair for me to be doing the same amount of work now as I did before I started working full-time. I want us to decide how to divide up the jobs more evenly. I would like us to start out by listing everything that has to be done around here."

Michelle, the daughter still at home, and I (after some initial grumbling) agreed to join Linda in making the list, which, to our utter amazement (not Linda's, of course), grew to twenty-six different jobs.

Then we started coming up with different ideas. **Step II: Generating Alternative Solutions.** "Let's each first pick jobs we'd most like to do," and "How about combining certain jobs, like cooking dinner and cleaning up afterward, or washing and feeding Katie [our dog]." Coming up with many such solutions took somewhere around a half hour, followed by a lot of testing and evaluating of the various solutions we had generated.

Step III: Evaluating the Alternative Solutions. "I don't think it's fair for me to be in charge of arranging the repair work on both cars," or "Watering all our plants doesn't take nearly as long as doing all the shopping," or "Cleaning up after dinner should include sweeping the kitchen and the dining room floor," or "Who's going to clean up the breakfast dishes?" Step III took nearly another half hour, as I recall.

Finally, we felt we were ready to finalize our decision. Because I had assumed the job of taking notes, I began reading off the various jobs and to whom each had been assigned by us, checking frequently, "Is this what we decided?" **Step IV: Decision Making.**

We still weren't finished, however, because there were some sticky matters of implementation we needed to deal with: "How often should Katie be washed?" "How soon after dinner should the dishes be put into the dishwasher and the floors be swept?" "What if we're invited out to dinner or decide to eat out on somebody's night to cook?" "Who makes the grocery list?" Handling these implementation issues to everyone's satisfaction—**Step V: Implementing the Decision**—took another ten minutes or so.

One final issue had to be dealt with at a subsequent meeting—namely, "How are we going to know whether our decisions are good ones or whether they are working out?" **Step VI: Follow-up Evaluation.** "What if one of us changes his or her mind about wanting to do a particular job?" We finally agreed to give our first decisions a trial run of several weeks. Then, if any one of us had a complaint or wanted a change of jobs, that person would call a meeting at which we would all discuss it. As I recall, the only problem brought up at the second meeting was Linda's comment that on my two nights of preparing the dinner and cleaning up I frequently had forgotten to sweep the floors. I argued that the floors seemed clean to me, but she countered by announcing that twice she had come up with plenty of dust and crumbs in the dustpan. I had to admit that I had found the sweeping part of my job distasteful and either forgot or consciously skipped doing it, hoping it wouldn't be noticed.

Our decisions about chores remained unchanged for several years until one day Michelle brought up that she didn't like cooking anymore. She didn't like preparing meals on her two nights a week, so she wanted to know if Linda and I would each add one night of cooking to our two, provided she would take over the total job of cleanup for all six nights. Without hesitation, Linda and I agreed. Later we confided to each other that we felt the two of us got the best end of that bargain, because we had grown somewhat tired of Michelle's serving either ham or hamburger on nearly every one of her nights to cook.

It should be said now that not all effective problem solving proceeds in an orderly fashion through the six steps. Often someone luckily comes up with such an elegant solution in Step II that no other solutions need be generated, and the evaluation step, Step III, can be very brief. Also sometimes when people find it's hard to come up with a mutually acceptable decision (Step IV), they'll find it necessary to go back to Step II and generate some more solutions, or go back to Step I and define the problem differently.

See if you can identify and locate each of the six steps in the following problem-solving process, one submitted by a father and mother with two children, age seven and nine. Here is how one of the parents described their meeting:

> TV was interfering with the dinner hour. The children wanted to run to the TV with their plates and wouldn't come to the table. There had been a lot of

hassling about this. At a family problem-solving session, I brought up the problem. My wife and I shared I-messages with our kids. The TV watching troubled us, the parents, because:

1. I enjoyed talking with my kids at dinnertime—hearing about their day, sharing mine. I was hurt when I couldn't do this.
2. For my wife, preparing dinner was a problem—keeping it hot, knowing when to serve.
3. If we tried to enforce their eating at the table, there was a hassle, hurt feelings, and then no one enjoyed the meal; if they ate in front of the TV, dishes were left there, and my wife and I were both uneasy because we couldn't share our days with them.

In response, the kids expressed *their* needs:

1. The very best programs for their ages came on from 6:00 to 7:00 P.M.
2. They would get started on a program and get interested and then we called them for dinner. They felt this was unfair.

We began to search for solutions:

1. Dinner could be at a more regularly scheduled time. This was okay with my wife. The kids would avoid programs at that time.
2. There were usually two nights per week when I was working. My wife said it was okay with her if they watched during dinner hour when I wasn't home. This was okay with me.
3. The children volunteered to avoid all TV during weekdays. I nearly fell through the floor. My wife and I responded that this was not acceptable to us because we thought it went too far. It was a proposal they probably couldn't keep.
4. They responded that they would limit them-

selves to one TV program each evening from
Sunday through Thursday. This was agreed
to—with exception for "specials."

OUTCOME: The TV hassle at our home really stopped.
The children selected their programs carefully and
stuck to their limit of one. This was an agreement we
never even anticipated—but it was beautiful. We had
evening time for family games. The kids had time
for homework and they got to bed earlier. This
mutually acceptable plan went on for one and a half
to two years. By this time habits were formed, the
kids were older, and there was not a need for any
rules on this. The problem just ceased to exist. The
TV at our home continues to be used sparingly.

Interviews with parents after they had taken P.E.T. have
provided us with many different examples of parents involving
youngsters in problem solving. Using the same six-step method,
families have set policies and made agreements for watching
TV, for setting times to go to bed or to come home at night,
for letting each other know where they are, for getting home
safely should the kids have too much to drink, for proper use
of the phone, for safe use of the swimming pool, for dealing
with strangers coming to the door, for handling complicated or
dangerous equipment, for where to go on vacations—for solutions to every kind of problem imaginable.

It's important to point out that in our courses we are not
advocating or prescribing any specific or "best" solutions to
problems. Rather, we offer only a procedure, a methodology—
our Six-Step Problem-Solving Process—that will help each family
find the solutions *most appropriate to that unique family*. Families
come up with a variety of different solutions to the same problem.

I also want to emphasize that the six-step methodology does
not always produce the *best* solution or one that solves a problem
for all time. Families may find their first solution didn't do the
job, and have to get together again and find a better solution.
Conditions may change, or the kids get older, or the family may
move into a new house—any of these changes may require

setting new rules or finding new solutions. Undoubtedly, one of the principal strengths of this problem-solving process is its flexibility and adaptability to new situations.

CONFLICT RESOLUTION: THE NO-LOSE METHOD

Mutual rule setting is meant to *prevent* conflicts, and it certainly does this better than rule setting done exclusively by adults. However, in both families and classrooms, conflicts inevitably come up for which there are as yet no rules. This means something has to be done to resolve these conflicts, or relationships will be endangered. How are conflicts usually dealt with in human relationships?

As I've stressed before, most parents and teachers view dealing with children in terms of being either strict or lenient, tough or soft, authoritarian or permissive. Locked into this either-or thinking, they tend to see their relationships with children as a power struggle, a contest of wills, a fight to see who wins and who loses. A father early in his P.E.T. course states:

> "You have to start early letting them know who's boss. Otherwise, they'll take advantage of you and dominate you. That's the trouble with my wife—she always ends up letting the kids win all the battles. She gives in all the time and the kids know it."

Two mothers of teenagers tell it in their words:

> "I try to let my child do what he wants, but then usually I suffer. I get walked on. You give him an inch and he takes a mile."

> "I don't care how she feels about it, and it doesn't make any difference to me what the other parents do—no daughter of mine is going to wear spiked hair. Here's one thing I am not going to back down on. I am going to win this fight."

Children, too, see their relationship with parents as a win-lose power struggle. Cathy, a bright fifteen-year-old whose parents are worried because she won't talk to them, told us in one of our interviews:

> "What's the use of arguing? They always win. I know that before we ever get into an argument. They're always going to get their way. After all, they are the parents. They always know they're right. So, now I just don't get into arguments; I walk away and don't talk to them. Of course it bugs them when I do that. But I don't care."

Ken, a high school senior, has learned to cope with the win-lose attitude of his parents in a different way:

> "If I really want to do something, I never go to my mother, because her immediate reaction is to say no. I wait until Dad comes home. I can usually get him to take my side. He's a lot more lenient, and I usually get what I want with him."

Typically, parents and teachers want to handle conflicts by demanding a solution by which *they win*. Other parents and teachers, far fewer in number, consistently give in to children out of fear of "frustrating the child's needs"—in which case *the child wins* and the adult loses.

In our courses, we refer to these two win-lose approaches simply as *Method 1* and *Method 2*. Here is how Method 1 works:

When a conflict between an adult and a child occurs, the adult decides what the solution must be, hoping the child will accept it. If the child resists, the adult threatens to use (or actually uses) power—Authority P—to coerce the child into compliance. *(Adult wins, child loses.)*

Here is how Method 2 operates:

When a conflict between an adult and a child occurs, the adult may try to persuade the child to accept the adult's solution. But when the child resists, the adult gives up or gives in, permitting the child to get his way. *(Child wins, adult loses.)*

It will be clear to everyone that Method 1 is an approach that depends on the adult having Authority P and the willingness to use it if necessary. The effects of this power-based method on the loser are quite predictable: resentment, low motivation to carry out the solution, and a reaction expressed by one or more of the *fight, flight,* or *submit* coping mechanisms. Adults pay a heavy price for using Method 1—they spend a lot of time enforcing the decision (nagging, reminding, prodding, threatening), they risk alienating the child, and they deny the child the opportunity to be involved in problem solving and to contribute to finding a solution.

Method 2 involves giving in, being falsely permissive, sacrificing one's needs in favor of the child's. Children of Method 2 parents seldom have any reason to be rebellious, hostile, or aggressive, nor will they be conforming or subservient. However, these children tend to use temper tantrums to get what they want, they learn how to make parents and teachers feel guilty, and they say nasty and deprecating things to try to get their way. They will grow up thinking that their needs are more important than anyone else's; life to such children is get-get and take-take, and they are uncooperative and inconsiderate of the needs of others. These kids are not very likable.

Children who get their way all the time at home will expect to have it the same way with peers. But their peers will see them as "spoiled." So will their teachers (most of whom are accustomed to getting *their* way in the classroom).

Method 2 produces resentment and anger in the *adult.* It's difficult for parents or teachers to feel loving toward a child who has become inconsiderate, uncooperative, and unmanageable. Parents who use Method 2 generally feel that being a parent is a burden and they look forward to the time when the kids are old enough to leave home. Parenthood for Method 2 parents is seldom a joy. How sad that is. Fortunately, we've found that less than 10 percent of parents are predominantly Method 2 users.

Because few adults experienced in their childhood anything other than Method 1 or Method 2 in conflicts with their parents or teachers, it comes as a surprise when in our P.E.T. or T.E.T. classes we offer a third method for resolving conflicts—a win-

win or no-lose alternative to the two win-lose methods. Here is how *Method 3*, the No-Lose Method, works:

When a conflict between an adult and a child occurs, the adult asks the child to participate in a mutual search for some solution acceptable to both. Either may suggest possible solutions, which are then evaluated. A mutually acceptable decision is made as to the best solution. Then they decide how it is to be carried out. No coercion is required, hence no power is used. Authority C is utilized.

There is nothing harmful about conflict itself. In fact, all relationships generate disagreements and differences. If there is no conflict, it may mean that children are too frightened to challenge a parent or teacher. What makes conflict destructive is using the "I win, you lose" approach or vice versa, both of which involve competition.

Psychologist Morton Deutsch, an outstanding thinker and researcher on the cooperation-competition issue, makes this distinction quite clear in his 1985 book, *Distributive Justice*:

> A cooperative process leads to the defining of conflicting interests *as a mutual problem to be solved by collaborative effort*. It facilitates the recognition of the legitimacy of each other's interests and of the necessity of searching for a solution that is responsive to the needs of all. In contrast a competitive process stimulates the view that the solution of the conflict can only be one that is imposed by one side or the other . . . through superior force, deception, or cleverness.

Cooperation is not the opposite of conflict. Rather, it establishes a climate in which conflict can happen but can also be resolved creatively and productively by avoiding the poisonous effects of the win/lose and power-struggle posturing most people employ at such times in their relationships. It is in the spirit of such cooperation that graduates of P.E.T. and T.E.T. use our No-Lose Method to find solutions mutually acceptable to both the adult and the child.

It's not a method to use only with older youngsters; the No-Lose Method works surprisingly well with very young children, too. Here is a brief conflict-resolution session with three-year-old Jan and her mother, who submitted the dialogue as she recalled it:

JAN: I don't want to go to my babysitter's anymore.
MOTHER: You don't like going to Mrs. Crockett's house when I go to work.
JAN: No, I don't want to go.
MOTHER: I need to go to work and you can't stay at home alone, but you are sure unhappy about staying there. Is there something we could do to make it easier for you to stay there?
JAN: [silence] I could stay on the sidewalk until you drive away.
MOTHER: But Mrs. Crockett needs you to be inside with the other children so she'll know where you are.
JAN: I could watch you from the window when you drive away.
MOTHER: Will that make you feel better?
JAN: Yes.
MOTHER: Okay. Let's try that next time.

The No-Lose Method can be utilized even with infants, the only difference being that the problem solving has to be primarily nonverbal. I remember well an incident in my own family when my daughter Judy was an infant.

When Judy, my first daughter, was only five months old, we went on a month's vacation during which we lived in a cabin beside a fishing lake. Before this trip, we had felt lucky because she had never needed a feeding from 11:00 P.M. until 7:00 A.M. But the change in surroundings brought a change in our luck—she started waking up at 4:00 A.M. for a feeding. Getting up to feed her at that hour of the morning was painful. In northern Wisconsin in September, it was freezing in the cabin, and all we had was a wood-burning stove. This meant we either had to take the time to build a fire or, equally bad, wrap up in blankets and try to stay warm for the hour it took to prepare the formula, warm the bottle, and feed her. We truly felt this was a "conflict-of-needs situation," requiring some joint problem solving.

Putting our heads together, my wife and I decided to offer the infant an alternative solution in the hope that she would find it acceptable. Instead of waking her up and feeding her at 11:00, the next night we let her sleep until 12:00 before we woke her and fed her. That morning she didn't waken until 5:00 A.M. So far, pretty good progress.

The next night we made a special effort to see that she drank more than her usual amount of milk, and then put her to bed around 12:30 P.M. It worked—she "bought" it, so to speak. That morning, and subsequent mornings, she didn't waken until 7:00, the time we wanted to get up anyway to get out on the lake when the fish were biting best. Nobody lost; we all won.

Even nonverbally, the problem-solving process usually moves through the six steps, as in the following incident written up by the parent of a small baby:

My baby was crying and screaming in the playpen, rattling the slats and putting up a fuss as if to try to get out. I didn't want him underfoot because I had to clean up the house before friends arrived [**Step I: Identifying and Defining the Problem**]. I thought I'd try Method 3, so I began thinking of different solutions. First, I gave him his bottle, half full of milk [**Step II: Generating Alternative Solutions**]. But he threw the bottle down and kept crying even more loudly [**Step III: Evaluating the Alternative Solutions**]. I then tried putting a rattle in the playpen [back to Step II], but he ignored it and kept crying and rattling the side of the playpen [again Step III]. Finally, I remembered a little colored trinket I'd bought and wrapped up some time ago. I went to the closet, took it out, and handed him the ribboned box [back to Step II]. Immediately he stopped crying and started to play with the box, trying to get the ribbon off [**Step IV: Decision Making**]. He occupied himself happily for half an hour while I did my housework [**Step V: Implementing the Decision**]. Every time I came back in the room to check on him, he was still involved with the trinket [**Step VI: Follow-up Evaluation**].

Mother didn't lose, child didn't lose—both won! All accomplished nonverbally.

These first few examples of the No-Lose Method involve very young children. I've done this deliberately, to show that the technique works even with infants.

The early use of the No-Lose Method can also be viewed as strong *preventive action*—that is, the biggest payoff will come a number of years down the road. By starting with the easier problems of young children, you'll do better when you come to the more difficult ones of older youth (such as conflicts about allowances, use of the car or phone, loud music, clothes, etc.). And an even greater payoff: there will be fewer—*far* fewer— conflicts with your teenager than is typical. Instead of the storm and stress, and sometimes the tragedies, that many parents experience as their children go through adolescence, the probability is high that this period will bring you satisfaction and joy in your relationship with your teenagers. How can I make such a prediction?

As with most activities, practice makes perfect. So it is with resolving conflicts by reaching mutually acceptable agreements and solutions. By starting when children are young, you are setting a pattern, establishing a practice of resolving each conflict so nobody loses. And the more you do it, the easier it will become for both of you. Whenever a new conflict arises, the attitude of each of you will be, "I want to find a way to get my needs met, and yours too." And having been successful in doing this in the past, you'll both feel confident (and competent) in doing it again.

Being successful over a long period of time with the No-Lose Method, neither you nor your son or daughter will likely react to each new conflict by assuming an adversarial posture and engaging in a power struggle. You've learned a completely different attitude and a set of ground rules. You've learned how to resolve your conflicts by talking, not by fighting; by negotiating, not by competing; by both persons winning—not by one losing. Now you'll find most conflicts don't get to the bargaining table; instead they are quickly solved, informally and with little heat. We call this "stand-up" problem solving. Problems will rarely get to the "we have a conflict" stage.

Instead of seeing you as an adversary, as so many adolescents view their parents, your son or daughter will see you as a friend and helper. And there will be much more mutual affection, respect, and love in your relationship.

DEALING WITH VALUES COLLISIONS

There are some conflicts that occur in all families that may not get solved by the No-Lose Method. These are the innumerable conflicts over issues involving children's cherished values, beliefs, personal tastes, style of dressing, philosophy of life, choice of friends. Think of such conflicts as *values collisions*. The No-Lose Method is sometimes not appropriate for resolving values collisions, because youngsters usually feel their values are constants, and not subject to negotiation. They think they have a right to choose their own values, beliefs, and preferences. It's a question of their civil rights, and today's youth, like those of previous generations, will defend such rights tenaciously. They will rebel against adults' attempts to force them into the adults' mold, rebel against adults' forcing them to act according to what *they* think is right. They will resist entering into a negotiating process because their values are seen as nonnegotiable.

Youngsters are usually willing, however, to enter into the No-Lose problem-solving process when it is very clear to them that their behavior does in fact tangibly interfere with someone else's life. In those cases, they are generally willing to problem solve and are open to the possibility of changing behavior that is unacceptable to the other person; and they are willing to respect the needs of the other person. They will *not* be willing to problem solve and negotiate when they can't see that it affects you in any tangible or concrete way.

Children are no different from adults in this respect. How many adults are willing to modify their behavior just because someone thinks they ought to? For adults to be willing to enter into problem solving, they, too, must be convinced their behavior is tangibly affecting the other person.

The lesson here is that the No-Lose Method for resolving conflicts is not the method of choice for changing the values and beliefs of young people to suit adults. For a child to change a value, parents must be able to make a good case for the child's behavior having a concrete negative effect on their lives. Without such a case, the youngster will take the position that his behavior is nonnegotiable.

Here are some behaviors parents have told us their children considered nonnegotiable:

Having pierced ears
Wearing miniskirts, tight jeans, beat-up sneakers
Having spiked hair
Having a friend parents didn't like
Wanting to quit college and become a rock musician
Joining a church of a different denomination from the
    parents'
Smoking cigarettes
Failing to do homework
Having dates with a member of another race or religion
Staying up too late before going to bed
Spending allowance on foolish things
Smoking marijuana

Consider one of the above. Suppose my daughter has spiked hair. Can I be convincing that spiked hair tangibly or concretely affects me in some way? Well, spiked hair won't get me fired, it won't reduce my income, it won't stop me from having friends of my choice, it won't hurt my tennis game, it won't make me gain weight, it won't prevent me from writing this book, it won't cost me money or time.

The truth of the matter is that I probably couldn't ever convince my daughter that wearing spiked hair tangibly affects me or deprives me of need satisfaction in any way. So why would we expect her to be motivated to stop doing what she obviously wants to do and values doing?

Does this mean that there is no hope for teachers and

parents to have an influence on children's values—no way to transmit their most cherished values, no way to teach what they strongly believe? Fortunately, adults *can* have an influence on children's values—and a strong influence at that.

First, parents and teachers are *always* teaching their values simply by living their own lives according to what they value—teaching by example, being a model, practicing what they preach. And the better the relationship the parent has with the child, the greater the modeling influence. This is because children are more apt to adopt the values of adults they like and respect.

Parents and teachers can also influence children sometimes by sharing their knowledge, experience, and wisdom much as a consultant does with a client. To be most effective in this consulting role, however, parents and teachers need to follow the same principles used by successful consultants:

- Be sure you are "hired" by your child or student; that is, be certain he or she has asked for your services and wants your Authority E. Ask children if they want to hear your facts or opinions.
- Be sure you know what the *real* need or problem of your child or student is. This will help you decide what information or experience will be appropriate and whether you actually have that information or experience.
- Share rather than preach; offer rather than impose; suggest rather than demand.
- Don't keep hassling your youngsters to try to persuade them to accept what you offer; don't shame them if they don't buy; don't keep pushing if you detect resistance.
- Leave full responsibility with your kids for either buying your expertise or rejecting it.
- Use your most valuable tool: Active Listening.

Most adults are guilty of the "hard sell," which makes kids respond with, "Get off my back," "Stop hassling me," "It's my life," "I already know what you feel about it—too much!"

A father reported how he tried out what he had learned about effective consulting:

My son had decided to grow a plot of marijuana with two neighbor kids. One of the kids had been growing the stuff a lot—he has pretty severe emotional problems. So I shared with my son one time, and one time only, how I felt about that: "I think growing grass is your decision as long as it's not on our property, where we could get in trouble. And you must think about the fact that if this kid gets caught, it could involve you. More than likely, he's going to be dealing in it to make money and that could make you a dealer too, which is a felony." And that's all I said; one time, right out loud how I felt about it. Haven't said a word since. I don't know what happened, but I feel I've done my consulting job—it's about all I could do. . . . Before P.E.T. I would have hassled him to death about it.

Whether the a value collision is about homework, smoking, premarital sex, style of dress, grades, choice of friends, or drugs, you may have to concede that neither modeling nor being a good consultant has resolved the conflict between you and your child. Despite the pain of the continuing values collision, a deeper pain would be to take action that would ruin your long-term relationship. Your only alternative, then, will be to accept the fact that you won't change the youngster. Readers may remember this profound prayer, which is appropriate when values collide:

Lord, grant me the courage to change what I can change,
The serenity to accept what I cannot change,
And the wisdom to know the difference.

Parents, and teachers, too, sometimes will need the serenity to accept what they find they can't change, because they will inevitably encounter values collisions they'll never resolve, when even their modeling and best consulting efforts are not good enough to influence a youngster to change what he or she values highly.

eight

Helping
Children Solve
Problems Themselves

The focus of the last two chapters was on influencing children to be more considerate of adults' needs—how parents and teachers can get kids to be willing to change unacceptable behaviors and how to get them to comply with rules and keep their agreements. As we have seen, influence-based methods are much more likely than control-based punitive methods to motivate children to *want* to change their behavior to help adults get their needs met.

Nevertheless, it must be understood that even influence-based methods will often fail, if parents or teachers do not respect the children's equal right to get their own needs met and if the adults do not put forth the effort to help them do so. I'll put this in the form of a principle that I wish every adult would memorize: *Children won't want to be helpful to you when you tell them you have a problem with their behavior, unless they feel you've generally tried to help them when they have had problems.*

In other words, only if the child feels the relationship to be reciprocal—fair, two-way, just, equitable—will he want to take the trouble to change his behavior to please you.

Cooperative, considerate youngsters who appear sensitive

and responsive to the needs, feelings, and problems of adults are those whose teachers and parents have frequently demonstrated sensitivity and responsiveness to the needs, feelings, and problems of the youngsters. When kids are told that things they're doing or not doing are unacceptable and upsetting, they won't feel like changing or accommodating if that adult consistently has been unwilling to help, or has not known how to help, when the shoe was on the other foot. Therefore, it is of the utmost importance for parents and teachers to learn how to be effective helpers when children have problems.

There is another compelling reason for parents to become skillful in helping their children solve problems and get their need met. Kids who are frustrated, needy, troubled, or unhappy because they have been unsuccessful in solving *their* problems are much more likely to engage in antisocial or self-harming behaviors that are unacceptable to their parents and teachers—behaviors that in turn cause adults serious problems; that hurt others; that bring on "disciplinary action"; that get labeled as "rebellious," "antisocial," "disruptive," "pathological," "wild," "self-destructive," "uncontrolled," "delinquent," "undisciplined."

By learning and using effective helping skills, parents and teachers will *prevent* such deviant behaviors. Unfortunately, most parents don't realize how critical their behavior is in preventing (or in causing) the very behaviors in children they dread the most: aggression, drug or alcohol abuse, failing or dropping out of school, depression, premarital pregnancy, stealing, violence, suicide, and so on.

It is tragic that so many parents fail to understand that antisocial and self-destructive behaviors are not genetically programmed in children; that they do not occur because of bad luck, watching television, or a "decline in respect for authority." These behaviors are youngsters' ways of coping with unsolved problems. They are frantic attempts to compensate for unmet needs and frustrations, a way of trying to belong and feel significant in relationships with others. They are their vengeful way of paying others back for hurts and deprivations, as well as a challenge to those who have tried to control them, a desperate attempt to get people to sit up and take notice.

Far too many parents, even well-educated ones, believe that failure and deprivation are good for children, while success and need-satisfaction will weaken or spoil them. There is in fact abundant evidence that solving one's problems successfully and getting one's basic needs met are the *major* ingredients of healthy, cooperative, considerate, self-responsible, self-disciplined individuals. It follows, then, that adults who have the capabilities of helping children learn to solve their problems and get their basic needs met will greatly increase the probabilities of developing the kind of youngster every parent wants. Similarly, teachers who learn the skills of helping students solve their problems and get their needs met will *greatly* reduce the number of disciplinary problems in their classrooms.

But aren't most parents and teachers helpful to children when they have problems? My experience has convinced me that most are not. Many *try* to be helpful, of course, but most are so ineffective at it that what they actually do or say is perceived by children as not helpful or as downright detrimental. Most parents and teachers, through no fault of their own, don't get high marks as counselors for children, which is why so many children complain that adults aren't good listeners or don't understand them.

Do specific methods and skills exist that have been proven effective in helping others solve their problems? If so, can they be taught to parents and teachers? My answer to both questions is a resounding yes. We now have a large body of knowledge about effective ways of helping people solve their problems. Professionals who are using this new knowledge in their occupations have come to be called "helping professionals." They work as counselors or therapists in social service agencies, churches, mental health institutions, and business organizations; they may also be private practitioners. They include psychologists, psychiatrists, social workers, pastoral counselors, marriage and family counselors, personnel counselors, and so on. In recent years, in addition, we've proven that parents and schoolteachers can learn what the professionals do.

These effective new methods are called "basic helping skills," "counseling skills," or "facilitative skills." How they were first identified is an interesting story in itself.

In the early 1940s, a number of graduate students in psychology, myself among them, stimulated by counseling courses taught by psychologist Carl Rogers, who had just taken a new position on the faculty of Ohio State University, became interested in finding out what really went on when people took their troubles to professional counselors. What did counselors do behind the closed doors of their offices? What helped troubled people solve their problems? What hindered?

All trained in the scientific method, these graduate students realized at the outset that they first needed to tape-record a number of counseling sessions, which they did at the Ohio State Psychological Clinic. This had never been done before anywhere. At first we thought the taping would have to be secret in order not to inhibit the counselees. But this was contrary to our professional ethics. So we decided to put the microphone in full view of the counselees, inform them that the taping was needed for research purposes, that all identifying passages would be deleted, and that each counselee had the final choice of whether to be taped or not. Not only did nearly every client permit the taping but it didn't seem to inhibit the counseling process in any way.

The typed transcripts of hundreds of taped fifty-minute counseling sessions provided our group of graduate students with the rich raw data we needed to find out what good counseling was all about. These studies, most of them Ph.D. theses, ushered in a new field of scientific inquiry—the study of the process and outcomes of helping people with personal problems. With the creative support and guidance of Rogers, our faculty sponsor and inspirational leader, these graduate students* became pioneers in a new field that came to be known as client-centered (or person-centered) psychotherapy.

The boundaries of this new field have since been greatly expanded. From the initial focus on the process by which a *professional* counselor helps a troubled client, the field now

---

* Elias Porter, Julius Seeman, Bernard Covner, Elizabeth Sheerer, Dorothy Stock, William Snyder, Virginia Axline, Victor Raimy, Nathaniel Raskin, Nicholas Hobbs, Donald Grummon, Arthur Combs, George Muench, Thomas Gordon.

includes the study of the helping process in parent-child relationships, teacher-student relationships, boss-subordinate relationships, couple relationships, doctor-patient and nurse-patient relationships, and so on.

We have discovered that the very same skills professional counselors learn to facilitate their clients' problem solving will facilitate problem solving in these other important relationships. This discovery eventually led to the development of new programs to train nonprofessionals in these facilitative skills. In my own Effectiveness Training courses, our instructors have trained nearly a million parents, teachers, school administrators, nurses, social workers, physicians, dentists, and organizational managers. And there are other such training programs based on sound principles whose effectiveness has been proven by research studies.*

I will describe and illustrate the basic helping skills in this chapter. But first it's important to understand the process of problem solving itself—what is the process people go through when they successfully solve problems of living?

HELPING CHILDREN USE THE PROBLEM-SOLVING PROCESS

When people successfully solve problems brought on by some unmet need, usually they have utilized a certain process, consciously or unconsciously. This problem-solving process is the same as the six-step process discussed in the preceding chapter, which can be summarized this way:

Step I   Identifying and Defining the Problem
Step II   Generating Alternative Solutions
Step III   Evaluating the Alternative Solutions

* Gerald Egan's Human Relations Training; George Gazda's Multiple Impact Training; Bernard Guerney's Relationship Enhancement; Norman Kagan's Interpersonal Process Recall; Robert Carkhuff's Human Resources Development Model; Gerald Goodman's Shasha Tapes; Eugene Gendin's Focusing; Luciano L'Abate's Social Skill Training.

Step IV   Decision Making
Step V   Implementing the Decision
Step VI   Follow-up Evaluation

We found it's very useful for parents and teachers to keep these steps in mind when called on to help a child with a problem. Obviously, the adult is only a facilitator of the child's problem-solving process; these are the steps you want the *child* to go through, not the adult. However, when dealing with very young children, who have limited resources and undeveloped verbal ability, helping them with their problems is somewhat more complicated, as I will now explain.

With infants and preverbal children, the adult has to be more than a *facilitator* of the process, because very young children can't always define what the problem is (Step I), can't always know what the alternative solutions might be (Step II), don't always have the experience to evaluate alternative solutions (Step III), and consequently can't choose the best solution (Step IV). Nevertheless, infants do have an important role to play in the process: they give nonverbal clues to the adult.

Adults usually must have a high level of involvement in the problem-solving process of infants and toddlers, because they are almost completely dependent upon adults for providing the means for getting so many of their needs met. As children get older, however, they become increasingly more capable of doing the entire job themselves—defining what their problem is, generating their own alternative solutions, evaluating those solutions, and deciding on the best one. This is illustrated by the following incident, submitted by an elementary school teacher:

STUDENT: I forgot my math things at home.
TEACHER: Hmm, you have a problem.
STUDENT: Yeah, I need my math book and the paper I was working on.
TEACHER: Wonder what kind of solution we could come up with?
STUDENT: I could call my mother and have her bring them, but she doesn't hear the phone sometimes.
TEACHER: That may not work out, then, huh?

STUDENT: I could get a book from the math center to use and take a fresh piece of paper because I know what page I was on.

TEACHER: Sounds like you have the problem all solved.

STUDENT: Yeah.

The most desirable aim for adults in their role as helper is to keep the amount of their direct involvement in the content of children's problem solving to a minimum, so that the child becomes less and less dependent on adults. Often this creates a dilemma for parents and teachers. They don't want to intervene and get involved so much that they keep the child dependent, yet they hesitate to withhold their help and thus give too little. Probably the best policy is to withhold your involvement in a child's problem solving until you are fairly sure the child doesn't have the resources to solve the problem without your active involvement. And, too, as everyone knows, children will differ greatly in their level of independence and problem-solving capability, even at the same age level.

Adults sometimes can be helpful to older children, too, by involving themselves in the youngster's problem solving as a "process guide." In this role, the adult sensitively guides (you might say, "leads") the child through the six steps of the problem-solving process. The adult must be careful not to rush the child. In fact, a child *might* move through the steps without *any* guidance from the adult. Should the child need guidance, listen for clues the child gives when ready to move on to the next step. Here are some typical things the adult can say when he thinks the child is ready to move from one step to the next:

From Step I to Step II:	"Do you feel you understand clearly enough what the problem is to start thinking now about possible solutions?" "Are you ready to think about things you might do to solve this problem?"
From Step II to Step III	"Have you reached the bottom of the barrel of possible solutions?" "Do you feel you have enough ideas to begin evaluating them?"

From Step III to Step IV	"Sounds like maybe you know which so-lution sounds best." "Does any one of the solutions stand out as your choice?"
From Step IV to Step V	"Now that you've decided on the best solution, what do you need to do to put it into action?" "Are you ready to plan who does what by when?"
From Step V to Step VI	"Maybe you could think now about how you'll know if your solution really works out." "It might be good now to set a time to evaluate how good your decision turns out to be."

Clearly, as a *process* guide, the adult doesn't get involved in the *content* of the youngster's problem, but merely helps the problem owner identify the stages leading to its resolution. Never forget that the child owns the problem—don't make it yours by taking over the problem-solving role yourself, which only keeps the youngster dependent and denies him or her the opportunity to be an effective problem solver.

Many parents who have taken our P.E.T. course have later submitted written incidents, often with actual dialogue, illustrating their efforts in facilitating a child's problem solving. Some have told us how they were amazed to discover how resourceful and creative their kids were, once given the chance (and the full responsibility) to solve their problems on their own and in their way. One mother, a graduate student in psychology who took P.E.T. when her daughter Alice was only two years old, submitted this incident when Alice was ten:

> Alice is pretty well behaved in school, but the teacher had been moving her around to sections in the room where there were a lot of boys causing a lot of trouble. . . . She came home in tears the other day—a real flood that lasted fifteen minutes. "It wasn't fair"; "I hate my teacher"; "He's terrible"; "He doesn't listen

to anybody." . . . He'd moved her one final time and she was really angry about it. She tried talking to him but he wouldn't listen. After she got all the anger out she calmed down. I said, "If he won't listen, what ways can you think of that might get his attention . . . ?" She said, "Well, I might write him a note." So she sat down and wrote a note saying it made her feel angry, it wasn't fair treatment for being good, and she wanted to be given a choice of where she sat for a while. She wrote that she realized how hard it was for him to listen to everybody with so many kids in the class. She took it in and, my God, that teacher read it. And he let her choose where she wanted to sit! I couldn't believe it.

The following dialogue illustrates how another parent participated actively in Step II but then stepped back while the child completed Steps III, IV, and V on his own:

JERRY: Mom, what would happen if someone was playing in someone's yard and they broke their clothesline?

MOM: Sounds like you're worried, Jerry.

JERRY: Yeah, I didn't know the person, I just ran away.

MOM: You're worried because you ran away?

JERRY: No, I'm scared! What can they do to me?

MOM: You're afraid of what they might do to you for breaking their clothesline.

JERRY: Not just me, Alan was there too. We were playing on the clothesline next door to Teddy's house and it broke, so we just ran away. And now I'm afraid they'll find out it's broken.

MOM: Wow, sounds like you're really upset, Jerry!

JERRY: Yeah, Mom, what should I do?

MOM: You'd really like it if I would tell you what to do.

JERRY: Oh, I know you won't. It's my problem. . . . But, Mom, if you were me what would you do, Mom?

MOM: Well, Jerry, if I were you, I guess I'd have several choices. I could just forget it ever happened; and, since you don't know them, they'd probably never find out who did it. Or I could ask Dad to help me fix it. Or I could go and tell them I broke their clothesline and would be glad to try and fix it. Then again, I could ask Alan to help me fix it. There are many things I guess I could do, but at this point, Jerry, I'm not sure just what I would do.

JERRY: Oh. [Silence]

Jerry then went into the living room and began watching television. I assumed he was going to forget about doing anything. A lot of time passed and Jerry got up and went outside. About fifteen minutes later Jerry came running in the door, very excited.

JERRY: Oh, Mom, I decided to go over and tell those people that I broke their clothesline and that I was sorry it happened and that I could try and fix it. Well, Mom, the man was so nice, he said, "Oh, that thing always breaks, don't worry about it, but thanks for telling me." Isn't he nice, Mom?

The mother added a postscript:

When Bill came home, Jerry felt so good about himself he repeated the whole story to his dad. That was a very exciting moment for Jerry. He felt so good about himself, and both Bill and I felt so good about him. He was able to make a decision on his own— one that had not been forced on him.

Parents and teachers are not always witnesses to all the steps of the child's problem-solving process. It frequently happens that a child will ventilate his feelings and define his problem (Step I), but then decide to stop the process, as if all he needed was someone to hear his feelings and acknowledge his problem. This happened with Tommy, age two, as described by his mother:

He'd gotten to be a big crier about being hurt. In preschool he hangs out with other little kids that have a habit of coming in and saying, "I got an Ow-wy, got an Ow-wy," yelling and crying loudly, you know, waiting for those hugs and sympathy. Tommy was picking this up. The next time he came in with one of those little Ow-wy's—and it wasn't severe—I said, "Wow, it looks like that really hurts." La-di-da, he just went off. That was it. And I've used that since on him. Something does happen inside a child when he feels, "I've been heard." But what is it? Because we can't see it, we can only hypothesize.

This mother is recognizing that at times a child needs only to be accepted as a person—one who momentarily hurts or is scared, disappointed, sad, lonely. Children often need only to be acknowledged or affirmed by another—whether it is for something satisfying: "Look, Ma, no hands!" or "Hey, Dad, I can stand on my head!"—or when they have a problem—"I'm scared of thunder" or "I cut my knee."

THE LANGUAGE OF UNACCEPTANCE

Conventional wisdom has it that if you genuinely *accept* a child, he or she will remain the same. It is also nearly universally believed that the way to help children do something better or change to something better in the future is to point out their faults or what is unacceptable about them now. Consequently, in dealing with children most parents and teachers rely almost exclusively on "correcting messages"—on judging, criticizing, preaching, moralizing, admonishing, name-calling, blaming, lecturing, threatening, ordering, and directing—all messages that convey *nonacceptance* of the child. This "language of unacceptance" is also the method of choice of other caretakers of our children.

In recent years, this deeply ingrained belief in correcting children with messages of unacceptance has been seriously challenged by the research and clinical experience of people in the helping professions. We have found ample evidence that a necessary condition for helping others change is accepting them the way they are. An interesting contradiction, is it not?

In our effectiveness-training classes we find that most parents and teachers are totally unaware of how often their everyday communication with children conveys nonacceptance and an intent to change them. Even adults who *think* that they are accepting and affirming are surprised to find out how frequently they communicate judgment and criticism. A simple exercise we use in every P.E.T. and T.E.T. class usually convinces parents and teachers that the language they typically use with children is in fact the "language of nonacceptance."

In the exercise, the instructor successively plays the role of each of several children who are having problems. Participants are then asked to write down, word for word, how they would respond to each of these children. Instructors collect these responses and categorize them for the group. Over the years we found that well over 90 percent of the responses fall into twelve basic categories of communication. Because these twelve categories so often convey nonacceptance and act to block further communication with children, we've come to call them "The Twelve Roadblocks" or "The Dirty Dozen."

How might *you* respond to the following typical problem? It involves a fourteen-year-old boy who is having a problem with his homework. He might say to you:

"I just can't get down to doing my homework. I hate it. And I hate school. It's boring. They teach you nothing important to your life—just a bunch of junk. When I'm old enough, I'm going to quit school. You don't need schooling to get ahead in this world."

In the left-hand column I've listed the typical responses of our class participants. In the right-hand column I've indicated our name for the category in which such a response (and those similar to it) falls:

Typical Response	*Roadblock*
"No son of mine is going to quit school—I won't allow it."	ORDERING, DIRECTING, DEMANDING
"Quit school and you'll get no financial help from me."	THREATENING, WARNING

"Learning is the most rewarding experience anyone can have."	MORALIZING, PREACHING
"Why don't you make a schedule for yourself to do your homework?"	ADVISING, GIVING SOLUTIONS
"A college graduate earns over fifty percent more than a high school graduate."	LECTURING, TEACHING, GIVING FACTS
"You're being shortsighted and your thinking shows immaturity."	JUDGING, BLAMING, CRITICIZING
"You've always been a good student, with lots of potential."	PRAISING, BUTTERING UP
"You're talking like one of those punk dropouts."	NAME-CALLING, RIDICULING
"You don't like school because you're afraid to put out the effort."	INTERPRETING, ANALYZING
"I know how you feel, but school will be better your senior year."	REASSURING, SYMPATHIZING
"What would you do without an education? How would you make a living?"	PROBING, QUESTIONING, INTERROGATING
"No problems at the dinner table! How's basketball going?"	WITHDRAWING, DIVERTING, DISTRACTING

These typical responses carry a high risk of producing certain negative effects on children. In reaction, the children may:

Stop talking.
Become defensive, resistive.
Argue, retaliate.
Feel inadequate or inferior.
Become resentful, angry.
Feel wrong, bad, guilty.
Feel unaccepted as they are.
Feel you are trying to change them.

Feel you don't trust them to solve their own problem.

Feel you've taken over their problem.

Feel they are not understood.

Feel their feelings are not justified.

Feel interrupted, cut off.

Feel misunderstood, frustrated.

Feel they're on the witness stand, cross-examined.

Feel you're not interested, that you want to get rid of the problem.

I have found that parents and teachers, with rare exceptions, use one or more of the Roadblocks when children share a problem with them. Some are typically "advice givers," some "judges," some "lecturers," some "reassurers," some "moralizers," and so on. Do you find yourself fitting into a particular category?

Parents we've interviewed have also told us about their experiences with Roadblocks. One parent shared this story about the effect of Roadblocks on her son, Timmy:

When Timmy started nursery school, he'd come home with nothing to say about the morning's events. I'd question him directly, and he wouldn't respond. . . . Then I began to notice that he rarely answered any of my direct questions. It was very frustrating to a schoolteacher mom like me to have a child who wouldn't speak up when questioned. . . . One of the first things I discovered was that my habit of questioning Timmy directly put him in a very vulnerable position. He hated to be wrong, so, rather than answer a question in a wrong way, he wouldn't answer at all. I listened to myself for a week and heard the stridency in my voice. It was a humbling revelation. The strict objectivity and prosecutor's pose which worked well in the classroom were overwhelming to my tiny five-year-old. His only defense was silence. Then I began to find that I could get answers by gentler means. If I'd be patient and listen carefully, I would eventually hear him mention something about his day at school.

. . . Little by little he began to open up and let me have a glimpse of his inner self.

When kids say, "My parents don't listen to me" or "Teachers don't try to understand kids" or "I can't ever discuss my problems with my parents," it's a sure bet those particular parents and teachers, like most, are in the habit of responding with some of the Twelve Roadblocks when they hear kids' problems. Evidence of teachers' heavy use of the language of nonacceptance is found in several studies by David Aspy and Flora Roebuck of the National Consortium for Humanizing Education (Aspy and Roebuck, 1983). Their principal findings:

- The average level of empathic understanding, genuineness, and respect for students among teachers was about the same as that of the general population.
- The average level of competence in interpersonal helping skills of teachers and administrators was below the *minimally effective threshold of 3.0* on the researchers' measuring scales for empathy, genuineness, and respect for students.

The investigators conclude that most teachers and principals generally operate at a low level of interpersonal helping skills.

ACCEPTANCE: THE BASIC HELPING ATTITUDE

As I mentioned earlier, the genuine acceptance of a person, just as he or she is, is *the* critical factor in fostering that person's constructive change, in facilitating the person's problem solving, in encouraging movement toward greater psychological health or productive learning. It is a beautiful paradox of life that when people feel genuinely accepted by another as they are, they are free to think about how they want to develop, grow, change, be more of what they are capable of being.

Acceptance is like the fertile soil that permits a tiny seed to develop into the lovely flower it is capable of becoming— acceptance enables a person to actualize his or her potential.

I think the greatest reward in my own professional life has

been discovering that parents and teachers can be taught how better to communicate genuine acceptance of children. When they learn how to show acceptance, they find they're in possession of a remarkable skill for helping children solve for themselves the many problems that life inevitably brings.

Obviously, it is not enough to feel accepting toward another or just to avoid the Roadblocks. Acceptance must come through the other person, it must be *felt* by him. This means that you must *demonstrate* your acceptance, actively *transmit* it, and overtly *communicate* it. How to do this most effectively is my next subject.

HOW TO DEMONSTRATE YOUR ACCEPTANCE

There are three basic ways to demonstrate acceptance, the first two of which are familiar to most people, though the third may not be: (1) Nonintervention, (2) Attentive and Passive Listening, and (3) Active Listening.

Nonintervention
Adults can show acceptance by refraining from intervening in a child's activity. Children interpret that to mean that what they are doing is acceptable to their parents or teachers, because they don't pick up any messages of disapproval from them. Too often, however, adults find it hard to keep out of a situation. Imagine a child trying to build a castle of sand at the beach. The parent says with the best of intentions, "Build the castle farther from the water," "You need to get the sand wetter," "Not that wet," "You'll have to pat it harder," "Shouldn't your castle have a moat?" "It's going to fall if you build it," "Here, I'll help you." The child hears this as evidence that he isn't good enough to be the "engineer" of his own project. Saying nothing, on the other hand, will convey acceptance. The child will feel, "What I'm doing is okay; it's acceptable to Dad for me to build my castle my own way, to solve my problems by finding my own solutions."

Attentive and Passive Listening
Allowing another person to express feelings or share a problem by remaining silent but attentive is a second way of communi-

cating acceptance. One shows attentiveness by certain postures and by steady eye contact. Here is a dialogue that illustrates attentive and passive listening:

CHILD: I got sent down to the principal's office today.

PARENT: Oh?

CHILD: Yeah. Mr. Frank said I was talking too much in class.

PARENT: I see.

CHILD: I can't stand that old fossil. He sits up there and talks about his troubles or his grandchildren and expects us to be interested. It's so boring you'd never believe it.

PARENT: Mm-hmm.

CHILD: You just can't sit in the class doing nothing! You'd go crazy. Jeannie and I sit there and make jokes when he's talking. Oh, he's just the worst teacher you can imagine. It makes me mad when I get a lousy teacher.

PARENT: [Silence]

CHILD: I suppose I'd better get used to it, 'cause I'm not always going to get good teachers. There are more lousy ones than good ones and if I let the lousy ones get me down, I'm not going to get the grades I need to get into a good college. I'm really hurting myself, I guess.

The mother's attentive and passive listening facilitated her daughter's moving far beyond admitting she'd been sent to the principal. Her mother's silent acceptance helped her feel safe enough to say why she was punished, to release her anger, to face up to the consequences of her negative reactions to bad teachers, and finally to conclude she was hurting herself.

Contrast the mother's passive listening above with responses that parents typically make:

"You what! Oh, no! You weren't really talking too much again!"

"Well, you asked for it, sister."

"Who made you an expert on teaching?"

"Honey, you have to learn to take the bad with the good."

Such nonaccepting Roadblocks, as you can imagine, probably would have stopped the daughter's communication cold and thus prevented her constructive, self-directed problem solving.

Active Listening

While attentive passive listening can be facilitative and convey acceptance, it does not prove to the sender that he or she has been accurately *understood*. However, there exists a remarkably effecive way of communicating proof of accurate understanding. In our courses we devote a lot of time to teaching what we call *Active Listening*, a method first used by client-centered counselors and therapists and sometimes called "reflection of feelings" or "reflective listening." Using Active Listening, the receiver doesn't remain silent but rather gets deeply involved with the sender in a special kind of two-way communication. First the receiver focuses attention exclusively on *understanding the message* being sent and what it means. Then the receiver puts what he has understood *into his own words and mirrors it back* to the sender (we say *gives feedback*) to get verification or correction of what the receiver understood the message to be. With this simple feedback procedure, the listener can give positive proof to the sender that he or she has been accurately understood. *Without feeling understood, people will seldom feel accepted.*

The following diagrams illustrate these techniques. *Note:* Everything I say from here on about the communication process between a child and a parent is applicable to the process between any two people.

Whenever a child communicates a message to a parent, it's almost invariably because the child has an unmet (unsatisfied) *need*. The child feels discomfort; needs company; is upset, frightened, hungry, cold. You might say that the child is in a state of *disequilibrium*. For example, a child is scared when she sees blood from a cut finger. The child can't communicate her actual fear—that's a complex physiological process going on inside the child. To tell her father about the feelings inside, the child must first choose a symbol or code that she hopes her father might know stands for being scared. This process is called *coding* (or encoding). It's the code, not the fear, that is actually communicated:

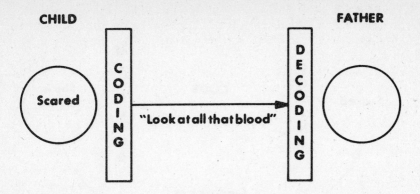

When Dad receives that coded message, he has to decode it to understand what the child is experiencing inside. *Decoding* is a form of translating, sometimes even guessing. Dad guesses accurately here when he senses that the child is feeling afraid. But

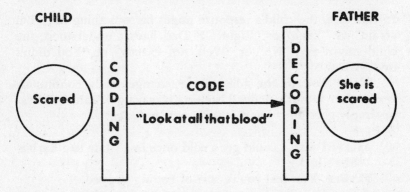

still, Dad can't know for sure that it's fear going on inside the child. To check on the accuracy of his decoding, Dad feeds back what he thinks he hears. *He does not send a new message of his own, but rephrases and feeds back the child's message, as in the last diagram.*

This feedback process, essential to what we call Active Listening, does two things: (1) it enables the child to know for sure whether she's been understood accurately, and (2) from the child's subsequent response to the feedback, Dad will find out whether he has understood the child's message accurately.

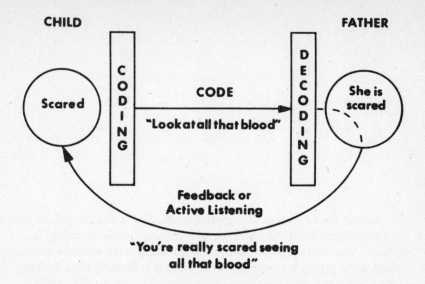

"You're really scared seeing
all that blood"

In this case, the child's response might be something like "I'm afraid" or "Yeah" or "Right." If Dad hadn't understood, the child might say, "No" or "Well, not exactly" or "You didn't understand."

Note how, in the following exchange, Sally continually verifies her father's Active Listening by saying "Yeah" or "Yes" or simply goes ahead and sends a new message:

SALLY: I wish I could get a cold once in a while like Barbie. She's lucky.
FATHER: You feel you're sort of getting gypped.
SALLY: Yes. She gets to stay out of school and I never do.
FATHER: You really would like to stay out of school more.
SALLY: Yes. I don't like to go to school every day—day after day after day. I get sick of it.
FATHER: You really get tired of school.
SALLY: Sometimes I just hate it.
FATHER: It's more than not liking it, sometimes you really hate school.
SALLY: That's right. I hate the homework, I hate the classes, and I hate the teachers.

FATHER: You just hate everything about school.

SALLY: I don't really hate all the teachers—just two of them. One of them I can't stand. She's the worst.

FATHER: You hate one in particular, huh?

SALLY: Do I ever! It's that Mrs. Barnes. I hate the sight of her. I got her for the whole year, too.

FATHER: You're stuck with her for a long time.

SALLY: Yes. I don't know how I'll ever stand it. You know what she does? Every day we get a long lecture. She stands up there smiling like this [demonstrates] and tells us how a responsible student is supposed to behave, and she reads off all these things you have to do to get an A in her class. It's sickening.

FATHER: You sure hate to hear all that stuff.

SALLY: Yeah. She makes it seem impossible to get an A, unless you're some kind of genius or a teacher's pet.

FATHER: You feel defeated before you even start, because you don't think you can possibly get an A.

SALLY: Yeah. I'm not going to be one of those teacher's pets. The other kids hate them. I'm already not very popular with the kids. I just don't feel too many of the girls like me. [Tears]

FATHER: You don't feel popular and that upsets you.

SALLY: Yeah, there's this group of girls that are the top ones in school. They're the most popular. I wish I could get in their group. But I don't know how.

FATHER: You really would like to belong to this group, but you're stumped about how to do it.

SALLY: That's right. I don't honestly know how girls get into this group. They're not the prettiest—not all of them. They're not always the ones with the best grades. Some in the group get high grades, but most of them get lower grades than I get. I just don't know.

FATHER: You're sort of puzzled about what it takes to get into this group.

SALLY: Well, one thing is that they're all pretty friendly— they talk a lot and, you know, make friends. They say hello to you first and talk real easy. I can't do that. I'm just not good at that stuff.

FATHER: You think maybe that's what they have that you don't have.

SALLY: I know I'm not good at talking. I can talk easily with one girl, but not when there's a whole bunch of girls. I just keep quiet. It's hard for me to think of something to say.

FATHER: You feel okay with one girl but with a lot of girls you feel different.

SALLY: I'm always afraid I'll say something that will be silly or wrong or something. So I just stand there and feel kind of left out. It's terrible.

FATHER: You sure hate that feeling.

SALLY: I hate to be on the outside, but I'm afraid to try to get into the conversation.

Can you feel the movement as Sally digs deeper, redefines her problem on her own, develops insights about herself, and makes a good start at solving her problem? Did you also notice that Sally's father, like a good counselor, put aside whatever thoughts or feelings he had? You'll find Active Listening demands this, because one's full attention is required to listen carefully, decode accurately, and then finally feed back what you decoded. Note, too, how the father's Active Listening responses generally began with "You," indicating that he was attending to *Sally's* thoughts and feelings, not *his own* (they would come out as I-messages).

Here is a second example of Active Listening and its effect, this one involving a teacher and student in a brief verbal interaction.

STUDENT: Are we going to have a test real soon?

TEACHER: You're worried about having an exam soon?

STUDENT: No, it's just that I don't know what kind of a test you're going to give and I'm afraid it'll be an essay type.

TEACHER: Oh, you're worried about the *kind* of test we are going to have.

STUDENT: Yes. I don't do well on essay tests.

TEACHER: I see, you feel you can do better on objective tests.

STUDENT: Yeah, I always botch up essay tests.

TEACHER: It'll be a multiple-choice test.
STUDENT: What a relief! I'm not so worried now.

In this case the teacher's first feedback was not on target so the student knew he had to restate or recode his message until ultimately he was understood.

I can't emphasize enough that without the proper attitudes or intentions behind it, Active Listening may sound mechanical, insincere, gimmicky. It should be viewed only as the vehicle, an ingenious one nonetheless, for communicating an accepting message: "I really understand what you are experiencing and I accept your feeling or thinking that way." For this message to come across, these conditions are important:

1. You must want to hear what the child has to say. This means you are willing to take the time to listen. If you don't have time, you need only say so.

2. You must genuinely want to be helpful to the child at this time and with this particular problem. If you don't want to, for whatever reason, be honest and say you can't.

3. You must genuinely accept his feelings, however different they may be from your own feelings or from the feelings you think a child should feel. You must not want to change the child.

4. You must have a deep feeling of trust in the child's capacity to handle her feelings, to work through them, and to find solutions to her problems. You'll acquire this trust over time, watching your child get better at solving problems on her own.

5. You must appreciate that feelings are transitory, not permanent. Feelings change—hate can turn into love, discouragement may quickly be replaced by hope. Consequently, you need not be afraid when feelings get expressed; they'll not become forever fixed inside the child. Active Listening will demonstrate this fact to you.

6. You must be able to see your child as someone separate from you—a unique person no longer "joined" to you, an individual having his own life and identity. Only by mastering

this will you be helpful to the child. You must be "with" him as he experiences his problems, but not responsible for him.

7. You must want to understand with empathy how the child feels from her point of view. Put yourself momentarily in the child's shoes and see the world as the child sees it, putting aside your own perspective. This quality makes Active Listening the best vehicle for communicating genuine empathic understanding.

8. You must be willing to take the risk of having your own opinions, attitudes, or values changed by what you hear. By deeply understanding another, you invite a reinterpretation of your own experience. A defensive or needy person cannot afford to listen to views too different from his own; it's too destabilizing. One must have a rather "full cup" to open up to others in that way.

When these conditions are met, I promise you that your Active Listening will communicate *empathic understanding, acceptance, and respect for the individuality of the other person.* And you'll be greatly rewarded by the experience of seeing children solve their problems themselves. Equally rewarding, you'll find that children you've listened to will feel more like listening to you when you have problems.

The remarkable effectiveness of Active Listening as a counseling tool has been shown in many research studies. In his classic book, *Client-Centered Therapy* (1951), Carl Rogers reviewed a number of studies of the outcomes of listening-based counseling. He summarized their findings, the most important of which were:

- Increasing frequency of positive self-references and self-regarding attitudes.
- Decreasing frequency of negative self-references and self-regarding attitudes.
- At the end stages of counseling there are more positive self-references than negative ones.
- Acceptance of self increases during counseling—that is, the person perceives himself or herself as a person of worth, worthy of respect.

- After successful counseling, people see themselves with less emotion and more objectivity, as more independent and more able to cope with life problems, more integrated and less divided.

Let me summarize the key points I've made in this chapter and their importance to a discussion about discipline.

All children sometimes behave in ways that are unacceptable to their parents, as I've emphasized repeatedly. Understandably, parents want to try to eliminate or change those behaviors. They want to *influence their children* to change out of consideration for the needs of the parents. However, to acquire such influence, a parent must be seen by the child as someone who usually is helpful to him when he or she has problems. In other words, the relationship must be felt by the child as reciprocal and fair. When parents demonstrate a willingness to listen when their children have problems, it follows that the children will be much more willing to listen when the parents confront them with "Your behavior is causing me a problem."

Parents benefit from becoming competent helping agents in another important way. The effective helping skills described in this chapter will actually *prevent* a lot of behaviors parents don't like to see in their children. Kids who have unsolved problems, unmet needs, or troubles that won't go away often react to their frustration with self-destructive and antisocial behaviors. Likewise, students who feel a lot of frustration in school are generally the ones who give teachers fits. However, if parents and teachers acquire the skills to spot troubled children, and then help them solve their problems, those unacceptable behaviors will be defused considerably. Discipline can become a non-issue.

chapter

nine

Active Listening: The All-Purpose People Skill

In the last chapter I presented Active Listening primarily as a counseling skill for helping children solve problems. However, by no means is this the only time it is useful and effective. In fact, communicating warm, empathic understanding and acceptance has such general usefulness, it might be called the "all-purpose people skill." Its versatility in facilitating communication has been proven in a wide variety of situations: mediating conflicts between children, ensuring good group discussions, and adding warmth and mutual caring to teacher-child relationships.

MEDIATING CHILD-CHILD CONFLICTS

A useful application of Active Listening is helping children when they get into conflicts with each other, as illustrated in this incident submitted by a New England teacher during her T.E.T. class. It seems that Ann, a fourth-grader, was disliked by other children because she was a pest. No one wanted to be seated with her as a partner. Laura, too, had been trying to avoid being Ann's partner:

ANN: Mrs. T., Laura won't sit with me and help me with the map project.

LAURA: It's because Ann doesn't want to work. She just wants to talk and fool around and she writes on my papers.

ANN: I'm just pretending to write on your papers.

MRS. T.: Girls, it seems to me that you both have a problem. I think that I could listen to both sides of the situation and perhaps we could come to some conclusions and even find a solution.

GIRLS: All right. What do we do?

MRS. T.: Just tell me how you feel and I'll listen very carefully.

ANN: Laura said she wanted to sit beside me and now she doesn't. She doesn't really want to anyway. She just did it so you'll like her and think she's nice. I really want her to work with me.

LAURA: I did want to work with you, but you're spoiling my work and I want to get it passed in on time. You don't care about your own work and you want me to be the same as you.

MRS. T.: Ann, I hear you saying that you'd like Laura to be your partner on this project, but you two aren't getting along together. Laura, I hear you saying that you'd like to work with Ann but getting along together is difficult because she's not working seriously. Let's list all the possible solutions to this problem.

ANN: Laura could be more patient and help me.

LAURA: I could leave Ann and we could work separately.

ANN: You could move our desks far apart.

LAURA: [Not really serious] You could send a note home to Ann's mother saying she's a big pest.

ANN: [Serious retaliation] Tell Laura's mother that she thinks she's perfect.

LAURA: Ann could settle down and do her work and stop fooling around.

ANN: Laura could wait till I catch up to the part she's working on.

LAURA: We could try again together.

MRS. T.: I'll read these possible solutions as I've jotted them down. Which of all these do you think is the best solution? [Reads solutions.]

ANN: We could try again . . . and if it doesn't work we could separate our desks.

MRS. T.: May I suggest something? Now that you know what bothers each of you about the other, why not try again for a day and try hard not to do the things that bother each other. Come and tell me at the end of the day how it worked. We can all talk again then, but really try to make this work. I know that desks can be moved far apart, but I think that's the easy way out and I also think you girls are grown-up enough to handle this map project and this problem together.

Here is Mrs. T.'s subsequent write-up of the outcome of this brief conflict-resolution session:

> The girls are now working together. So far, two days have passed without a request for separation. Ann's pattern has always been to "test" her friends to the extreme to ensure their true friendship (or maybe because her friendships so often terminate and she wants to get the hurt over with). But for now, Ann has a friend and a working partner.

I cannot resist drawing an exciting inference from this real-life situation. As you observed, in just a few minutes Mrs. T. offered Ann *a new model* for all her interpersonal relationships. With several repetitions of this model, Ann might radically change her ineffective methods of relating to her peers. Should that happen, Mrs. T. will have been an educator in the truest sense of the word—not just as a teacher of subject matter, but as one who facilitates the development of "the whole child," something educators theorize about but is seldom done in schools.

ENSURING GOOD GROUP DISCUSSIONS

Teachers are known to complain that they can't get their students to participate in meaningful discussions about things the class is studying. As a consequence, the teachers either give up trying and fall back on giving lectures, or they have discussions in which only a few students talk. In either case, many of their students, bored with lectures or uninvolved in discussions, engage in disruptive behaviors. Kids at home often act up at dinnertime or on trips with parents, because they are not interested in the conversation.

However, most youngsters get turned on by a good discussion of something that interests them. Unfortunately, not many adults have the skill to facilitate absorbing and meaningful group discussions.

Active Listening has proven to be an invaluable skill for teachers and parents to get kids to participate actively in meaningful discussions. It communicates acceptance and respect for what each group member contributes, thus encouraging shy members to make contributions. And, because it provides a model of respectful listening, participants gradually start listening respectfully to each other, something rare both in classrooms and in families.

A teacher of upper-elementary-grade students told about his experiences using Active Listening to facilitate student-centered discussions:

> They were really helpful. I'd forgotten how hard it is for eleven- and twelve-year-olds to make sense out of the world. I was surprised at the amount of nonsense they believed in, and, at the same time, how much insight they have. Some of the things they talked about have been low-level things like how the food in the cafeteria could be improved. But they tackled a few really tough issues, too. Things like "What is honesty?" and "Do people ever have the right to control other people for their own good?" Really heavy stuff, things I didn't work on until I was in college, or later. I don't know a better way to let

kids sort through all the conflicting information and feelings than these class meetings.

Here is a classroom group discussion where the teacher relies almost entirely on Active Listening to clarify and restate:

TEACHER: You've been reading about the Spanish-American War. I'm wondering what you've learned and what your reactions are to your reading.

BRET: I thought it was going to be dull, but it wasn't. Henry and I were talking on the bus yesterday about how surprised we were that the book told the truth. Most of the history books I've read before made the United States out to always be, you know, good guys.

HENRY: [Interrupting] Like the ones we had on the Civil War that said Lincoln freed the slaves and all that bull.

TEACHER: These books seem different to you. You don't feel you're being lied to by these authors.

MARCIA: I don't think the other books exactly lied. They just told one side of the story or left out some things that happened.

HENRY: If that's not lying, what is? If I told people that our football team scored two touchdowns, gained a hundred and eighty-five yards, intercepted a pass, and blocked a punt last Friday against Central, they sure wouldn't get the whole picture, right? [Central won the game 45–15.]

GROUP: [Laughter]

TEACHER: Henry, you maintain that withholding information is the same as lying and that some of the references we have had seemed to do that.

HENRY: Yes. It's true! When we compared some of the different books you'd think they were talking about different wars.

NANCY: Well, how does anybody get to be a historian anyway? After all, they're just people who write books about things that happened a long time ago. They're bound to be prejudiced.

VICKY: You're right. My sister says that historians are all male chauvinist pigs writing stuff like "Brave men traveled west and some even took their families." Nobody ever wrote about brave women, or if they did, it was like they were surprised that women could shoot a gun or put up with hardships.

TEACHER: If I understand, you are all questioning the ability of anyone to write an unbiased history—you're saying that writers' opinions will influence their views of history.

NANCY: That's the problem, so why even bother to read the stuff?

BRET: You're missing the point, Nancy. The point is not to believe something just because it's written in a book. I think we ought to read more books, not less.

NANCY: Fewer. Say "fewer" books, not "less" books.

BRET: Chalk up one for you. Anyway, get more books.

HENRY: Yeah. I wonder what Spanish history books say about the Spanish-American War?

VICKY: If they were written by men they're probably just as chauvinistic as ours.

MARIE: Who ever heard of a woman historian?

VICKY: Nobody. That's why all the books talk about history as if the only important things that happened were done by men and the only important people were men. One book I had, I think it was in eighth grade, had about three pages called "Great Women in American History." It made me sick.

TEACHER: It's your experience, Vicky, that women have been treated pretty lightly by historians.

VICKY: Yes.

HENRY: Well, what did women do in the Spanish-American War? I don't see what this thing about women has to do with what we're talking about.

MARCIA: I think it has a lot to do with it. You were the one that was griping about not telling the whole story, Henry. Well, not telling about the things women did is like leaving out part of the story.

HENRY: Yeah, but women never did anything. They never wrote treaties, or formed governments, or were captains of ships, or explorers, or anything.

VICKY: That's just the attitude I was talking about. You read the books that men write and you get the idea that men do everything. I don't claim that women were generals or anything. It's just that women are put down in the books. You know, the things they have done are sort of sneered at.

TEACHER: You seem very interested in how history is written, especially how biases, like the one Vicky sees regarding women, show up in what you read. This seems a change from the general feeling I got earlier that you liked the books you were reading on the Spanish-American War.

VICKY: It was Henry and Bret that said that.

BRET: Said what?

VICKY: That you liked the books. You were talking about how they gave a fair description of the war and didn't try to make the U.S. look good when they didn't deserve it. Well, these same books aren't so fair to women. My sister is taking a women's studies course at the university and she's got some materials that show how to evaluate the language of books to see how slanted they are against women. I'll get her to help me look through these books and then next week I'll show you.

BRET: Okay, but how about other slants?

TEACHER: You're interested in finding out how to read between the lines and get the real truth when you read history—not just about women, but about any bias that happens. Is that right?

HENRY: Yes. How do we evaluate the stuff we read?

TEACHER: Vicky has promised to share some ways to evaluate. Bret, you suggested reading a variety of books, and, Henry, I believe it was you who suggested getting foreign books so we could compare. Are there any other ideas?

MARIE: I think we need an expert. We could get a historian to come here and tell us what to do or answer questions. My neighbor teaches history at the university and maybe he'd come to our class.

VICKY: Another male historian. [Shrugs]

MARIE: I think he's fair. In fact, we could ask him about sexism in history books.

NANCY: You could get us some of the references listed as source books in the bibliography.

TEACHER: You mean in the textbook we're using?

NANCY: Yes.

MARCIA: I think we ought to put off talking about the Spanish-American War until after we do this other stuff. It blows my mind that maybe all the stuff I've read could be, you know, not true. When Vicky was talking I got to thinking, and she's right, none of the books I ever read ever made women out to be important even when they were, so how do I know about the rest of the things they wrote?

TEACHER: You can see some advantage to studying the writing and evaluating of history books before doing any more reading.

MARCIA: Yes. [The group agrees.]

TEACHER: Okay. Let's set a time schedule for who is going to do what kinds of things. I'll get the source books from the library by next Tuesday. Vicky, when will you be able to make your report? [Arrangements are made to define the tasks of the members of the study group.]

In less than fifteen minutes, this class completely changed from having a discussion of what the students got out of a book on the Spanish-American War to exploring historical source materials and developing a set of criteria for evaluating the texts and other books used in history courses at the school. Active Listening played a vital and necesary role in this deep and meaningful learning experience.

Most teachers tell us that they are reluctant to break away from the lecture model, even though most of them know it's overused and ineffective, because they've had nothing but unrewarding experiences trying to get students to talk. In fact, most teachers don't know how to facilitate student talk. Many have never heard of Active Listening as a teaching tool. Educational researchers David Aspy and Flora Roebuck (1983) found that teachers talk 80 percent of the time in secondary-school classrooms. Until teachers learn how to get students actively involved in the classroom, schools will never get rid of the discipline problem. And Active Listening is indispensable for fostering involvement in productive classroom discussions. This is reinforced by what one teacher reported during his T.E.T. class:

I think one of the things that may be hanging us up here is that we aren't viewing Active Listening as a teaching tool. In my department we have been urged to use all kinds of new inquiry approaches and to hold discussion groups. We have been given special training in these techniques for two years. But only in the last few days, after I learned about Active Listening, has any of these approaches ever worked for me. Now I see why my discussion groups always turn into bull sessions or I end up lecturing as usual— the only difference being that the students are seated in a circle instead of rows. In other courses, they told us we had to be "nonevaluative" but never showed us how. Since I've been trying Active Listening, discussions are really discussions. I'm enjoying it, and the kids in my classes are really turned on.

As this teacher found out, Active Listening is a powerful tool for getting kids to talk and think—for clarifying ideas, promoting inquiry, creating a climate where students feel free to use their minds, generate questions, and explore ideas. Such a climate, unfortunately, is a rarity in school classrooms. With systematic training, however, teachers can reach high levels of skill in facilitating student-centered participation in the classroom and, as a result, eliminate a lot of discipline problems.

TOWARD WARMER RELATIONSHIPS
BETWEEN TEACHER AND STUDENTS

Think back to when you were a student and try to recall the teachers you really liked or loved. Most of us remember one teacher, sometimes two; very few remember more than that. It is a sad commentary on our schools that teacher-student relationships are so universally poor.

"Kids don't learn from people they don't like" claims the title of a book by David Aspy and Flora Roebuck (1977). It is also common knowledge that the quality of the teacher-student relationship has a lot to do with how much kids learn. As students, we somehow put forth the effort to do our best when we had teachers we liked or loved.

Not only did we learn more, but we acted better in class with teachers we liked. Kids are less likely to hassle, sass, and make trouble for teachers they like. Kids who cause disciplinary problems, on the other hand, are usually acting out some kind of hostility toward their current teacher, or they are retaliating for the way they have been treated or talked to by former teachers.

While there are a number of different elements that contribute to promoting good discipline and good relationships between teachers and students, none is more effective than a classroom climate where students are encouraged to express their ideas and opinions and are made to feel those ideas and opinions are understood, respected, and accepted by the teacher.

Parents and teachers alike generally turn kids off by failing to listen when youngsters express strong or "far-out" opinions, especially on controversial topics, as kids often do. But because Active Listening dramatically changes the way adults and children hear each other, it often dramatically changes adult-youth relationships.

Youngsters who are understood and respected by adults invariably experience a sense of greater self-worth and importance. The satisfaction of being understood, coupled with increased self-esteem, causes them to develop positive feelings toward their parents and teachers. Adults who listen empathically also will get a broader understanding of young people and begin to see what it's like to be in their shoes. Listening in this way means walking a few steps with a youngster on his or her life journey, which is truly an act of caring, respect, and love. Most children have never experienced it before, which increases its impact on them even more when they feel truly understood and accepted for the first time. They learn that their feelings and opinions are acceptable, that it's all right to be who they are, that talking about things that are interesting and important to them is both exciting and worthwhile.

Whether a teacher uses Active Listening to listen empathically to a single child with a problem, to two children with a conflict, or to a classroom of students discussing the bias of history books—the effect on students is much the same. They feel good about themselves; they feel good about their teacher. Because their teacher demonstrates an interest and a respect for their ideas and feelings, the students feel more valued, have more self-worth. They like these feelings, and therefore grow to like the person who has helped produce them. Over time, the relationship with their teacher becomes one of mutual caring, mutual respect.

In such relationships, not only will teachers have fewer discipline problems—fewer rebellious or retaliatory children—but their students will also be more self-controlled, responsible, and self-disciplined.

These assertions are not universally believed at first. Teachers enrolled in our T.E.T. classes initially question the need to learn how to listen empathically. They argue, "We are supposed to be teachers, not counselors, and our job is to provide students with information and knowledge, not listen to the 'collective ignorance' of student discussions."

School administrators and members of school boards use similar arguments to justify turning down proposals for teacher training in the helping skills. They, too, see no direct relationship between teachers' effectiveness as listeners, helpers, and facilitators and their effectiveness in promoting the acquisition of knowledge. "It's nice to be nice, but you gotta teach them something" seems to be the conventional attitude.

Nevertheless, there exist considerable "hard data" that show conclusively that the student-centered, empathic, facilitative skill I've described actually helps teachers achieve even the traditional goals of our schools, such as scholastic achievement, good attendance, creative thinking, strong learning motivation, and self-discipline.

RESEARCH SUPPORTING FACILITATIVE SKILLS TRAINING

In a major study by Aspy and Roebuck (1983) involving six hundred teachers and ten thousand students from kindergarten through grade twelve, the students whose teachers were trained in the skill of communicating empathic understanding, acceptance, respect, and regard for students as persons were compared with students whose teachers were not trained in these facilitative skills. The teachers who got the training had students who were found to:

- Miss fewer days of school during the year (four fewer days per child)
- Make greater gains on academic achievement measures, including both math and reading scores
- Be more spontaneous and use higher levels of thinking
- Increase their scores on IQ tests (from kindergarten through fifth grade)
- Make gains in creativity scores from September to May
- Show increased scores on self-esteem measures
- Commit fewer acts of vandalism to school property
- Present fewer disciplinary problems

The study also found that teachers who were trained in the helping skills had classrooms in which there was:

- More student talk
- More student problem solving
- More student verbal initiation
- More verbal response to teacher
- More student asking of questions
- More student involvement in learning
- More eye contact with teacher
- More physical movement
- Higher levels of cognitive thinking
- Greater creativity

Students of the *untrained* teachers, on the other hand, suffered an actual *decrease* in their self-esteem scores. To paraphrase the investigators, teaching a child to like himself *less* is not what should be going on in schools.

In several other studies conducted by the staff of the National Consortium for Humanizing Education (Aspy and Roebuck, 1975; Roebuck, 1975; Roebuck and Aspy, 1974), it was found that teachers who provided high levels of empathic understanding in their classrooms also tended to provide:

- More response to students' feelings
- More use of students' ideas in ongoing instructional interactions
- More discussion and dialogue with students
- More praise of students
- More "real" and genuine (less ritualistic) teacher talk
- More tailoring of instructional content to the individual student's immediate needs
- More smiling with students
- More emphasis upon productivity and creativity than upon evaluation
- Less emphasis on grades and tests
- Learning goals that were derived from cooperative planning between teacher and students

In yet another study by Roebuck (1980), it was shown that one of the most important benefits of learning the facilitative skills is a reduction of disruptive behaviors in the classroom. This study involved eighty-eight classes in grades two through six. The researcher measured the teachers' empathic understanding, their respect for their students, and the degree of student involvement provided by the teachers. She also collected the number of disruptive behaviors occurring in each classroom for a month. Her findings: More disruptive behavior occurred in classes whose teachers were *low* in empathy, respect, praise, and acceptance of students' ideas and thinking.

I've said it before: When relationships between teacher and students involve mutual caring, respect, and love, discipline problems decrease significantly. Kids won't want to hassle and make trouble for teachers who respect and care for them— teachers they grow to love. Classroom time usually spent dealing with discipline problems will instead be available for teaching and learning.

OTHER BENEFITS FROM LEARNING THE FACILITATIVE SKILLS

Another benefit of learning the facilitative skills is that you will greatly increase your ability to influence children at those

times when you want them to change behaviors that are interfering with your getting *your* needs met—when their behavior
is causing you some kind of a problem. In Chapter 8, I presented
a principle: *Children won't want to be helpful to you when you tell
them you have a problem with their behavior, unless they feel you've
tried to help them when they have had problems.*

This kind of reciprocity exerts a great influence in all
relationships. You'll find this out when you use your new
facilitative skills; and as you acquire more influence you won't
be tempted to use power-based discipline to try to change
children's behavior. Consequently, you'll avoid having to deal
with rebelling and resisting behaviors ("fight" responses) or
withdrawing or escaping behaviors ("flight" responses). And
you'll be helping your children or your students become more
self-disciplined, self-controlled, and responsible. They'll also
show a new respect for you—not respect (fear, really) for your
Authority P, but a respect for your right to get your own needs
met, because you have shown them the same respect.

Perhaps the greatest benefit of learning to be an effective
listener is that the kids in your home or your classroom will
have fewer unresolved problems. As we've learned, children
who feel unhappy and deprived usually engage in disruptive or
destructive behaviors to a much greater degree than children
who do not have unmet needs. Troubled, unhappy, unfulfilled,
needy children are the ones who invite disciplinary action.
Children whose parents or teachers become helping agents may
not have fewer problems, but they'll certainly have fewer *unresolved* problems. Your facilitative skills will help them acquire
more of that all-important problem-solving ability, which will
also help them feel, overall, more self-confident and less helpless.

Why Adults
Don't Give Up
Disciplining Children

Despite the innumerable difficulties in employing rewards and punishments in the everyday life of families and schools, despite the failures that parents and teachers obviously experience when they try to control children with rewards and punishment, and despite the profusion of research studies that confirm both the ineffectiveness and the damaging effects of power-based discipline, most parents, teachers, and educators cling to the belief that you must discipline children. Even some of the most progressive advocates of "humanistic education" and "child-centered parenting" defend rewards and punishments in some form or another as necessary for children's healthy development. In fact, I have found it difficult to identify more than a handful of psychologists or educators who support the position that I have espoused for over a quarter of a century—namely, that discipline is an ineffective, outmoded, and harmful way to rear and educate children.

A questionnaire study of active members of the Northwestern Pennsylvania Psychological Association found that the *majority* of those psychologists spanked their own children, and half felt that school personnel should have the option to spank them, too.

Another study in the same state found the following percentages of various personnel who favored corporal punishment in the schools (Reardon and Reynolds, 1975).

School board presidents	81 percent
Principals	78 percent
Administrators	68 percent
Teachers	74 percent
Parents	71 percent
Students	25 percent

What are the possible reasons for this nearly universal reluctance to cease disciplining children? In the next sections, I shall try to identify the various sources of this resistance.

THE DOCTRINE OF "SPOILING" CHILDREN

One of the most prevalent myths about bringing up children is the doctrine that if adults focus on helping children get their needs satisfied they will "spoil" them. People who believe this notion view children as having wants and needs that are both unlimited and insatiable and as wanting far more need satisfaction than is good for them. "Spoiled" is certainly a strange term in this context, but its meaning suggests that children will become self-centered, selfish, inconsiderate, undisciplined, demanding, incapable of tolerating frustration, and any other undesirable characteristics you can think of if they are "coddled."

Fears and anxieties about spoiling children ("Spare the rod and spoil the child") have caused many parents and teachers to resolve not to give in to children's wants. One study found that 69 percent of New Zealand mothers believed it was possible to "spoil" children. Because of this fear, the mothers in this study admitted to holding back natural feelings of love and warmth, and repressing desires to provide their offspring with what they needed to thrive and to develop a feeling of well-being (Ritchie and Ritchie, 1970).

It apparently does not occur to parents that children's desires for affection, attachment, touching, attention, play, cuddling, and the like might operate on the same principle as other biological drives such as hunger or thirst—namely, that when children have had enough, they're satisfied (as opposed to the notion that their needs are insatiable). Nor do many adults understand that gratification of needs actually leads to contentment, satisfaction, well-being, and health.

THE BELIEF THAT
CHILDREN ARE BAD BY NATURE

Resistance to abolishing the disciplining of children is based, too, on the widespread belief that children can't be trusted because they are born wicked. This attitude toward children has had a strong influence over the years on child-rearing philosophy in Western culture. Hence the practice of "beating the devil out" of children and the belief in "breaking children's will." This unusually negative view of their nature has deep roots in our history. John Wesley, in a 1742 sermon entitled "On Obedience to Parents," quotes a letter from his mother saying:

> In order to form the minds of children the first thing to be done is to conquer their will. . . . Heaven or hell depends on this alone. So that the parent who studies to subdue it [self-will] in his children, works together with God in the saving of a soul. The parent who indulges it, does the devil's work. . . . This, therefore, I cannot but earnestly repeat: Break their wills betimes; begin this great work before they can run alone, before they can speak plain, or speak at all. Whatever pains it costs, conquer their stubbornness; break the will, if you would not damn the child. I conjure you not to neglect, not to delay this! Therefore, (1) Let a child, from a year old, be taught to fear the rod and to cry softly. (2) In order to do this, let him have nothing he cries for; absolutely nothing, great or small; else you undo your own

work. (3) At all events, from that age, make him do as he is bid, if you whip him ten times running to effect it. . . . Break his will now, and his soul will live, and he will probably bless you to all eternity.

Similar ideas appeared in John Calvin's teachings about infants: "Their whole nature is a sort of seed of sin and therefore it cannot but be hateful to God." And in an early edition of *The Mothercraft Manual*, the main publication of a parenting movement popular in England in the last century, we find this same picture of children (Cook, 1978):

> Self-control, obedience, the recognition of authority, and, later, respect for elders are all the outcome of the first year's training. . . . The baby who is picked up or fed whenever he cries soon becomes a veritable tyrant, and gives his mother no peace when awake; while, on the other hand, the infant who is fed regularly, put to sleep, and played with at definite times soon finds that appeals bring no response, and so learns that most useful of all lessons, self-control, and the recognition of an authority other than his own wishes. . . . The conscientious mother has to be prepared to fight and win all along the line, in matters small and great.

Though most parents these days may not go so far as to consider a child "wicked," many do still tend to believe kids will always try to get away with something if they can, act selfishly, and so forth.

Peter Cook, a New Zealand psychologist and an early P.E.T. instructor now living in Australia, has stressed more clearly than anyone I know the effects of this astonishing, widespread view of children as base, perverse, even wicked, which he calls the "basic distrust orientation" to child rearing. He writes:

> These ideas also lead to a concern to control the older infant's behavior by training, often reinforced with threats and punishment. Teaching "right" from

"wrong" and securing obedience is often a dominant objective. This approach may apparently succeed, sometimes at considerable cost, but it frequently leads to increasing conflict, emotional disturbance, and rebelliousness. . . . The theory [the basic distrust orientation] . . . tends to become a self-fulfilling prophecy. . . . When naughtiness is seen as the result of failure to control natural tendencies which are considered to be primitive, animal, and therefore bad, [the mother's] conviction may be reinforced that these must be eliminated by appropriate training, lovingly if possible; but coercion and threats may be needed if resistance is encountered. If this becomes pronounced, *violence is justified in what is, after all, seen as a good cause.* If this doctrine and the related training processes produce a "naughty" or "disturbed" child, this can still be seen as confirming the premise that the original tendency to naughtiness was strong, and the difficulties may be attributed to *"insufficient training and punishment"* [italics added]. (Cook, 1978)

The influence of this disparaging and denigrating view of children appeared as recently as 1946 in a paperback published by evangelist John R. Rice, entitled *Correction and Discipline of Children.* It is still being sold. The author advocated that good old-fashioned thrashing should begin at birth and continue until wedding vows are recited.

A good old-fashioned thrashing. That works even in the cradle. Many, many times I've seen a child scream and howl for his own way and yell defiance for half an hour at a time. Then finally have seen mother or father with a few vigorous blows settle the whole matter. The spanked child would suddenly give up his rebellion, would cling in penitence to his mother or father, and when assured of forgiveness would peacefully go to sleep within a minute of time (Rice, 1946).

Rice also believes that children are naturally wicked; that "parents, like God, must punish and reward"; that God holds parents to account for discipline; that "lack of discipline leads to public shame"; and that "whipping children keeps them out of Hell."

If people believe that children come into the world with built-in tendencies toward maliciousness, it logically follows in their minds that kids must be set straight, purged of their baseness, socialized, shown the light, controlled, restricted, bridled, checked, curbed, kept in line, restrained, disciplined. Physical punishment, even severe punishment, can easily be justified with this extremely distorted view of the nature of children and the sacred duty of their parents.

EITHER-OR THINKING
ABOUT ADULT-CHILD CONFLICTS

Another source of resistance to giving up power-based discipline is the commonly held belief that when conflicts arise in adult-child relationships, as they inevitably will, one has to win and the other has to lose. Of the many thousands of parents and teachers who have attended our Effectiveness Training classes, a very high percentage—I would estimate over 90 percent—are locked into thinking in win-lose terms, what could be called *either-or thinking.* "Either I get my way, or the child will get his or her way"; "If I lose, the child wins." And because nobody feels good about losing in a one-on-one conflict, the only acceptable approach is to employ power to get one's way, assuming one has the power, as most parents and teachers do.

As I've mentioned before, it is a revelation to parents and teachers to learn that there is a third alternative: *Nobody* needs to lose. The No-Lose Method, Method 3, where the parties in conflict join together in a search to find a solution acceptable to both, is a solution that *meets the adult's as well as the child's needs.*

I think either-or thinking is one of the principal reasons why so many parents and teachers never give up the power required by Method 1 (I win, you lose). They wrongly assume that the only alternative (and it is a distasteful one) is Method

2 (I lose, you win). Resistance to giving up Method 1 usually dissolves, however, when people comprehend that moving to Method 2 is not the only alternative. They have available Method 3, in which *the child gets his or her needs met, but the adult makes sure to get his or her needs met as well.* No one loses.

THE BIBLICAL DEFENSE
OF PUNITIVE DISCIPLINE

A rather large sector of the Christian community, the one that is more conservative, fundamentalist, and literal in its interpretation of the Bible, takes the position that the Bible provides parents with the authority and with sufficient instruction on how to discipline children:

> Foolishness is bound in the heart of the child, but the rod of correction shall drive it far from him. (Proverbs 22:15)

> Withhold not correction from the child, for if thou beatest him with the rod, he shall not die. (Proverbs 23:13)

> Thou shalt beat him with the rod and shalt deliver his good soul from hell. (Proverbs 23:14)

Scores of books have been published in recent years advising parents to adopt what is called the biblical approach to raising children. James Dobson is perhaps the most popular author of these books. He calls his the "Judeo-Christian approach": "My purpose has been nothing more ambitious than to verbalize the Judeo-Christian tradition regarding discipline and to apply those concepts to today's families." (Dobson, 1978)

A backward look at the two-thousand-year-old Judeo-Christian approach to child rearing, however, reveals a history of widespread and severe child abuse—excessive beatings, imprisonment in closets, the withholding of food, the use of torture, and even the sale of children. In his comprehensive book, *The*

History of Childhood, Lloyd De Mause (1974) reports the findings from his research on methods of discipline over the years. His conclusions provide a grim picture of violence and abuse:

> The evidence which I have collected on methods of disciplining children leads me to believe that a very large percentage of children born prior to the eighteenth century were what would be today termed "battered children." Of over two hundred statements of advice on child rearing prior to the eighteenth century which I have examined, most approved of beating children severely. . . . The further back in history we went, the lower the level of child care we found and the more likely children were to have been killed, abandoned, shipped, sexually abused, and terrorized by their caretakers.

In addition to using the Bible as the authority for the physical punishment of children, many authors add another argument in support of raising children to obey. They fear that if the child is "allowed" to disobey his or her parents, that will inevitably lead to disobeying teachers, police, relatives, neighbors, and eventually God.

It puzzles me that those who take this position never consider the possibility that punitive discipline may more often *cause* disobedience than *cure* it. Children "willfully defy" adults who do a lot of commanding, dictating, demanding, coercing, or prohibiting; children can't rebel against a parent who has learned to replace power-based authority with nonpower methods of influence and instruction; children can't disobey parents' rules if parents don't make rules for them unilaterally. In short, it seems to me that disobedience occurs as a reaction to the use of coercive power.

Despite his conviction that biblical discipline is loving, as a parent Dobson seems anything but a loving leader:

> When a youngster tries this kind of stiff-necked rebellion, you had better take it out of him, and pain is a marvelous purifier. . . . You have drawn a line in

212 DISCIPLINE THAT WORKS

the dirt, and the child has deliberately flopped his big hairy toe across it. Who is going to win? Who has the most courage? Who is in charge here? (Dobson, 1978)

Whether the dare-to-discipline advocates have the one and only interpretation of the teachings of the Bible seems a relevant question. Other Christian authors find passages that support a nonpunitive, gentle, loving, nurturing philosophy of interpersonal relations and child rearing. Jesus challenges his disciples to "feed my lambs," not beat them; in the twenty-third Psalm "thy rod and thy staff they comfort me"; the Golden Rule teaches, "Treat others as you would like them to treat you"; Jesus said, "Suffer little children to come unto me, and forbid them not"; "Thou shalt love thy neighbour as thyself"; "And whoso shall receive one such little child in my name receiveth me, but whoso shall offend one of these little ones which believe in me, it would be better for him that a millstone were hanged about his neck, and that he were drowned in the depth of the sea"; "Judge not that ye be not judged"; and so on.

Passages such as these are far different from those selected by the dare-to-discipline advocates. Other examples can be found in a book by Earl Gaulke,* Lutheran pastor and Christian parent. In *You Can Have a Family Where Everybody Wins: Christian Perspectives on Parent Effectiveness Training* (1975), parents are shown that the specific skills taught in P.E.T. are in fact congruent with the Christian faith and that the "P.E.T. skills relate to—and become even more effective as they are powered by—God's love in Christ."

* Earl Gaulke is also one of more than a thousand ordained ministers, priests, and rabbis who have chosen to be trained and authorized to teach the P.E.T. course. Within this large group are ministers of many different Protestant denominations, as well as priests from many different orders of the Catholic church. The P.E.T. and T.E.T. courses have also gained the full backing of the national headquarters of two of the Lutheran Church denominations (Missouri Synod and American Lutheran Church), with instructors available throughout the United States under the umbrella organization: Effectiveness Training for Lutherans.

THE PERMISSIVENESS MYTH

There exists a widespread belief that everything that is wrong with kids today has been caused by overly permissive parents. I call this the "permissiveness myth." It blames permissiveness for all the worst things that youngsters fall into— juvenile delinquency, drug abuse, violence, premarital sex, alcoholism, dropping out of school, vandalism, rebellion against authority.

Blame for permissive parenting is usually placed on Dr. Benjamin Spock, renowned author of *The Common Sense Book of Baby and Child Care* (1957). In my opinion, this is totally unjustified, and Dr. Spock has been grossly misrepresented to the public. Careful reading of his book and magazine articles clearly finds Dr. Spock advocating "setting limits," warning against "parental submissiveness" and an "inability to be firm." He advises parents that "the way to get a child to do what must be done or stop what shouldn't be done is to be clear and definite . . . keeping an eye on her until she complies" (Spock, 1974).

Eventually, history will affirm Dr. Spock's momentous contribution to parents. He shared with them much of his pediatric knowledge and experience, which gave them more confidence, reduced their anxieties, and, most important for their children's well-being and emotional health, increased their *acceptance* of their children. In the terminology of our Effectiveness Training courses, Dr. Spock helped millions of parents enlarge the No-Problem area of their behavior rectangle (see p. 108)—that is, Spock enabled parents to greatly reduce the number of behaviors that they ordinarily would find troublesome and unacceptable in their children. As parents become more accepting, their lives with their children in turn become more pleasant and their relationships more loving.

This to me is a contribution of great magnitude, and one for which he has my respect and admiration. However, I wish more people would understand that because Dr. Spock practiced pediatrics, a medical specialty, the knowledge he shared with readers was primarily *medical* knowledge. That kind of knowledge helped parents deal more effectively with problems of health, diet and nutrition, sleep, hygiene, common ailments, diseases, and so on. Understandably, he gave parents very little psychological knowledge, nor did he deal much with family governing methods, counseling skills, parent-child relationships, communication skills, problem solving, conflict-resolution methods, authority and power, coping mechanisms, resolving values collisions, rewards and punishment, democratic parenting styles, and so on. With respect to the issue of permissiveness, Spock was downright uninformative; he certainly does not deserve the label of "permissivist."

What does *permissiveness* mean? In the minds of most people it is usually associated with a *lack of control* over children—allowing them too much freedom, being too lenient. Believing that permissive parenting has caused everything they fear the most, adults understandably conclude that the only remedy for permissiveness is to be strict, to exercise *a lot of control* over their children, to severely restrict their freedom, to make and enforce rules, to use parental power. This line of either-or thinking can be found in most of the dare-to-discipline parenting books. I believe the authors of these books commit serious errors of logic. First, they mistakenly hold up permissiveness as the evil culprit; then they scare parents into believing the only thing they can do to overcome it is to exercise strong parental authority—that is, be strict, lay down rules and vigorously enforce them, set firm limits, use physical punishment, and demand obedience.

Let me explain why the concept of permissiveness is simply a myth. In the first place, we now have abundant statistical evidence that, contrary to common belief, only a handful of permissive parents exist in our society. Most parents, in fact, use physical punishment, as I pointed out earlier. The authors of *Behind Closed Doors* estimate that between 3.1 and 4 million children have been kicked, bitten, or punched at some time in their lives, and between 1.4 and 2.3 million have been beaten while growing up (Straus, Gelles, and Steinmetz, 1980).

Does this sound like we're a permissive society? It would be more accurate to say that we are predominantly a society of authoritarian parents, trying to control our children by physical punishment.

If not permissiveness, then what *does* cause so many kids to go wrong? As I documented in Chapters 4 and 5, the evidence clearly points the finger at harsh, punitive, power-based punishment. Numerous studies found that delinquents had been subjected to a lot of power-assertive punishment by their parents, that schools using a lot of physical punishment have more vandalism than schools using little physical punishment, and that violent criminals were far more likely than law-abiding citizens to have been subjected to a great many beatings from their parents.

Clearly, it is not permissive parents who produce the antisocials, delinquents, and criminals in our society. It is strict, authoritarian, punitive parents. Kids who get into serious trouble are invariably those who are reacting to, rebelling against, or escaping from being neglected or mistreated at home. The unhappy, resentful, rebellious, angry, and retaliatory young people in our society have not had too much *freedom*; quite the contrary, they have had too much control, too much discipline, too much pain and deprivation.

Let me be clear about my position. I am as strongly opposed to permissiveness in raising children as I am to strict discipline. First, I see permissiveness in child rearing or in the classroom (what little there is) as equally harmful and detrimental to the *adults*. When children are permitted to do whatever they want whenever they want it, they end up treating their parents or teachers shamefully, showing no consideration for their needs and rights. They often refuse to pull their weight and do their share of the work in the home. So it's the *parents and teachers* who are the real losers; and understandably it is *they* who feel resentful, angry, unhappy, deprived.

The children of permissive parents and teachers don't fare so well either. They can develop guilt about the way they treat others; they often feel unloved because it's hard for adults to love (or like) inconsiderate, selfish kids; and they often have trouble making friends with other kids because they try to get their way all the time with them, as they have with their parents and teachers.

I hope it's clear now why I feel that parents should not be *either* lenient or strict, *either* soft or tough, *either* permissive or authoritarian. It is not an either-or question at all. Both styles of parenting can be harmful to children and to parent-child relationships.

To summarize: Most people have been hoodwinked into believing that everything wrong with kids today is the fault of permissiveness and the only remedy is strong authority and strict discipline backed up by punishment. But there are two problems with this belief: first, permissiveness is rare, not rampant; second, all the hard evidence shows that it's authoritarian, punitive treatment that is damaging to children and causes them to go wrong, not permissiveness. What is needed then, is a completely new and different way to deal with children—one in which parents are neither dictators nor doormats.

ATTITUDES AGAINST DEMOCRATIC LEADERSHIP

One reason why many people resist giving up power-based disciplining of children and students is the strong bias they have against democratic groups and democratic leadership styles. In our Effectiveness Training classes, all of our instructors have been struck by the high percentage of parents, teachers, school administrators and company managers who carry strong negative judgments of democratic leadership. In our classes we consistently hear statements such as these:

Groups can't make decisions.
Because leaders know more, they *must* make the final decision.
A camel is the result of a committee trying to make a horse.
Our three kids would outvote their mom and dad.
Group decisions end up as a pooling of ignorance.
Democracy doesn't work in business.
Democratic groups are inefficient.
Someone has to be boss.

As a way of governing families, classrooms, work groups, or organizations, democratic leadership is widely distrusted. Interestingly, there is also widespread distrust throughout the world of the ability of a democratic system to govern nations effectively. Although many countries in the world claim to be "democratic," a very large number of the member nations in the United Nations are one-party autocratic systems or dictatorships. Leaders of many of the third-world countries reject democracy in favor of harsh, punitive, autocratic discipline as the only hope for their societies. Even some of the more modern Western societies are governed by the military or by powerful religious groups who use harsh physical punishment as the principal means to conrol their people.

In our own country, we teach about democracy in our schools as a value and as content, but have failed to teach it as a process. There is a difference between *what* we teach and *how* we teach it. As a result, youngsters rarely, if ever, directly experience being in a democratically functioning group—either at home or in the classroom. Instead, they move from family to classrooms, each one always having someone "in charge" who unilaterally makes the rules and uses rewards and punishment as the principal means of enforcing compliance with those rules. No wonder most children pass into adulthood and parenthood without ever experiencing what it's like to participate in a democratic group.

In an article recommending democratic practices in schools as a way to teach self-discipline, educators Floyd Pepper and Steven Henry write:

> The democratic principles and values basic to the teaching and training of self-discipline include equality, mutual respect, shared responsibility, and shared decision-making. In a democratic classroom, the students and teachers work together in planning, organizing, implementing, and participating in the business of teaching, learning, thinking, and living harmoniously in the classroom. (Pepper and Henry, 1985)

Unfortunately, probably not more than one out of one thousand students in our schools has ever experienced a classroom like that.

RESISTANCE TO TRAINING

Few professionals would disagree that parents and teachers need first to see some alternatives that really work before they'll give up the idea that kids must be disciplined. And, with few exceptions, they will need some kind of practice before they feel competent enough to use these more effective nonpunitive methods and skills. Yet there is still widespread resistance among parents and teachers to the idea of "taking a course" to become more effective at these jobs.

The notion of achieving greater parent effectiveness through special training flies in the face of many traditional views about parenthood. For as long as I can remember, when parents have encountered minor difficulties in rearing their children, they have blamed their troubles on the child—Jimmy is a "problem child," Sue is "maladjusted," Dave is "incorrigible," Kevin is "hyperactive," Linda simply will not "accept authority," Ray is "emotionally disturbed," Peter is "bad."

Rarely have parents of such children asked whether the problem of their children might have something to do with their own ineffective parenting methods. So when serious breakdowns in the parent-child relationship occur, parents first think about taking the child someplace to be fixed up—"counseled," "adjusted," "disciplined," or "straightened out."

Most parents likewise blame changes in our society for their family problems: ubiquitous television, the breakdown of authority, the availability of drugs, the disappearance of the extended family, the increase in the divorce rate, lack of child care, the questioning of basic moral values, increasing affluence, and so on. Although I don't completely discount any of these factors as having some possible influence on family life, I do feel that focusing on them encourages a limited way of thinking about what causes kids to go wrong, and about why parent-child relationships deteriorate as frequently as they do. Such traditional thinking has tended to divert parents from the idea that their own lack of skill in parenting could be the most significant factor in bringing on problems with their children.

In our P.E.T. program, we encounter many other reasons why parents do not seek out training for parenthood. Among them:

Loving your children is enough. Love is certainly important, but feeling love for a child is certainly not all that is involved in being an effective parent. Other factors are: how much time is spent with the child; the ability to use empathic listening; how much of the child's behavior is accepted, how much is not; sending I-messages as opposed to destructive You-messages; knowing that there is a way to resolve conflicts without someone ending up a loser; and so on. Besides, love is not some medicinal substance parents have in unlimited supply and can dispense daily. My experience is that if parents don't have the skills to change unacceptable behaviors of their children, they become resentful and angry because their needs are not being met. Over time they can grow to dislike (yes, even hate) their children, a situation not unlike what happens in a marriage where one partner feels deprived and unsatisfied.

We don't have any serious problems now. Resistance to most preventive efforts stems from this belief. If you have no serious symptoms of illness, why eat properly, exercise regularly, or quit smoking? Parent training is acquiring knowledge and skills to *prevent* problems—training *before* trouble. After parent-child relationships begin deteriorating, it can be too late to repair them.

Other parents need training more. Usually those "other parents" are thought to be the poor, the uneducated, or the "culturally deprived." Many parents believe that only in such families do children become delinquents, dropouts, suicides, or drug abusers. The evidence refutes this—serious trouble can occur in all kinds of families.

We've got plenty of time—our kids are still young. This attitude fails to recognize that it's while children are young that they begin to develop their patterns of behavior, such as thoughtfulness toward others, self-esteem, a sense of responsibility, self-confidence—or their opposites. Parents need effectiveness skills when their children are very young—when the skills pay off the most.

Troubled kids come mostly from broken homes. Not so, in my opinion. In fact, divorce can even be *caused* by troubles with kids. We also know that people who lack the skills to be effective in the marriage relationship are likely to be ineffective in the parent-child relationship too. Troubled kids and broken homes may indeed occur together, but it does not follow that broken homes *cause* troubled kids.

We're not emotionally sick people. Unfortunately, the idea of training for parent effectiveness may carry the same stigma as getting psychotherapy, especially if parents see anything "psychological" in the training program. Actually, going to a parent training class doesn't mean a person is "sick" any more than going to Sunday school means a person is sinful. Parent training is an educational experience. It's not therapy; it is primarily prevention, not treatment.

Nobody is expert enough to tell me how to raise my kids. This attitude reflects a misunderstanding of what parent training is all about. It does not tell parents what they should teach their children, nor does it offer pat solutions to the hundreds of different problems families have. Rather, it teaches parents proven skills and methods for fostering effective two-way communication, for getting kids to solve their problems in their own way, for resolving conflicts between parent and child so nobody loses. These are the same skills you need to have good relationships with anyone—with your spouse, your friends, your coworkers, your in-laws.

FEAR OF CHANGE IN THE AMERICAN FAMILY

Another source of resistance to giving up power-based discipline is the fear that the American family will be changed. We see this clearly among Christian authors supporting authoritarian parenting who are also strong champions of a much larger conservative agenda for families. This agenda includes opposing feminism, birth control, sex education, legal abortion, humanistic education, and homosexuality. It also includes support for the death penalty, capitalism, strong military defense and nuclear armaments, and military aid to pro-American and anti-Communist repressive governments.

Ann Eggebroten, writing in the magazine *The Other Side*, calls our attention to the "strongly political context" of the dare-to-discipline authors:

> Basically, these conservative goals revolve around protection of the American status quo—as measured on a suburban sunny day in about 1951. The main commonality to be protected is the Family, and the main danger to be avoided is One-World Government (a communist takeover). . . . These conservative authors generally refer to "the Judeo-Christian tradition" . . . "the way of our forefathers." For example, Dobson has written in defense of a vague "Judeo-Christian concept of manliness," which he argues "has been blurred by the women's liberation movement." He implies that Jesus calls us to defend some clearly biblical model of manliness—a topic which Jesus neglected to discuss. (Eggebroten, 1987)

I have occasionally encountered strong criticism of the P.E.T. course by those who see parent training as a threat to the hierarchical family, as undermining the father's position of authority, as stressing the equal rights of women and children, as encouraging openness and uncensored communication between child and parent. In fact, P.E.T. (as well as most of the other nationwide successful parent-training programs) may indirectly pose a threat to nondemocratic families simply by showing a model of a democratic family and how effectively it can function.

History has shown us often that fear can move people (and nations) toward authoritarianism—toward wanting more controls over others, toward advocacy of strong punishment of criminals, toward restricting the freedoms of people. Witness the beguiling appeal, spearheaded by Ronald Reagan, to return to "good old-fashioned discipline" in the schools. Authoritarian power has often been regarded hopefully as a means of protection against things we fear—a permanent and dependable shield. Marilyn French compellingly underscores this phenomenon in her scholarly book *Beyond Power*:

Power has been exalted as the bulwark against pain, against the ephemerality of pleasure, but it is no bulwark and is as ephemeral as any other part of life. Coercion seems a simpler, less time-consuming method of creating order than any other; yet it is just as time-consuming and tedious and far more expensive than personal encounter, persuasion, listening, and participating in bringing a group into harmony. (French, 1985)

Reading this passage I am impressed by the similarities between French's alternatives to coercive power and those I advocate in relationships, though we use different terminologies:

Her "personal encounter" is my "confrontive and preventive I-messages."

Her "persuasion" is my "influence" based on Authority E.

Her "listening" is my "Active Listening."

Her "participating in bringing a group into harmony" is my "No-Lose Method 3" for conflict resolution.

Men particularly seem to resist giving up the power position in the family—power over wives as well as over their children. One of their strongest fears, as I have pointed out earlier, is that children will disobey if given the chance, and be spoiled or otherwise ruined unless families stick with the "tried and true," biblically based, "father knows best," "father as the head of the family" model. Yet my experience is that this approach seriously impairs the relationship of fathers with their wives and their children, among other consequences. Most professionals who work with families would agree, I believe, that by and large men are not good fathers. Their emphasis on power-based control prevents them from having warm, supportive, loving relationships with all family members.

In our P.E.T. classes, far fewer fathers than mothers enroll (one for every three mothers). And we also find that among mothers who report difficulties putting their P.E.T. skills into practice, many cite the opposition of autocratic husbands toward the new methods as a primary stumbling block.

RESISTANCE TO CHANGE IN SCHOOLS

The strong resistance to giving up disciplining children in schools derives from some of the same sources of resistance found among parents. After all, teachers and school administrators were once children raised on power-based discipline and provided with a model of heavy use of rewards and punishment.

Also, most teachers in their student days had teachers who managed *their* classrooms autocratically, who "taught by the tune of the hickory stick." And school board members and administrators too have been exposed to far more authoritarian principals and assistant principals than democratic ones. I suspect that there are very few teachers or administrators who ever encountered a democratic, nondisciplinarian-type teacher or principal whom they could use as a model for their professional role.

Not to be overlooked is the resistance to changing our schools because they are such *traditionalist institutions*. Charles Silberman, in his classic *Crisis in the Classroom*, points out some of the traditional practices that have stubbornly endured over time:

> The "necessity" that makes schooling so uniform over time and across cultures is simply the "necessity" that stems from unexamined assumptions and unquestioned behavior. The preoccupation with order and control, the slavish adherence to the timetable and lesson plan, the obsession with routine qua routine, the absence of noise and movement, the joylessness and repression, the universality of the formal lecture or teacher-dominated "discussion" in which the teacher instructs an entire class as a unit, the emphasis of the verbal and de-emphasis of the concrete, the inability of students to work on their own, the di-

chotomy between work and play—none of these are
necessary; all can be eliminated. (Silberman, 1970)

I concur with Silberman's list of current practices in schools that
have stubbornly resisted change. I believe that each of these
practices contributes significantly to creating the serious discipline problem found in schools throughout the country. However, I would add a few more practices to his list: the universal
system of grading students, which is rewarding to the few and
demeaning to the majority; those extracurricular practices that
provide rewards only to those who excel in either beauty or
brawn; and the traditional practice of requiring that almost all
students take the same courses, expecting that all have equal
mental capability of mastering those subjects.

Carl Rogers, the only psychologist to be given both the
Distinguished Professional and the Distinguished Scientific
awards from the American Psychological Association, once said
to a group of us assembled to talk about schools, "When I visit
the schools my grandchildren are now attending, what I see
there is almost identical to what I experienced as a child sixty
years ago." I think most other professionals who have seriously
studied our school system would agree with Rogers's observation.

Let me summarize this examination of the sources of
resistance to giving up disciplining and controlling children. I'm
tempted to make a broad generalization that much of the
resistance can be traced back to a single cause—namely, an
almost universal distrust of, and lack of experience with, how
democratic groups function. It is something of a truism that
people hold on to what is familiar and strongly resist changing
to what is unknown. I've come to believe that, to most people,
democracy is an unknown.

In the next chapter, I'll try to explain what democratic
families and schools—as opposed to those that are autocratic—
can do for their members' health and well-being.

eleven

How Democratic Relationships Foster Health and Well-Being

This investigation of the concept and practice of discipline has given me a deeper understanding of its precise nature, a wealth of data as to its ineffectiveness, and a surprisingly large amount of evidence regarding how it harms children and youth. My investigation has also led me to discover some effective new alternatives to discipline, particularly some innovative procedures being used in schools. This investigation has both confirmed and strengthened my belief in the validity of the skills we have been teaching in our P.E.T. and T.E.T. courses worldwide—namely, the interpersonal skills of accurate two-way communication, of problem solving, of conflict resolution, of consulting and facilitating.

But even more rewarding to me, this task has brought into clearer focus an idea I have been thinking about and informally discussing with colleagues for several years. The core idea is that democratic relationships and groups make people "healthy," while nondemocratic relationships and groups make people "unhealthy." One produces "wellness"; the other produces "illness."

It has become increasingly evident that organizations whose

managers use a participative style of leadership—group decision making, high employee involvement, two-way communication—have workers with higher productivity, lower turnover, higher morale, fewer grievances, less absenteeism, better physical health. These workers also feel better about themselves, like to go to work, and have more self-esteem and self-confidence and less sense of powerlessness. As we saw in Chapter 7, these were precisely the findings of the study of fifty companies by John Simmons and William Mares (Simmons and Mares, 1983).

Where participative, democratic leadership has been introduced and practiced in schools, students made significant gains in study habits and scholastic achievement, improved their social skills, produced closer relationships with students of different color and background, increased their level of moral reasoning maturity, had fewer disruptive behaviors. These were the findings from other studies described in Chapter 7.

Do parents who learn how to create democratic family environments foster the good health and well-being of their children? My answer to that question is yes, and quite a large number of research studies support that answer.

The effects of the P.E.T. course have been evaluated in a number of studies, all done by researchers outside the P.E.T. organization. In 1983, Boston University psychologist Ronald Levant published a review of twenty-three such studies. While he found that many had serious methodological problems, he selected three that fully met the standards of methodological adequacy. Each study compared P.E.T. parents to a non-P.E.T. control group and used before- and after-the-course measurements. Out of 35 comparisons, 24 (or 69 percent) favored P.E.T. over the control group, none favored the control group, and 11 (31 percent) showed no difference (Levant, 1983).

Levant's specific findings were that the P.E.T. course produced positive improvements in parents' attitudes and behaviors: they became more accepting, more confident as parents, more understanding. The children of the P.E.T. parents showed an increase in self-esteem and received more positive evaluations of their classroom behaviors by their teachers.

Later, a student of Dr. Levant, R. Bruce Cedar, used a new statistical technique for combining the findings from twenty-six different studies and reanalyzing the combined data (1985). This technique, called a "meta-analysis study," produced these findings:

- P.E.T. had positive effects on both parent attitudes and parent behaviors and these effects endured for up to twenty-six weeks after the parents completed the course.
- The better, more scientifically designed studies showed greater positive changes in parents and children than did the more poorly designed studies.
- Parents showed improved scores on tests measuring "democratic ideals," acceptance of their children, and understanding of their children.
- The greatest effect on the P.E.T. parents' children was an increase in child self-esteem. (Cedar, 1985)

Dr. Levant, who sponsored Cedar's research, commented on the results of his graduate student's reanalysis: "P.E.T. comes out with a clean bill of health, though more high-caliber research is still required."

The effects of our T.E.T. course on teachers have been evaluated in eight studies reviewed and summarized by Edmund Emmer and Amy Aussiker of the University of Texas at Austin. Their conclusion:

> Studies that assessed teacher behavior after training generally found evidence that teachers increased their ability to use recommended T.E.T. skills. Effect sizes ranged from small to large, with large effects common. . . . The results support the conclusion that T.E.T. training can change teacher attitudes and behavior in a direction more consistent with the assumptions of the T.E.T. model: toward a more democratic view of the use of authority and more concern for student perceptions and feelings, and toward behavior that reflects acceptance of students. (Emmer and Aussiker, 1987)

Several other research studies show the positive effects of democratic parenting (not P.E.T. parents) on children's self-esteem:

- Stanley Coopersmith's study (1967) of fifth- and sixth-grade boys showed that the parents of high-self-esteem boys (by contrast with parents of low-self-esteem boys) favored reasoning over coercive methods of discipline and fostered a democratic style of family decision making in which children participated and were allowed to question parental viewpoints.

- After reviewing a number of studies of the antecedents of high-self-esteem children, Eleanor Maccoby and John Martin (1983) summarized as follows: "The weight of the evidence would appear to be that neither authoritarian control nor unalloyed freedom and permissiveness is the key to the development of high self-esteem in children. Rather, a pattern of interaction in which parents make reasonable and firm demands that are accepted as legitimate by the children, but in which *parents do not impose restrictions*, but make demands and give directions in ways that *leave a degree of choice and control in the hands of the children*, is the control pattern most likely to foster high self-esteem" [italics added].

I found two studies that related parenting styles with children's physical health:

- In the first study, the behaviors of mothers whose children had disorders that may have a psychosomatic origin (bronchial asthma, arthritis, ulcerative colitis, peptic ulcers, and atopic eczema) were compared with a control group of mothers whose children had nonpsychosomatic illness (polio, congenital heart disease, nephrosis, hemophilia). *Finding:* Mothers of the psychosomatic group were more dominating and comparatively argumentative with their children than mothers of the nonpsychosomatic group (Garner and Wenar, 1959).

- A second study reported similar characteristics in mothers of asthmatic children who had a *low* allergic predisposition to this illness as contrasted with a control group of mothers with children with a *high* allergic predisposition to asthma (high somatic causal factors). Maternal criticism and rejection were higher in the families in which the children had developed asthma even with a low allergic predisposition (Block et al., 1964).

A classic study done many years ago provides the strongest and most convincing evidence for the health-giving potential of democratic family environments. It was a study done at the Fels Institute in Antioch, Ohio. In it, three types of families were located and identified: autocratic, permissive, and democratic. The children of these families were given an extensive battery of tests and then retested periodically until they reached adolescence. The most surprising finding from this study had to do with changes in the IQs of the children. Over the years, the IQs of the children with autocratic parents decreased slightly, while those of permissive parents remained almost the same. However, the IQs of the children of the democratic parents increased significantly over the years. The mean increase was over eight IQ points. The investigators concluded, "It would appear that the democratic environment is the most conducive to mental development." The democratic parents surrounded their children with an atmosphere of freedom, emotional rapport, and intellectual stimulation. The children in those families also were given higher ratings by their teachers in originality, planfulness, patience, curiosity, and fancifulness. And they held more leadership positions in school and scored higher in emotional adjustment and maturity. In the words of the researchers:

By the time the child from the democratic home has become of school age, his social development has progressed markedly; he is popular and a leader; he is friendly and good-natured; he seems emotionally secure, serene, unexcitable; he has had close attachments to his parents and is able to adjust to his teachers. (Baldwin, Kalhorn, and Breese, 1945)

230 DISCIPLINE THAT WORKS

In earlier chapters, I cited other convincing research evidence that nonauthoritarian, nonpunitive families produce healthier and more effective children. Children from such families were found to be "healthier" in a variety of ways. They showed:

Less aggressive behavior
Less vandalism
Less child-child violence
Higher self-esteem
Fewer suicidal tendencies
Better relationships with classmates/peers
More social initiative
More internal locus of control
Fewer depressions; less crying
More satisfactory love affairs
Less worry; less anxiety
Less guilt
Fewer quarrels
Less shyness

Further support for my belief that relationships that involve persons using power over others produce ill health comes from a pioneering investigation into the root causes of mental and emotional problems in our society. In the first full-length book dealing with primary prevention of psychopathology, psychologists Marc Kessler and George Albee provided an extensive review of the existing literature (381 articles and books) on what causes and what might prevent mental and emotional disturbances. At the end of their review, they concluded:

It is tempting to suggest an extension to the human environment of Lord Acton's dictum: "Power tends to corrupt—absolute power corrupts absolutely." Everywhere we looked, every social research study we examined, suggested that major sources of human stress and distress generally involve some form of excessive power. The pollutants of a power-consuming industrial society; the exploitation of the weak by the powerful; the overdependence of the automotive culture on powerful engines (power-consuming symbols of potency); the degradation of the environment with the debris of a comfort-loving impulse-yielding society; the power struggle between the rich consuming nations and the exploited third world; the angry retaliation of the impoverished and the exploited; on a more personal level the exploitation of women by men, of children by adults, of the elderly by a youth-worshiping society—it is enough to suggest the hypothesis that a dramatic reduction and control of power might improve the mental health of people. (Kessler and Albee, 1977)

While research studies strongly support that democratic families do provide an interpersonal climate conducive to healthy, creative, and fully functioning youngsters, how does it happen? What goes on that makes these families different? The research studies give us some clues, but we've learned much more from parents who have taken our P.E.T. course.

Less Deprivation and Humiliation

Probably the most common characteristic of what I've been calling democratic families is the absence of punishment, physical or otherwise, as a method of dealing with unacceptable behaviors. In the traditional family, power-based autocratic control, as we have seen, requires the frequent use of punishment to try to bring about compliance and obedience. And, because punishment by definition often results in humiliation and deprivation of children, the ensuing frustration is bound to be damaging to their psychological and/or physical health. Abraham Maslow, one of the founders of the large international Association of Humanistic Psychologists, stated this principle strongly and clearly:

Let people realize clearly that every time they threaten someone or humiliate or hurt unnecessarily or dominate or reject another human being, they become forces for the creation of psychopathology, even if these be small forces. Let them recognize that every man who is kind, helpful, decent, psychologically democratic, affectionate, and warm is a psychotherapeutic force, even though a small one. (Maslow, 1970)

Parents who treat their children as Maslow describes, who make a practice of using the nonpower-based methods that I have described in some detail in Chapters 6 and 7, and who respect the equal rights of all family members to get their needs met, will have children who won't have to use self-harmful coping mechanisms, won't need to employ extreme reactive behaviors— angry rebellion, lawbreaking, drinking excessively, escaping through drugs, overeating, aggression, shyness—for the simple reason that in their families there will be nothing to fight against, or escape from, or submit to. They won't experience nearly the degree of need deprivation, low self-esteem, and hopelessness that provoke youngsters to use these coping behaviors. This is not to say their lives will be a bed of roses or that they will not run into problems or experience disappointments. But as I distill my years of professional work with families in therapy or in parent training and read the growing body of research evidence on what makes kids healthy or unhealthy, effective or ineffective, winners or losers, I'm convinced that those who are brought up with warm, accepting, and nonpunitive parental leadership will have sufficient resources (their own, *plus* the support of their parents) to deal constructively with the usual out-of-home problems, conflicts, and disappointments they encounter.

Less Stress, Less Illness
Other positive effects can be found in families where parents have successfully used a P.E.T. type of democratic leadership. From the widely publicized scientific studies of stress conducted by the famous physiologist Hans Selye, we know that illness frequently follows high levels of stress—stress from grief, unrequited love, depression, financial losses, humiliation, emotional deprivation, and other painful events. As anyone whose mother or father was punitive and autocratic knows, life in such

a family always produces a great deal of stress. It stems variously from the pain and humiliation of being physically punished, from the fear and anxiety that you *may* be punished, from the tension of frequently trying to escape punishment, from the anger and resentment triggered by giving in to someone with power over you, and from carrying inside you the mixed feelings of love and hatred for your parents.

In contrast to such stress-generating, autocratic families, those families in which parents have learned how to function democratically will enjoy a climate conducive to cooperation, job sharing, equitable conflict resolution, mutual need satisfaction, and consideration for others—without parental coercion, without punishment, without fear. It follows then that the children of parents using P.E.T. methods will experience less stress, and therefore less illness. It's not surprising that some P.E.T. graduates have reported that their children have had fewer colds, fewer digestive upsets, fewer allergies. In fact, in my book *Parent Effectiveness Training* I cite the story of the asthmatic child who never had another attack following an intense Active Listening session with his mother, during which the child eventually revealed that he was afraid of dying in his sleep should he close his mouth when his nose was stuffed up (Gordon, 1970).

So, the idea that parents and teachers can actually make their children sick is not really surprising in light of the intricate relationships, established by research, between emotional stress and illness. Domination, punishment, criticism, restrictiveness, and rejection typically produce in children fear, anger, apathy, and frustration—common behavioral symptoms of physiological stress. Certainly it is logical to assume that where adults are less dominating, punishing, and restrictive, children will have a greater chance of growing up free of stress—thus, physically healthy and more resistant to physical illness.

More Problem-Solving Competence

Life is often harsh and complicated, and all children are bound to encounter difficulties in their lives in getting essential needs met. Overcoming these difficulties requires effective problem-solving skills. The model of parenting and teaching

I've described here encourages children to be active participants in the problem-solving process, as opposed to being handed adult-imposed solutions. In such democratic environments children experience firsthand how to use problem solving to set family and classroom rules, to plan projects, to resolve all kinds of conflicts. When parents and teachers give up being solution givers, decision makers, and lawmakers, they bring children into these processes as equal participants, an experience that provides them with problem-solving competence they can use in all areas of their lives, and for a lifetime. And this is bound to increase their confidence, self-esteem, independence, and sense of control over their lives.

Less Anger and Hostility

When youngsters (and adults, too) feel deprived, frustrated, or defeated, they often become angry, either turning their anger inward and hating themselves or outward and hating others. Such anger and hostility are common reactions of those who feel like have-nots or consistent losers. The skills we've reviewed in this book greatly decrease the probability of kids' losing in their conflicts with parents or teachers, of feeling like second-class citizens. Satisfied, need-fulfilled youngsters are not likely to turn into hostile, retaliatory members of society.

Freedom from Fear

Power-based, punitive discipline, on the other hand, depends upon keeping children in a state of fear of their parents or teachers. Punished dogs become cowed, nervous, vigilant—and so do some children in authoritarian environments. Living in a climate of constant potential danger is damaging to a person's psychological health, as we have learned so well from studies of Vietnam veterans, an admittedly extreme example. But children in democratic families and classrooms have nothing to fear; they are free of the fear of punishment, of deprivation, of being a loser, of failing.

More Responsibility, More Fate Control

Clinical evidence has shown that the feeling of not being responsible for one's life, one's destiny, can be a cause of poor mental health—particularly of depression, anxiety, and stress. At the core of both the P.E.T. and T.E.T. courses is the principle of promoting children's self-control versus adult control, inner control versus external control. Psychologists have recently become interested in this issue, using the term "fate control." Autocratic teachers and parents, relying heavily on external control of children, foster feelings of dependence and lack of fate control. Democratic teachers and parents, who give children a lot of freedom and responsibility, make children feel they can be trusted to be responsible for their own destiny. In Chapter 5, I described Stanley Milgram's (1974) experiments on obedience to authority. Recall his conclusion: "The disappearance of a sense of responsibility is the most far-reaching consequence of submission to authority."

Fewer Self-Harming Behaviors

Self-destructive, risk-taking behaviors of young people usually exist in clusters. Kids who feel deprived or who experience a lot of pain and injustice in their lives may react by employing a variety of health-compromising behaviors—smoking, using drugs, reckless driving, driving under the influence of drugs or alcohol, premature sexual activity. In families or in schools where youngsters' basic needs are respected, where no-lose solutions are the rule, where fairness is valued and injustice is avoided, children have far fewer reasons to engage in such reactive, health-damaging behaviors.

Better Social Skills

Many parents who have learned how to employ P.E.T. skills in their family life report that their children eventually acquire competence in the same skills, undoubtedly through modeling their parents' behaviors. Having experienced their parents' listening to them, they learn to listen empathically. Having experienced their parents' I-messages, their communication is open, honest, and nonblameful. And, because they have been participants in many such sessions with their parents, they learn how to problem-solve with others and to resolve conflicts so that no one loses.

We have learned from P.E.T. parents—and often have seen

firsthand—that their children develop many close and warm friendships; that friends bring their problems to them; that when they have conflicts with their friends they work them out amicably; that younger children love them, look up to them, and emulate them; that adults are drawn to their friendliness and sociability; that they do not exploit others, and characteristically are willing to pull their weight and do their share; and, as found in the Fels Institute studies, that these children gravitate into leadership positions in school and church organizations.

Because of these positive experiences, children from democratic families make friends and keep them, seldom experience loneliness and rejection, develop self-confidence and high self-esteem, and feel loved and often admired by others. In short, a health-giving family life has provided them with the person-to-person skills that will bring them even more health-giving relationships and health-giving success experiences in their life outside the family.

Both from research findings and from case histories of families that have learned to function more democratically, we are beginning to understand the precise processes by which children in democratic families acquire high self-esteem, become responsible, develop confidence, learn to discipline themselves, and develop close friendships—that is, become healthier mentally, physically, and socially.

Discovering such a cause-and-effect relationship is not surprising, in a way, considering that it is commonly accepted that citizens of democratically governed countries by and large feel more contented, satisfied, fortunate, uncoerced, and self-directing than do those who are ruled by authoritarian governments.

The same is true in the workplace. While only a few persons have had truly democratic managers or supervisors, who hasn't experienced the frustration, constraint, fear, insecurity, and deprivation that results from having an authoritarian boss? Fortunately, those who find themselves in that situation generally have the freedom to escape from such a relationship and seek a new job.

Not so with children. Until they reach adolescence, they are stuck with their parents and stuck with their teachers. This being so, it seems more important than ever to intensify our efforts to democratize our families and schools, to remove the causes of psychopathology in our children before they take root, as opposed to treating youngsters after they have been psychologically damaged.

Take drug abuse and alcoholism as an example. I'm convinced that finding ways to democratize families and schools would be a far more effective strategy for reducing the frequency of these self-destructive behaviors among our young people than strategies to change the child—such as the "Say No" approach, courses for kids that present the physiological dangers of alcohol and drugs, psychological counseling and other treatment programs, campaigns to teach parents to recognize the various signs that their children are taking drugs or abusing alcohol, and so on. Marc Kessler and George Albee, in a pioneering book, *Primary Prevention of Psychopathology*, stress prevention rather than treatment.

> It is public health dogma that no widespread human disease is ever brought under control by the treatment of afflicted individuals. Smallpox was not conquered by treating smallpox patients; neither was treatment of the individual the answer to typhoid fever, polio or measles. Every plague afflicting humankind has been controlled when discovery of the cause led to taking effective steps to remove it. The process is primary prevention. (Kessler and Albee, 1977)

I firmly believe that we have discovered at least *one* of the principal causes of psychopathology and antisocial behavior in young people: our heavy reliance on power-based punitive discipline for the purpose of controlling their lives at home and at school. This discovery in itself is encouraging, but we can find even more encouragement from the fact that we already have viable alternatives to discipline that are readily available, work better, and produce demonstrably better results. They produce the kind of youngsters we want, the kind our society needs.

How we treat children is far more critical to the kind of

society we have than most people think. In his book *Cosmos* (1980), noted astronomer Carl Sagan describes a study done by neuropsychologist James Prescott on a cross-cultural analysis of 400 preindustrial societies. Prescott found that cultures in which children are physically punished and deprived of overt affection tend to be characterized by such institutions as slavery, frequent killings, torturing and mutilation of enemies, a strong belief in the inferiority of women, and a strong devotion to one or more supernatural beings who intervene in daily life. Prescott concludes that such cultures are composed of individuals who have been deprived of the pleasures of the body in at least one of two critical stages of life—infancy and adolescence. In contrast, cultures in which physical affection of children is encouraged and premarital sexual behaviors are tolerated tend to be disinclined toward the use of violence and theft, organized religion, and individual displays of wealth.

It is tempting to conclude this analysis of discipline and its alternatives by indulging in some speculation about what the long-term consequences in our society might be were we able to democratize most families and schools—in effect free our children of control by power-based discipline. Based on the findings of research studies I've cited in previous chapters, we can be relatively certain to find some of the following consequences. Others are more or less conjectural. None of them, however, is without some basis in fact or experience. And many of the consequences I foresee are quite profound and would be strongly felt in our society:

1. Children would be healthier, both physically and emotionally.
2. We would see a substantial decrease in those self-harming and high-risk adolescent behaviors that are so detrimental to society: juvenile delinquency, alcoholism, drug abuse, reckless driving, vandalism, truancy, suicides, rape, gang violence, premarital pregnancies, homicides.
3. Fewer young people would be thrown out of their homes by their parents or leave home on their own to become teenage "street people."

4. All students, regardless of their various innate intellectual capabilities, would be given the opportunity to learn at their own pace and be freed of the onerous and shameful experience of failing subjects, dropping out, remaining illiterate.

5. The almost universally adversarial nature of teacher-child relationships would become more like those of friends or colleagues. Children would like their teachers and like going to school.

6. We would see a drastic reduction in family violence, whether parent-child, child-child, spouse-spouse, or child-parent.

7. Most children would be motivated to learn, feel a sense of achievement and accomplishment, and develop self-esteem.

8. Adolescence would not be a period of such storm and stress, for either parents or the teenagers themselves.

9. We would see the elimination of the A-B-C-D-F grading system that is so destructive to the self-esteem of many students; instead, students would be evaluated on individual progress toward mastery of skills and subject matter. Thus, we would have schools without failure— where every student can learn to the best of his or her ability.

10. Young people would respect the needs and rights of others, because adults respected their needs and rights.

11. Graduates of our high schools, colleges, and professional schools will have learned the skills necessary to work cooperatively with others, be participative managers, resolve conflicts amicably, and function effectively in democratic and nonpower relationships.

12. We would see fewer acts of injustice, fewer senseless and incomprehensible killings, fewer wars.

13. We would see fewer people who feel helpless and hopeless, who attribute their unfavorable conditions to factors outside themselves.

14. There would be less obedience and subservience to arbitrary authority.

15. More youngsters would grow to be adults with high moral and ethical standards.

I'm convinced we would gradually see in successive generations a whole "new species" of young people, discernibly different from the typical youth of today—youngsters who are healthier, happier, more spontaneous, more self-confident, more self-reliant, more considerate of the needs of others, and quite capable of disciplining themselves.

I have already known a considerable number of this new species of youth—sons and daughters of parents who learned the skills we teach in P.E.T., and the students of teachers who learned in T.E.T. how to manage their classrooms democratically and treat students with respect. Believe me, these youngsters are impressive.

References

Aschuler, A. *School discipline: A socially literate solution*. New York: McGraw-HIll, 1980.

Aspy, D. and Roebuck, F. *Kids don't learn from people they don't like*. Amherst, Mass.: Human Resource Development Press, 1977.

Aspy, D. and Roebuck, F. The relationship of teacher-offered conditions of meaning to behaviors described by Flanders Interactional Analysis. *Education*, 95 (Spring 1975).

Aspy, D. and Roebuck, F. Researching person-centered issues in education. In C. R. Rogers, *Freedom to learn for the 80's*. Columbus, Ohio: Charles E. Merrill, 1983.

Azrin, N. and Holz, W. Punishment. In W. Konig (ed.), *Operant behavior*. New York: Appelton-Century-Crofts, 1966.

Baldwin, A. Socialization and the parent-child relationship. *Child Development*, 1948, *19*.

Baldwin, A., Kalhorn, J. and Breese, F. Patterns of parent behavior. *Psychological Monographs*, 1945, *58*.

Barton, K., Dielman, T. and Cattell, R. Child rearing practices and achievement in school. *Journal of Cenetic Psychology*, 1974.

Baumrind, D. Child care practices anteceding three patterns of preschool behavior. *Genetic Psychology Monograph*, 1967, *75*.

Baumrind, D. Current patterns of parental authority. *Developmental Psychology Monograph*, 1971, *4*.

Becker, W. Consequences of different kinds of parental discipline. In M. Hoffman and L. Hoffman (eds.), *Review of Child Development Research*, Vol. I. New York: Russell Sage, 1964.

Block, J., Jennings, P., Harvey, E., and Simpson, E. Interaction between allergic potential and psychopathology in childhood asthma. *Psychosomatic Medicine*, 1964, *26*.

Bongiovanni, A. *A review of research on the effects of punishment: Implications for corporal punishment in the schools.* Paper presented at the Conference on Child Abuse, Children's Hospital, National Medical Center, Washington, D.C., February 19, 1977.

Burrows, C. *The effects of a mastery learning strategy on the geometry achievement of fourth and fifth grade children.* Unpublished doctoral dissertation, Indiana University, Bloomington, 1973.

Cedar, R. B. *A meta-analysis of the Parent Effectiveness Training outcome research literature.* Ed.D. dissertation, Boston University, 1985.

Combs, A. Achieving self-discipline. In W. W. Wayson (ed.), *Theory into practice: Teaching self-discipline.* Columbus, Ohio: Ohio State University, 1985.

Cook, P. Child-rearing, culture and mental health. *The Medical Journal of Australia*, Special Supplement, 1978, *2*.

Coopersmith, S. *The antecedents of self-esteem.* San Francisco: Freeman, 1967.

Cordes, C. Researchers flunk Reagan on discipline theme. American Psychological Association *Monitor*, March 1984.

Cuniberti, B. Hinckleys: After tears, a crusade. *Los Angeles Times*, February 23, 1984.

Davidson, H. and Lang, G. Children's perceptions of their teachers' feelings toward them. *Journal of Experimental Education*, 1960, *29*.

Deci, E., Betley, G., Kahle, J., Abrams, L. and Porac, J. When trying to win: Competition and intrinsic motivation. *Personality and Social Psychology Bulletin*, 1981, *7*.

De Mause, L., ed. *The history of childhood.* New York: Psychohistory Press, 1974.

Deutsch, M. *Distributive justice: A social-psychological perspective.* New Haven: Yale University Press, 1985.

Dobson, J. *Dare to discipline.* Wheaton, Ill.: Tyndale House, 1970.

Dobson, J. *The strong-willed child.* Wheaton, Ill.: Tyndale House, 1978.

Dollard, J., Doob, L., Miller, N., Mowrer, O. and Sears, R. *Frustration and aggression.* New Haven: Yale University Press, 1939.

Dreikurs, R. *Challenge of parenthood.* New York: Hawthorne, 1948.

Dreikurs, R. and Soltz, V. *Children: The challenge*. New York: Duell, Sloan, Pearce, 1964.

Duke, D. and Perry, C. Can alternative schools succeed where Benjamin Spock, Spiro Agnew and B. F. Skinner have failed? *Adolescence*, 1978, *13*.

Duke, O. *Managing student behavior problems*. New York: Teachers College, Columbia University, 1980.

Eggebroten, A., Sparing the rod: Biblical discipline and parental discipleship. *The Other Side*, Philadelphia, April 1987.

Emmer, E. and Aussiker, A. *School and classroom discipline programs: How well do they work?* Paper presented at American Educational Research Association Meeting, Washington, D.C., April 1987.

Farson, R. Praise reappraised. *Harvard Business Review*, September–October, 1963.

French, M. *Beyond power*. New York: Summit Books, 1985.

Garner, A. and Wenar, C. *The mother-child interaction in psychosomatic disorders*. Urbana: University of Illinois Press, 1959.

Gaulke, E. *You can have a family where everybody wins*. St. Louis: Concordia Publishing House, 1975.

Gilmartin, B. The case against spanking. *Human Behavior*, 1979, *8*.

Glasser, W. *Control theory in the classroom*. New York: Harper and Row, 1986.

Gordon, T. *Group-centered leadership*. Boston: Houghton-Mifflin, 1955.

Gordon, T. *Leader effectiveness training: L.E.T*. New York: G. P. Putnam's Sons, 1977.

Gordon, T. *Parent effectiveness training: P.E.T*. New York: Peter H. Wyden, 1970.

Gordon, T. *Teacher effectiveness training: T.E.T*. New York: Peter H. Wyden, 1974.

Gordon, T. *What every parent should know*. Chicago: National Committee for Prevention of Child Abuse, 1975.

Gordon, T., with Sands, J. *P.E.T. in action*. New York: Peter H. Wyden, 1976.

Holt, J. *How children fail*. New York: Delacorte, 1982.

Hyman, I., McDowell, E. and Raines, B. Corporal punishment and alternative in schools. *Inequality in Education*, 1975, *23*.

Johnson, D., Johnson, R., Tiffany, M. and Zaidman, B. Cross-ethnic relationships: The impact of intergroup cooperation and intergroup competition. *Journal of Experimental Education*, 1984, *78*.

Johnson, D., Maruyama G., Johnson, R., Nelson, D., and Skon, L. Effects of cooperative, competitive and individualistic goal structures on achievement: A meta-analysis. *Psychological Bulletin*, 1981, *89*.

Jones, V. and Jones, L. *Responsible classroom discipline*. Newton, Mass.: Allyn and Bacon, 1981.

Kadushin, A. and Martin, J., Physical child abuse: An overview. Chapter I in *Child abuse: An interactional event*. New York: Columbia University Press, 1981.

Kempe, C. et al. The battered child syndrome. *Journal of the American Medical Association*, 1962, *181*.

Kessler, M. and Albee, G. An overview of the literature of primary prevention. In G. Albee and J. Joffe (eds.), *Primary prevention of psychopathology*, Vol. I, University Press of New England, 1977.

Kohlberg, L. High school democracy and educating for a just society. In R. Mosher (ed.), *Moral education: A first generation of research and development*. New York: Praeger, 1980.

Kohn, A. *No contest: The case against competition*. Boston: Houghton Mifflin, 1986.

Krumboltz, J. and Krumboltz, H. *Changing children's behavior*. Englewood Cliffs, N.J.: Prentice-Hall, 1972.

Levant, R. Client-centered skills training programs for the family: A review of the literature. *The Counseling Psychologist*, 1983, *11:3*.

Lippitt, R. and White, R. The "social climate" of children's groups. In R. Barker, J. Kevnin and H. Wright (eds.), *Child behavior and development*. New York: McGraw-Hill, 1943.

Lombardi, D. and Corsini, R. C4R: A new system of schooling. *Holistic Education*, 1988, *1*.

Maccoby, E. and Martin, J. Socialization in the context of the family. Chapter I in P. Mussen (ed.), *Handbook of Child Psychology*, Vol. IV. New York: Wiley, 1983.

Mack, J. The juvenile court. *Harvard Law Review*, 1909, *23*.

Makarenko, A. *The collective family: A handbook for Russian parents*. Garden City, N.Y.: Doubleday, 1967.

Martin, B. Parent-child relations. In M. Hoffman and L. Hoffman (eds.), *Review of Child Development Research*. Chicago: University of Chicago Press, 1975.

Maslow, A. *Motivation and personality*, 2nd ed. New York: Harper and Row, 1970.

Maurer, A. *1001 alternatives to punishment*. Berkeley, Cal.: Generation Books, 1984.

Maurer, A. *Physical punishment of children*. Paper presented at the California State Psychological Association Convention, Anaheim, California, 1976.

McCord, J. and McCord, W. The effects of parental models on criminality. *Journal of Social Issues*, 1958, *14*.

McLaughlin, T. A comparison of self-recording and self-recording plus consequences for on-task and assignment completion. *Contemporary Educational Psychology*, 1984, *9*.

Milgram, S. *Obedience to authority*. New York: Harper and Row, 1974.

Newsletter of the Committee to End Violence Against the Next Generation, Berkeley, California.

Palmer, S. *The psychology of murder*. New York: Thomas Y. Crowell, 1962.

Parke, R. Effectiveness of punishment as an interaction of intensity, timing, agent nurturance, and cognitive structuring. *Child Development*, 1969, *40*.

Pepper, F. and Henry, S. Using developmental and democratic practices to teach self-discipline. In W. W. Wayson (ed.), *Theory into practice: Teaching self-discipline*. Columbus, Ohio: Ohio State University, 1985.

Peterson, R., Loveless, S., Knapp, T., Loveless, B., Basta, S. and Anderson, S. The effects of teacher use of I-messages on student disruptive behavior. *Psychological Record*, 1979, *29*.

Pogrebin, L. *Family politics*. New York: McGraw-Hill, 1983.

Power, C. *The moral atmosphere of a just community high school: A four-year longitudinal study*. Unpublished doctoral dissertation. Harvard University, 1979.

Power, T. and Chapieski, M. *Psychology Today*, November 1986.

Reardon, F. and Reynolds, R. *Corporal punishment in Pennsylvania*. Department of Education, Division of Research, Bureau of Information Systems, November 1975.

Rice, J., *Correction and discipline of children*. Murfreesboro, Tenn.: Sword of the Lord, 1946.

Risley, T. and Baer, D. Operant behavior modification: The deliberate development of behavior. In B. Caldwell and H. Ricciuti (eds.), *Review of Child Development Research*, Vol. III. Chicago: University of Chicago Press, 1973.

Ritchie, J. and Ritchie, J. *Child rearing practices in New Zealand*. Wellington: Reed, 1970.

Roebuck, F. *Cognitive and affective goals of education: towards a clarification plan*. Presentation to Association for Supervision and Curriculum Development, Atlanta, March, 1980.

Roebuck, F. *Polynomial representation of teacher behavior*. Presentation to AERA National Convention, Washington, D.C., March 31, 1975.

Roebuck, F. and Aspy, D. Response surface analysis. Interim Report

No. 3 for NIMH Grant No. 5, Northeast Louisiana University, September 1974.

Rogers, C. *Client-centered therapy.* Boston: Houghton Mifflin, 1951.

Rogers, C. *Freedom to learn for the 80's.* Columbus, Ohio: Charles E. Merrill, 1983.

Rosemond, J. *Parent power.* New York: Pocket Books, 1981.

Sagan, C. *Cosmos.* New York: Ballantine Books, 1980.

Sears, R. The relation of early socialization experiences to aggression in middle childhood. *Journal of Abnormal and Social Psychology*, 1961, *63*.

Sears, R., Whiting, J., Nowlis, V. and Sears, P. Some child-rearing antecedents of dependency and aggression in young children. *Genetic Psychology Monographs*, 1953, *47*.

Silberman, C. *Criminal violence, criminal justice.* New York: Random House, 1978.

Silberman, C. *Crisis in the classroom.* New York: Random House, 1970.

Simmons, J. and Mares, W. *Working together.* New York: Alfred A. Knopf, 1983.

Skinner, B. *Newsletter of the Committee to End Violence Against the Next Generation*, 1986–87, *15*.

Snow, C. "Either-Or." *Progressive*, February 1961.

Spock, B. How not to bring up a bratty child. *Redbook*, February 1974.

Spock, B. *The common sense book of baby and child care.* New York: Duell, Sloan and Pearce, 1957.

Straus, M., Gelles, R. and Steinmetz, S. *Behind closed doors: Violence in the American family.* New York: Anchor Press/Doubleday, 1980.

Summit, R. The child sexual abuse accommodation syndrome. *Child Abuse and Neglect*, 1983, 7.

Taylor, L. and Maurer, A. *Think twice: The medical effects of physical punishment.* Berkeley, Cal.: Generation Books, 1985.

Urich, T. and Batchelder, R. Turning an urban high school around. *Phi Delta Kappan*, 1979, *61*.

Wasserman, E. Implementing Kohlberg's "just community concept" in an alternative high school. *Social Education*, 1976, *40*.

Watson, G. A comparison of the effects of lax versus strict home training. *Journal of Social Psychology*, 1943, *5*.

Wright, L. *Parent power.* New York: William Morrow, 1980.

Index

acceptance:
  Active listening in, 180, 182–89
  attentive and passive listening in, 180–82
  how to demonstrate, 180–89
  nonintervention in, 180
  in Six-Step Problem-Solving Process, 179–80
  see also language of unacceptance
Active Listening, 190–203, 222
  as alternative to praise, 56–58
  conditions important to, 187–88
  effectiveness of, 188–89
  good group discussions insured by, 193–98
  to help children solve problems, 180–89
  in mediating child-child conflicts, 190–92
  parents in, 182–86, 193, 199
  Positive I-messages vs., 57
  research in support of, 200–202
  warmer relations between teachers and students facilitated by, 198–200
Acton, John Emerich Edward Dalberg, Lord, 74, 230
Adler, Alfred, 30–32
adult-child conflicts, 209–10
adult-child relationships:
  boss-subordinate relationships compared to, 102
  breakdown of, 85–86
  flight responses damaging to, 84

No-Lose Method and, 154–61
praise damaging to, 45
reward-and-punishment approach in, 23–24
undermining of, 85
aggression:
  discipline leading to, 4
  frustration and, 70–71, 88
  how punishment fosters, 70–72
  permitting free expression of, 47
  see also violence
Albee, George, 230–31, 237
alcoholism, 92–93, 237
American family, fear of change in, 220–23
American Psychological Association, xxvii, 224
American Psychological Association Monitor, xviii
anger, 126–30, 234
Aschuler, A., 143
Aspy, David, 179, 197–98, 200–202
Association of Humanistic Psychologists, 231
attentive and passive listening, 180–82
Aussiker, Amy, 227
authoritarian:
  definition of, 12
  parents as, 91
authority:
  based on expertise, 13, 16–18, 222
  based on informal contracts, 14–15, 18